Creating a Neurodiversity-Affirming Classroom

of related interest

Executive Function Essentials in the Classroom (publishing March 2025)
Strategies to Support Learning and Growth
Zoe Beezer
ISBN 978 1 80501 077 7
eISBN 978 1 80501 081 4

Learning from Autistic Teachers
How to Be a Neurodiversity-Inclusive School
Edited by Rebecca Wood with Dr Laura Crane, Francesca Happé, Alan Morrison, and Ruth Moyse
ISBN 978 1 83997 126 6
eISBN 978 1 83997 127 3

The Neurodiverse Classroom
A Teacher's Guide to Individual Learning Needs and How to Meet Them
Victoria Honeybourne
ISBN 978 1 78592 362 3
eISBN 978 1 78450 703 9

Creating a Neurodiversity-Affirming Classroom

Easy Ways to Achieve Access, Agency, and Wellbeing for All

Kara Dymond, Ph.D.

Jessica Kingsley Publishers
London and Philadelphia

First published in Great Britain in 2025 by Jessica Kingsley Publishers
An imprint of John Murray Press

1

A CIP catalogue record for this title is available from the
British Library and the Library of Congress

ISBN 978 1 83997 880 7
eISBN 978 1 83997 881 4

Printed and bound in the United States by Integrated Books International

Jessica Kingsley Publishers' policy is to use papers that are natural,
renewable and recyclable products and made from wood grown in
sustainable forests. The logging and manufacturing processes are expected
to conform to the environmental regulations of the country of origin.

Jessica Kingsley Publishers
Carmelite House
50 Victoria Embankment
London EC4Y 0DZ

www.jkp.com

John Murray Press
Part of Hodder & Stoughton Ltd
An Hachette Company

The authorised representative in the EEA is Hachette Ireland,
8 Castlecourt Centre, Dublin 15, D15 XTP3, Ireland (email: info@hbgi.ie)

For the wonderfully fascinating, endlessly curious Max, and for anyone who has ever felt unseen, unheard, or unsupported at school.

Acknowledgments

It is humbling to think of all of the people (and pets) who helped me to write this book. This process was made easier by friends who regularly checked in to ask if I was on track while writing.

I am grateful to my partner, Aurélien, for his boundless love and belief in me; and to my parents for always being in my corner.

Many thanks to all my family, friends, and cats (especially Gerrie, who is deeply missed). A special shoutout to my brother Danny, without whom I might never have become a teacher (or author or presenter or podcaster or...). Inspiration also came from students of all ages; and the incredible books and authors I referenced.

I am blessed to have a professional support system of colleagues whom I look up to and consider friends, such as Shelley Murphy; Sonia Tran; and my co-researchers on accessibility and Universal Design for Learning in higher education, Kathy Broad and Lincoln Smith.

This book is all the better for the insightful readers who gave feedback on early drafts or who helped with harder elements for me, like chapter summaries: Rozarina Md Yusof Howton, Andrea Liendo, Bruce Petherick, Lindsay Ryan, Craig Segal, Lincoln Smith, and Maja Toudal. Many thanks!

My manuscript was refined and vastly improved by Lynda Cooper, Pauli Roos, Laura Savage, Peter Dillon-Hooper, and the team at Jessica Kingsley Publishers.

Lastly, thank you to all the contributors whose examples and experiences breathed life into this book.

Contents

Introduction

How We Do Things Differently

The world expects the impossible of teachers, or so it can feel. It would be one thing if all we had to do was automate our schedule, engage students by the push of a button, teach them identical content, and give them all exactly the same things. However, as anyone on the inside really knows, educators have a loftier calling. We quickly realize that what one young person in front of us needs is different from their neighbor.

I remember my first school board interview in 2011. They asked me how I would support learners in a class where a handful of the students had "special needs." Rather precociously, I responded, "I truly believe all learners have special needs—but I think I know what you're trying to ask!" Given my rather original take, it probably won't be a surprise to readers to learn that I am autistic and have ADHD, although I was undiagnosed at the time. I often interpret questions differently than expected, and my filter isn't particularly good. I say what I believe, and what seems simple to me may not seem so simple to others (and vice-versa). Within this anecdote lies a seed of what would become a strongly rooted philosophy—one which continues evolving throughout my career as a teacher, author, lecturer, podcaster, and coach.

Teachers may have 30 young people in our care, all with unique needs. A classroom is more like a garden than an assembly line, where everyone flowers in their own way and time, and under the conditions appropriate for them. One may grow tall and seek the sunlight, while others quietly spread in the shade. On rare occasions, you might stumble upon a tropical orchid and wonder why it is not thriving. Some plants bear fruit multiple times a year. A handful blossom exquisitely at one time, and you'd better not miss it! It is a beautiful gift, to help to grow humans, and to grow right alongside them.

In the almost decade and a half I've been a teacher, I've learned that each of the students in front of us walks in with different skillsets, interests, developing areas, lived experiences, and beliefs about their own abilities that shape their learning readiness. All of these are like the specific soil conditions, climate needs, sunshine and water requirements that determine the health of the plant as an individual and in community with the rest of the garden. However, we don't always know what each plant is, what it needs to thrive, and there aren't apps to scan students to figure these things out, the way there are for plants!

If we're lucky, we'll have a heads-up in a student's file that gives us some background: whether they have an identified learning need; whether our instruction is in their first language; whether they've recently emigrated from a war-torn country; whether they have complex health issues; whether they are in foster care; or whether perhaps their family (and they, by extension) are struggling through a contentious divorce. (Like teaching, parenting is a challenging and oftentimes a heart-rending responsibility!)

Even without that folder of student information, we might realize—fairly quickly—that we have a student whose grasp of the material exceeds our own. (I once taught algebra to a class of gifted 12- and 13-year-old (grade 7) students, which was a stark reminder that my math skills tapped out in grade 5!) Or we might quickly flag a learner who needs more support and advocate for an assessment, knowing full well it is unlikely to happen that school year. We do our best to support them with the information we have.

We struggle when students struggle

The reality, however, is our students are fighting so many battles we cannot read about in the pages of manila folders. (Rarely does a clinical assessment contained within do justice to the student's experiences.) There are no magic glasses to help us to spot those who have experienced—or are experiencing—trauma; whose brains process information differently; who struggle with friendships; whose perfectionism and self-doubt get in the way of trying new things; and not to mention the scores of students whose learning needs go unidentified to both them and to us!

So, no, teaching isn't all fun and games. We grapple with limited resources, unsupportive systems, administrators who may not share our priorities, and our own self-pressure to be superheroes. (Reminder: You are not meant to be one. Give yourself grace!) There are times your attempts to help someone may feel a bit like Plinko, that gameshow gimmick where you drop a ball down a board in the hope it lands on the outcome you want. Sometimes, however, it doesn't ricochet through the rungs to where you aimed. Maybe that strategy helps someone else, but it wasn't what you wanted to achieve. Or to return to the gardening analogy, you turn on the automatic sprinkler and some of the plants bloom and others begin to wither. Perhaps it isn't precisely the care that is needed.

So, what do we do? Fortunately, here is where we can all toot our own horns a little: teachers are really good at spotting patterns in our students and collecting data. We talk to colleagues. We talk to parents and guardians. We analyze. We rely on our acute powers of observation and our strong hypothesizing abilities to plan a course of action to "get it right." (I take comfort in knowing there is no one correct way! Teaching is so much more than a science.)

The other collective strength we have as teachers is our resourcefulness. Once we've found something that works, we archive and recycle that idea for future use. We know that the good strategies we develop for one or two students will benefit others. However, we're so good at jumping to the problem-solving, that we sometimes waste time trying a sequence of things and watching to see what works—and ultimately our assessment needs a rethink. We jump to the conclusion *Oh, they're struggling with getting started*, when really they can't remember the steps in their head.

I'm a bit embarrassed to admit this, but for the first few years of my career, I came back to the drawing board more often than I'd like to admit. I considered myself a reflective practitioner, agonizing over every lesson or interaction in retrospect for how I could do things better. When I stumbled upon an orchid in the garden, I studied the student, I wondered about them, created observation logs, and analyzed every shared moment, gesture, exchange, and action to help me better understand them. I tried stopping the previous year's teacher at the photocopier, made calls home, initiated case conferences, invited the school psychologist to observe, and generally hounded every adult I could possibly think of for insights. If I piled up all the reward systems and behavior contracts I wrote back then, I could change a lightbulb without a ladder. There was a literal mountain of evidence that something wasn't working.

It took me far too long to realize an essential truth: students are our best resource. If you need to know what's going on with a student, ask them. As I say to my students, I'm not a mind reader, so I'm going to get curious about your experiences!

I know, I know. It seems so obvious! I've sat in many staff rooms and collaborated with enough teachers to I know I'm not alone in spending the bulk of my planning time (and much of my off-work hours) expending a feverish amount of energy to figure out why and under what conditions something is hard for a specific student. And the remarkably simple thing we too often forget? Just ask—and be prepared to listen.

Fortunately for us, students aren't plants! They have remarkable insights that can change how you teach forever. I'm going to share many of these moments in my career with you, and the questions I learned to ask. But first, we should talk about my garden analogy—and the concept of neurodiversity it intends to illustrate.

Classroom neurodiversity

Neurodiversity includes everyone. It comprises the incredible variety of brains and how they process, interpret, store, and think about information from the world around them. Our brains are remarkable— ever-changing, responsive to our environments, and completely unique. Given that no two brains share the same formative experiences, passions, or practice schedules, it's safe to say our brains are as individualized as our fingerprints. Anything we think or do repeatedly impacts our brains, building and strengthening neural connections. Our brains are shaped by the languages we speak; the hobbies we develop; whether we're right-handed, left-handed, or ambidextrous; our exposure to and affinity for music; and how much we read or are read to; to give a few examples. Ever efficient, brains also prune neural connections we don't utilize, which further differentiates our distinct brains.

Our classrooms, then, are teeming with neurodiversity; with a myriad of minds, all brimming with their own specialties, patterns of skills, and developing areas. Some brains are considered *neurodivergent*, as they learn and process information differently than the "standard" or *neurotypical* way (but certainly not the only way). If doctors spot these brains, they might give them a label like autism, ADHD, Tourette's, obsessive compulsive disorder, anxiety, depression, traumatic brain injury, gifted, dyslexia, dyscalculia, dyspraxia, or other brain-based differences. Newer labels for brain variations keep coming out of the woodwork, like misophonia (extreme distress at certain sounds, like someone chewing), aphantasia (thinking and remembering without conjuring up visual or other sensory information), or hyperphantasia (thinking and remembering using extremely vivid conjuring of visual or sensory information, almost like a 4-D movie). Even within brains sharing a label, there is tremendous variability. This book does not contain an exhaustive list, but I hope you'll learn a few cool brain facts—and marvel at ways of thinking and experiencing the world that are different from your own! (What a rich ecosystem in our garden!)

Growing as a teacher

I never planned on becoming a teacher. I was fascinated by people, by movies, and by theater, practicing scenes in the mirror as a child. I had a ceaseless yearning to understand what motivated people to do what they did, which I explored by writing short stories, half-finished novels, and plays. I have always loved contemplating different minds! My mother wanted me to go into teaching and possibly to my parents' chagrin, I pursued a Bachelor of Arts degree, with a focus on theater, history, and anthropology. I might have pursued psychology, but at my institution, you needed math courses to continue past the first-year introduction course. The math requirement was a disappointing barrier for me, especially after learning I was in the top 5% of students in the course! How sad, not to have various pathways. Upon receiving my degree, I announced to my parents that I was done with school—never suspecting I would return for two more degrees or that I'd choose to work in schools every day!

For a time, I worked in theater, though the unpredictability, the need to self-promote, and the scrutiny of auditions gnawed at my stomach. Fortunately, an opportunity arose to develop a drama program for autistic students. I found them to be creative, funny, and relatable (even though I did not yet know the extent of my own neurodivergences). I so enjoyed jumping into scenes with them and sharing imaginations (which completely flew in the face of the autism-related literature of that period, which inaccurately asserted autistics as a monolith had difficulty with abstract imagination). Those students and our drama classes propelled me to earn my Master of Teaching degree and pursue as much related learning as I could.

In 2011, I followed my mother's advice and entered the profession. Within a few months, I had settled into a unique position: teaching small groups of autistic elementary students from different schools who would come together, traveling to my school on their scheduled day. I also provided support to their families and mentorship to their general education teachers. This is still my role today. I have been enriched, personally and professionally, by these relationships and chances to extend my thinking via the perspectives of others. My learning has been off the charts because of these collaborations!

It's fair to say none of us are the same teacher we were on our first day on the job. I tried very hard to command a room the way my mother does (a former teacher, she has always been a brilliant powerhouse of a human, whose assertiveness skills I can only dream of matching). In my early years, I did all the things I'd been taught in autism trainings—you can see traces of these suggestions in my first book, *The Autism Lens* (Dymond, 2020), despite the central premise of listening to children. Fortunately for me, I did listen to children, and I've made some significant shifts in pedagogy—from teaching a variety of accessibility "Tools of the Day" to replacing reward systems with collaborative problem-solving and empowering students to set and assess their own goals. (I'll tell you more about those things later!)

Three powerful ideas have percolated over time, shaping me as an educator and person the way a trickle of water can carve out a cave:

- Labels are not the be-all and end-all.
- We need to normalize the idea that there is no "normal."
- It is important to create a neurodiversity-affirming classroom.

Labels are not the be-all and end-all

My earliest and most simplistic understanding of neurodiversity—that the world is made up of many equally valuable but different kinds of minds—developed in childhood, before the term was even coined. My parents told me and my siblings that our younger brother Danny was autistic with a cognitive impairment when I was 9. I intuitively learned to adjust my communication with him because asking too many questions or making a multi-step request would compel Danny to walk away, struggling to process too much information. Being asked to make a decision could trigger a complete freeze response. While I was successful in most academic subjects, Danny's tremendous struggles in the education system underscored for me how capabilities could so easily be overlooked, hidden behind overreactive nervous system responses to tasks and requests non-autistics find easy; or just as easily brought out through things like rapport and accommodations. I didn't know all those buzzwords then, so this was more of a feeling which developed over countless homework sessions with Danny, in which I added Mario, Luigi, and other Nintendo characters to math problems to pique his interest. Despite my unending belief in him, I was surprised to learn that inside Danny were whole galaxies, as for decades now he has imagined dozens of planets replete with their own biodiversity, living beings, mythologies, histories, customs, and more. The complexities of his thinking and his incredible memory for Nintendo release dates are a constant reminder: labels can be helpful as a schema of what domains may be hard for a student and why, but they are never the whole story.

Years before my own diagnoses, I had been labeled as gifted. This is another example of how a label is never a perfect fit—while my writing skills, boundless creativity, and ability to hyperfocus in courses that interested me helped me sail through high school, I experienced extreme difficulties with math, a complete lack of physical or written organization, a tendency to overthink multiple-choice or true-or-false questions to my detriment, and absolutely no idea how to study. Before I knew what impostor syndrome was, I had it. How could some things come so easily, and other things be so, so hard? References to my brightness felt like teasing—something that didn't fit and was at odds with the vast discrepancy between expectations and reality. University worked best for me, especially after first year when I could take smaller classes on specific topics that fascinated me. Better yet, assessments were often essays or performances where I could show what I knew, rather than multiple-choice high-stakes examinations.

There can be significant personal value in a label that fits. In grade school, I occasionally reflected year to year that my brain felt like it had grown over the summer, as I now could tackle material that had been unfathomable for me the previous year. I had no deep friendships in elementary school, and although I got invited to the occasional sleepover birthday, I didn't care about boy bands and had little to talk about. I spent most of the night during these sleepovers trying to stay awake in terror, as, I'm still not sure why, but somehow, we all knew I'd be the obvious target to prank.

After I found a book on autism on my mother's side table with a highlighted neon yellow passage on how siblings could have autistic traits, I began to wonder. As a teen, I occasionally googled autism tests online and repeatedly found I met the threshold, but then wondered if I was overthinking and rigging the outcome (Likert scales—rating statements from always, often, sometimes, rarely, and never—are notoriously difficult to answer precisely, when one cannot give context to qualify one's answers. Valuing precision, I have since discovered, can be an autistic trait). More recently, I engaged with autistic people online, learning so much more about autism than I had in books. I kept relating and making sense of my experiences. It wouldn't be until my late thirties and significant burnout that I would share these niggling suspicions with anyone and pursue answers. I was privileged to have access to a diagnosis, and this discovery has been overwhelmingly positive for me. Learning that I have both an autistic and ADHD mind released a considerable burden and opened up avenues for self-compassion and support.

The inverse can also be true. You can probably think of a dozen labels thrown out as insults and that children internalize. Children also intuit adult discomfort with certain words. They may jump to the conclusion that a label like *autism* is bad. To make matters worse, so does much of society! The way autism is talked about in the media suggests that it is incompatible with any future positive outcome or personal fulfillment (Chapman & Carel, 2022). Parents of autistic children quake in their boots at the horror stories told by professionals and their social circle alike and are left to navigate what to do on their own. Teachers may feel out of their depth about how to support an autistic student on their upcoming roster, though their comfort and belief in their abilities tends to grow with more experience (Dymond, 2019).

Labels are meant to be signposts suggesting a particular direction, but instead we've made this one seem more like a murderous scarecrow who sends you running for the hills! What was interesting to me—as I reviewed the literature for this book—was to find that other forms of neurodivergence are rarely discussed this way. Articles on dyslexia, dysgraphia, dyscalculia, aphantasia, and to some extent ADHD routinely mention that these labels are differences in how the brain is wired, without the fatalism. Another related problem: labels are limiting and fail to capture who we are holistically. I have friends, who are likely autistic, who have been told they don't qualify for an autism diagnosis because they have a successful career, or they have a high degree of empathy, or they have an incredible gift for storytelling. (One friend was told they had inflection in their voice so they could not be autistic. Unbelievable!) These things are not mutually exclusive. Cases in point: three famous autistics with these qualities are Dan Harmon, Morgan Harper Nichols, and Sir Anthony Hopkins.

All of this informed my decision to be openly autistic. My proclamation that "I am autistic" might be the first time students have heard that label discussed in a matter-of-fact or positive way. Along the way, I've met other autistic educators who have seen the value in disclosing their autism to students, like my dear friend Bruce.

INSIDER'S PERSPECTIVE

Bruce Petherick, Autistic Musician and Educator (mainly at the high school and college level)

After my official diagnosis, I made it a point to disclose this to every class I taught at the start of the year/semester. I wanted to model the presence of Actually Autistic adults in the teaching environment. What happened, after every class, was eye-opening for me. Every time after I disclosed to a class, there were a number of neurodivergent students who approached me, and often a distressingly large number, who told me that they didn't get any support, or minimal support, from the school because their support needs were too low. The students were "falling through the cracks." There was a feeling, from the administrative staff and often other teachers, that they had survived this long, and didn't need anything special for support. This made me realize that I needed to be more flexible in my own teaching style—that I may be missing neurodivergent students who were masking and to be more aware of that, and, more importantly, to be more open about my own diagnosis, and to encourage those students to self-advocate, with help from me or, especially important, from fellow students.

It is noteworthy that autistic people largely prefer identity-first language (such as *autistic person*) as a way of recognizing that autism shapes how we think, feel, exist, and experience the world. In teachers college, it was drilled into me to use person-first language (*person with autism*) as a reminder that the most important thing about someone is, in fact, their personhood. While I don't disagree with the intention, and I used both forms interchangeably in my first book for several reasons, including grammatical ones (such as when listing students with various labels in sequence), the more I thought about it, the more identity-first made sense to me as my personal choice. Autism is central to my perspective. Being autistic links me to a community. It got me to wondering, why do we use identity-first in some contexts but not others? What message does it send when we say "gifted student" but not "autistic student"?

There are no hard and fast rules, so if an autistic person says they prefer being called a "person with autism," listen! Whether you use one, the other, or both descriptors, either can be said affirmatively or pejoratively. Sometimes, with no malice aforethought, non-autistic adults might imbue these terms with fear or utter them in hushed, scandalized tones. Autism is my "normal," as natural as any other difference in human experience. Would you bawl your eyes out, lamenting to your daughter about what it means to have a period? Probably not. Would you hide information from her, so she wonders what on earth is wrong with her? Definitely not! Because, either way, it's something she will adjust to and live with, even if at times it's frustrating. Accept it and help her figure out how to manage more comfortably!

All this to say, how we talk about differences matters. Research shows this as well. A recent study of autistic doctors showed that those who had not worked with other autistic doctors were more likely to have considered suicide. Further, those who think of their autism as a disorder rather than as a difference, and who use person-first terminology like "doctor with autism," were also more likely to have attempted suicide (Shaw et al., 2023).

So, I'm of two minds. Generally, I think we need to talk about labels. The majority of students that I work with are relieved when they learn what autism is for the same reasons I was—provided they get the opportunity to feel a community connection and are in environments where that label is spoken of in all its complexities, with its inherent strengths and challenges, and not as a hopeless tragedy or something they can just work harder to overcome. Knowing they are not alone and learning strategies from other people who experience similar challenges can unravel layers of shame and internalized ableism. They can find workarounds that actually work for their specific needs.

It isn't just students with a label who may internalize negative messages. To revisit the garden analogy one more time, too many students think they're weeds. They look around the garden at the perennials in flower most of the time. They see the ease with which the ivy and clematis climb to the top. They compare themselves. They receive innumerable messages, intended and unintended, that they are less than. Whether or not they come with a little card that tells me they have specific care needs, each of them is entitled to care—in education speak, the appropriate level of choice, challenge, and support.

As every teacher knows, many more students go unidentified and unsupported, passed on from year to year. This underscores one of our biggest problems in education: school systems worldwide are designed so that support is contingent on labels—while simultaneously restricting access to labels. Which brings me to my second assertion: I don't—and shouldn't!—need a label to support a child. Having taught many students with complex needs beyond their original label, I've learned to look at how each child learns, and not so much at the label. From there, it's easy to get to the important part: changing how we—and students—think about supports!

We need to normalize the idea that there is no "normal"

Bell curve thinking has really done a number on education and on society in general. The idea that only a certain number of students will do exceptionally well, most folks are middle performers, and a small group inevitably trail behind has never sat well with me. It is based on the notion that achievement and intelligence are relatively fixed. It might make sense to have standards for height and weight for growing babies, but for intelligence? There are so many problems with capturing a person's intelligence in the first place. Metrics continue to be developed, debated, and revised due to problems of bias and subjectivity, and even what skills are considered aspects of intelligence.

IQ tests measure specific skills performed under specific conditions and often in a certain amount of time. Does one person's slower processing speed mean we should write them off, when they might have a brilliant take if given more time? Must a person be equally brilliant across all subjects, or can they struggle sometimes? Are they allowed an off day? Even if we don't question the validity of intelligence quotients (though we should!), this presumption that the bell curve is an accurate measure of human potential is illogical and doesn't hold water. Think of any old elitist post-secondary institution with impossibly high entry requirements, which looks for those top-of-the-curve applicants. Why on earth would professors be required to mark admitted students on a bell curve, and forced to re-mark if the grades are too high? If our supposed "intelligence" really were fixed, the distribution of ability should be allowed to skew toward the As and higher. So, I have to wonder, which is it? Either our supposed "intelligence" is fixed, which suggests our box is inescapable (and what is the point of continual grading!)—or as university grade quotas suggest, our intelligence needs re-measuring every time we walk into a room, in relation to who is around, which would mean it is dynamic, and boxes are overly simplistic.

If our achievements can so drastically fluctuate, like the weather, wouldn't that suggest that in some environments and conditions, anyone can thrive or fail to thrive? In which case, we should be mobilizing to find out what conditions make the difference. Instead, educational systems are premised on two devastating assumptions: (a) that students should fall into rigid boxes according to a quota; and (b) neither students nor teachers are expected to be able to change any student's projected "potential." What a dismal vision for education! Rather than categorizing and ranking students, we need to think more holistically about people, their abilities, and the many complexities of life impacting them.

Since 2019, I've been a sessional lecturer at an education faculty where, for several years, I taught a mandatory "special education" course. I've always raised an eyebrow at the term, but even more so after hearing from scores of teacher candidates that they weren't interested in going into special education. This course wasn't about teaching in a specialized setting! Every topic emphasized that old inclusive education chestnut, "necessary for some, beneficial for all." I was both relieved and inspired to see how their understandings evolved throughout the course, as they became empowered to meet needs and collaboratively problem-solve when they weren't sure what to do.

In 2022, I proposed my own course: Accessible Education & Classroom Neurodiversity. In one of the first classes, we discussed the concept of "normal" and how it is only about a century old (Waltz, 2020)—relatively recent in the grand scheme of things! Once you have "normal" as a construct, you begin to identify what or who may be considered "abnormal." Even worse, that bell curve thinking in education leads to an insidious complacency. Somehow the narrative perpetuates that it's only the students who leave for special education classes who learn differently and everyone else learns in exactly the same way.

Plenty of students learn and process information in their own way and time. We begin to say students with a label are served best by specialists, and we may see offering a different access point, more explicit instruction, or more time to practice as "extra" or "going above and beyond." And what about students who need a label and don't have one? Well, we could write them off as the obligatory quota of students at the bottom. If we're "supposed" to have so many students floundering, why should we change what we're doing? A teacher who believes their job is to mark on a bell curve will teach very differently than one who envisions their role as guiding all students toward success.

Now, I know you're reading this because you already know that our job is more than teaching the students who easily learn the way schools are traditionally designed—you know, the students who could learn well enough without us! You put great consideration into how you plan and set up your classroom. Please know, this isn't a criticism of teachers, who are always tasked with doing more with fewer resources and surging numbers of students; it is an indication of the prevalent and often unchallenged beliefs in education—and a call for reflection. How can we do things differently, at our classroom level? How can we advocate for change more broadly? Karen Timm, an autistic educator and advocate, shares her thoughts on the hallmarks of neurodiversity-affirming schools.

INSIDER'S PERSPECTIVE

Karen Timm, Autistic Advocate, Educational Leader, and Founder of Neurodivergent Infinity Network of Educators

I have often said that we cannot wait for policies, procedures, and processes to be updated before making neurodiversity-affirmative shifts in our schools. That is for one clear and present, yet disturbingly ironic, reason. Systems are driven by evidence, and before change can occur systematically, decision-makers need to see the benefits of investing in change. When it comes to neurodiversity-affirmative practice, the proof is in the people.

Time and time again, when neurodivergent educators feel understood, accepted, and appreciated by their supervisors and colleagues, they feel safe to be authentic and motivated to do their best work. The same is true of students, and this relational commitment echoes amongst families/carers as well. This is a pivotal aspect of neurodiversity-affirmative practice, and it all connects back to creating a sense of belonging in a learning community. When school communities follow the lead of practitioners who are modeling neurodiversity-affirming language, practice, and culture, it comes across in the emails, writing samples, student and staff involvement, and the evidence of collaborative leadership where everyone is a valued co-learner.

- In a school where neurodiversity-affirming practice is being established from the ground up, students and staff engage in deeper, more honest conversations, where they build their confidence to be risk-takers, because there are no experts.

- In a school where neurodiversity-affirming language is being established in classrooms and the yard, it can be seen in the posters, displays, and other environmental print. It can be heard in how conflicts are solved, and in how recognition is given. It can be felt in how students, staff, and visitors are greeted, included, and appreciated.
- In a school where neurodiversity-affirming content is being embedded, everything ties back to human rights, social justice, anti-oppression, and inclusion. Universal Design for Learning is not something to check for after planning; rather, it is the starting point for everything, and all stakeholders know this.

Neurodiversity-affirming practice is not just about including neurodivergent humans more actively; it is about shifting the defaults about notions of normal, so everyone is valued genuinely, and this extends to all layers of identity. Neurodiversity-affirming practice allows for and embraces differences consistently and establishes a culture of kindness in which the goal is not to force compliance on anyone but rather to shift the focus on seeking to understand.

There is a lot of damage to undo. The pervasiveness of "normal" trickles down to our students. Some who need help are afraid to ask, for fear they may look "stupid." Others who leave the room to access special education supports may fear they are less than their peers—and worse, that others will notice. What does that do to their confidence? I also see it in their classmates, who feel relieved not to be singled out or who simply feel smarter. How does any of this help society to become more inclusive? If we want to de-stigmatize needing different supports, we need to normalize the idea that there is no normal way to learn! In our next insider's perspective Joanna Maselli shares the need for greater teacher awareness and self-reflection around the needs and trajectories of neurodivergent students.

INSIDER'S PERSPECTIVE

Joanna Maselli, Secondary School Drama, English, and Special Education Teacher with ADHD and parent to a neurodivergent kindergarten student

What I feel we are lacking the most is a neurodiversity-affirming framework for education that needs to be applied much in the same way that we are applying frameworks related to CRRP [Culturally Responsive and Relevant Pedagogy] or culturally responsive practices... we need to acknowledge that neurodiversity is large. It encompasses a larger group of students than we realize, and it increasingly encompasses students in the mainstream. So, it's not just the fact that we are losing our specialized classrooms and spaces and programming and increasing inclusion for students who, even until the last couple of years would have been placed in withdrawal programming, where they're not in a mainstream class all day—or maybe at all—during their school day. But I'm talking even for the students who were always included in mainstream programming, such as myself. (I had some withdrawal services for giftedness. Looking back, I probably had some for ADHD as well but... My school board didn't really have a special education department in that way for those types of students.)

It is really important to be assuming competence. There will be all these neurodivergent students in your class. Some of them are going to be identified, and some of them aren't. They may not need special programming. They just need a neurodiversity-affirming space to learn and grow. That can be done through a lot of Universal Design for Learning, and it doesn't have to have any negative impact on anybody else. We also need to check our assumptions. I think sometimes we associate a student's need for a lot of reinforcement and reminders and revisiting of information with a lack of their ability to think complexly or to understand certain things. A student, for example, might need a reminder about certain rules of phonics for the rest of their reading life. That doesn't mean that they are not capable of understanding what we're saying when we're speaking in front of them. That does not mean that they are not capable of doing math at a higher level. My hope is that inclusion of neurodivergent students in mainstream classes will help mainstream teachers see and learn to appreciate the unique academic and social-emotional development patterns that neurodivergent students often experience—especially since those with high accommodation needs used to be hidden from view of the mainstream classroom teacher.

It is important to create a neurodiversity-affirming classroom

Imagine a whole-class approach to accessible education—one centered on the idea that there is no "normal," where everyone is planned for, expected, and welcomed from the outset. Where we plan for access, agency, and wellbeing for all learners. Students are taught about neurodiversity, metacognition, and self-advocacy alongside the curriculum. They are encouraged to think deeply about how they learn best and what works for their brain, diagnosis or not. We don't have to wait to provide support until a student hopefully works up the courage to tell us they are struggling. We make learning tools (often called "accommodations"—but I don't like that, as it sounds like something "extra"!) and strategies available to anyone who needs them. Sounds idyllic? Fanciful?

It's not. I've tested it out—in general education classes, in my own specialized classes, in graduate classes, and I've had colleagues test it out, too. Teaching teachers has put my own teaching under a microscope. It's made me even more intentional in what I say and do. I've experimented and discovered that the things I do in the elementary classroom—modeling my thought process out loud; being extraordinarily clear about my pedagogical choices so students understand the rationale; creating opportunities for inquiry and critical reflection; differentiating for the success of all; touching base with each student personally each week for check-ins; promoting whole-class mindfulness, stretch breaks, and use of fidget tools—all work equally well at the graduate level.

My work with adults has also informed my elementary classroom. Reading books by Alfie Kohn, Mona Delahooke, Ross Greene, Zaretta Hammond, and Stuart Shanker (among others) has inspired deeper thinking about other ways of engaging, relinquishing control, partnering with students, and considering what my long-term goals are for students. Emboldened by the literature, I piloted new methods I was scared to try with young and adult learners. We had candid conversations around questions like: What are your brain strengths? What's hard for your brain? What helps your brain in those situations? What does your brain need? I taught them all various accessibility tools they could experiment with to aid their own learning. As best I could, I threw out rewards and punishments for meeting or not meeting my expectations. I told them accommodations were available for anyone who needed them, with or without an Individualized Education Plan or institutional approval. I challenged them to set and assess their own goals, which has enabled me to coach, drawing out their ideas for steps forward, rather than critiquing and suggesting my own quick fixes. Descriptive feedback replaced grades along the way. But the best part? Regardless of age, we got to talking about how they learn. We came to see some struggle—productive struggle (Hammond, 2015)—as an inherent part of the process. We managed big feelings and gave ourselves grace. What a learning experience—for all of us!

None of this required labels. Instead, I taught students to think about how they perceived various parts of the learning process. We'd examine how we identified within broad categories of learner variability (listed below), connecting to experiences, rather than labels. (I'll include labels as examples here, but with students, I leave them out. Students who are neurotypical or unlabeled also experience differences in these domains. A student may fall in multiple domains or may have specific times and subjects when they fall into a domain.)

- *Activated attention systems*: Learners whose attention systems work differently, whether highly attuned all the time or some of the time, noticing everything, or those with monotropic hyperfocus. (Students in this category might be autistic or have sensory processing differences, ADHD, anxiety, and/or trauma.)
- *Alternative communicators*: Communicators who best express their knowledge in other ways than mouth words (whether they are nonspeakers, occasional nonspeakers, a speaker of sign language, have expressive language differences, and/or sometimes prefer to demonstrate their learning via other modalities).
- *Specialized processors*: Learners who encode and retrieve

information in a way that is less common than the majority (such as those with giftedness, autism, aphantasia, hyperphantasia, auditory processing differences, and/or receptive language difficulties).

- *Distinct decoders*: Learners who experience different barriers and access points when decoding and understanding written text (which may include folks with dyslexia, reading disabilities, hyperlexia, autism, ADHD, and Down syndrome, or multilingual students).
- *Measured movers*: Learners with fine and gross motor differences (like dyspraxia, dysgraphia, and apraxia).

I've spent a few years now problematizing with graduate students how we can be prepared to meet students of all kinds and with all minds. These adult learners have responded to reflection prompts of their choice in whatever way works for their brain (voice notes, typed, a photograph of handwritten responses, an infographic or video, etc.). They've imagined different ways of doing things, collaborating on long lists of ideas for neurodiversity-affirming classrooms. They've reflected on the personal impact of being in a course that practices what it preaches—having opportunities to have a voice, to be able to choose, and to engage in meaningful learning, even if it looks a little different for everyone. It just makes sense: if we want to create independent, confident problem-solvers and self-advocates, we have to give learners opportunities *to* problem-solve, reflect on, and voice what they need—at any age. These aren't "special" education techniques, but rather techniques which make education accessible to everyone. Imagine this mindset being instilled in all classrooms!

As you read, I may make suggestions that won't work for you or which you aren't yet ready to try. That's okay; there isn't just one pathway. We all draw on different teaching strengths, styles, and expertise, and our classroom dynamics vary based on the relationships and minds in front of us. You may realize you've taught sometimes in ways that didn't work for everyone—and I hope you know the same is true for me! We are all works in progress, looking forward, rather than backward in blame, to do better. I invite you to brainstorm how you might apply and extend the concepts in this book with compassion toward yourself and your students. You will find what works for you in your classroom context, too.

What to expect in this book

This book will help you figure out some lines of inquiry to build not only your understanding, but each student's. This is a book about forging partnerships with students to better understand what makes them tick and how they learn best. It's also a book about developing student metacognition so they can identify barriers and self-advocate for what helps them. It is grounded in my own experiences and research as well as the wisdom I've gleaned from colleagues, parents, and students along the way. And what a journey it's been!

Each chapter contains brain-based information and anecdotes from real teaching and learning experiences to illuminate WHY certain learners need different things and so teachers can better anticipate potential roadblocks.

I'm going to introduce you to some fabulous educators I've had the pleasure of learning from! You'll have windows into their classrooms and glimpses into how aspects of neurodiversity-affirming classrooms can look. This book also incorporates perspectives of neurodivergent learners who may think and experience the world differently than you do (or not!).

The bulk of each chapter is devoted to the HOW, offering lesson ideas and metacognitive prompts to support learners in understanding how their brains work best in this area and a list of practical strategies and tools for both whole-class and individualized approaches. These are highly transferable between grades and subjects. While each chapter builds on the previous ones, they don't need to be read sequentially. If there's an area you want to brush up on, simply flip to that chapter for immediate support. There is some repetition where information is relevant in more than one chapter to benefit readers using it this way.

- Chapter 1 suggests ways we can prepare an environment where students feel safe and seen and where we teach the emotional regulation tools that help them to work through the initial discomfort and self-doubt that sometimes come when learning something new. This is part of the learning journey!
- Chapter 2 considers how we can more effectively communicate with students and how information is processed by various learners.

- Chapter 3 focuses on attention, working memory, cognitive load, and strategies to help students learn information in a lasting way.
- Chapter 4 examines executive functioning, scaffolding, and how to help learners to confidently take steps on their own. It also gives considerations and questions to guide planning and assessments.
- Chapter 5 delves into problem-solving with students and becoming more aware of your own reactions and triggers. It presents empowering ways of thinking of the teacher–student dynamic.

A note to the reader: Long lists of strategies contained in each chapter may seem daunting. If you approached it as a checklist and checked off things you're doing, you'd likely see the many ways you have been supporting learner variability in your classroom already. I bet you could even add to these lists! Teaching is additive, so as things become second nature, we are ready to try out something new. Challenge yourself to think of two or three additions to test out over time and incorporate changes slowly. You're learning new skills, just as students are.

It is my hope that, in reading this book, you feel recognized for what you've already mastered. May the words within strengthen your resolve to continue doing all those great things you already do, and to be able to confidently express to parents, students, and other educators the rationale behind them. Perhaps it will also inspire you to think even more deeply about your pedagogical choices, your long-term goals for students, and whether your classroom gives them the opportunities they need to achieve those long-term goals. And even better, whether your room is a place where they can set their own goals.

If I had one wish to better the lives of teachers, it would be that when you come up against a barrier in a student's learning, you remember you are never alone. We've all had shining moments and some defeated moments we wish we could forget. We've all struggled, feeling powerless when faced with a student whom we can't seem to reach. I don't want any of you spending another lunch break or sleepless night wondering what is hard for Deshawn and why, what on earth compelled Charlie to take a bite out of Juan's sandwich, the reasons why Siobhan's homework never gets done, or what Skylar was thinking when they crumpled up their worksheet. Stop relying on sheer cognitive effort and willpower (even though, let's face it, you have those in abundance!). Instead, I urge you to remind yourself—as you will your students—that we're all learners, whether we're the youngest or the oldest person in the room. And when these feelings inevitably pop up, perhaps you'll pick this book up as a guide.

May it help you figure out how to partner with students when roadblocks occur and get curious about their experiences—from their perspectives rather than yours. Embrace the fact that problem-solving collaboratively builds an abundance of skills—and also leads to more powerful solutions. Selecting strategies at random is like dropping that zigzagging ball down that giant Plinko board. I want you to become a dart master instead—aiming and directing your energy in a targeted way alongside your students. That's the power of welcoming learner insights to inform and transform your practice.

You're in it, together.

How We Feel a Part of Things

In a course I took during my doctorate, peers and I brainstormed words related to education on post-its. We then laid out terms like "Curriculum," "Field Trips," "Multimodal," and "The Arts" onto a table, grouping related concepts and relationships together. Which words connected to others? We were challenged to sort and re-sort these as we walked around the table, silently, after examining changes made by colleagues. I brought words like "Disability" and "Special Needs" to the center, under "Constructivism," "Learning," and "Play." Each time I circled back, these words were relegated off to a corner edge of the table, linked only to "Schooling." This hit me in the gut, because even in an institution well known for its focus on equity and inclusion, and in a room I knew to be filled with compassionate educators, nobody else seemed able to conceptualize how or where these learners fit. It struck me as a microcosm of what we end up doing to many students with "special needs"—we warehouse them in segregated settings, assign them curiosity-killing worksheets, and deprive them of meaningful opportunities to engage or explore (Hammond, 2015). The niggling question that embedded itself in my brain: Why did nobody else see disability as a part of things—and how could I change that?

Inclusion is hard to do if you've never seen it done—at least, not truly. We often don't question practices that are commonplace, and it is difficult to envision different systems than the ones we experienced as students ourselves. That is precisely why we must question things; and so, I created a course. Graduate students and I devote ourselves to the questions: How can we expect, plan for, and be prepared to welcome everyone? How can we do things differently?

Anticipating the myriad of individual differences that make our classrooms and our world so much more interesting begins before students ever set foot in our classrooms. It starts with the planning of our classroom environment (where we are not "Schooling" but rather learning, co-constructing knowledge, and playing, all together!). It's essential that we acknowledge the interconnectedness of safety and learning, where the latter cannot exist without the former.

School and anxiety

Any student can feel singled out, embarrassed, excluded, or act like their differences are flaws to hide at all costs. This is true even in inclusive settings. A study of autistic teens showed that, despite their peers and teachers believing the setting to be inclusive, the teens supposedly requiring and benefiting from inclusion still felt left out (Locke et al., 2010). Similarly, children and teens with ADHD report feeling significant stigma from peers and teachers (Ringer, 2019; Wiener et al., 2012). We won't always know how students are internally experiencing our classroom and our community or who might be internalizing their difficulties as personal failures. However, we can assume everyone experiences stress at school at least some of the time. This is especially true for neurodivergent students, whose first-hand accounts can help us to better understand how our classrooms may be experienced differently than we intend—and what to do about it.

INSIDER'S PERSPECTIVE

Iain Morrison, late-diagnosed 41-year-old autistic Mature Student

School was a disorientating, alienating experience for me. Even today, at 41 years of age, I still have nightmares about losing track of my class schedule, struggling to absorb information presented to me in lessons, losing track of time daydreaming, and experiencing relentless bullying. All of these things were part of my experience at that tender age; a time when I had no idea I was autistic, only that I felt different. Teachers didn't understand me and neither did my fellow students. I was singled out in lessons, laughed at for missing crucial information in class, put on regular school report to chart my underperforming, and often punished with detentions for not completing homework assignments.

As a teacher candidate in my first practicum in a classroom of 6- to 7-year-olds (grade 1 in the US), I was shocked to see how anxious students were. In retrospect, the shift from kindergarten to grade 1 is as significant as the shift to middle or high school—and even post-secondary. They were nervous about sitting at desks all day. The thought of writing tests. The fear of failing (a societal pressure, no doubt instilled with best intentions but yielding devastating results). They came in with math anxiety, reading reluctance, and quaking in their boots, terrified to make a mistake. In creative writing, they watered down what they wanted to say, afraid to misspell a word. My mentor teacher, Mrs. Evans, was absolutely incredible at gradually making them—and me!—feel safe. I've never forgotten one of her lessons—beautifully designed, multimodal, hands-on, collaborative, which should have worked but for some reason just didn't that day—and she turned to me and said, "Kara, sometimes, a lesson will go like that. You shrug it off and try again another way tomorrow." It was a freeing realization. It's likely the reason to this day I often try new ideas or activities I've dreamed up, even if I'm not sure how it will go. It's not the end of the world if I (or you) have to pivot to something else or adapt on the fly!

Mrs. Evans was the kind of teacher who understood that children need to feel safe to be able to learn. She was sensitive to the deep, yearning hearts of children and intuitively understood our work can't begin until students feel seen, heard, and supported in our classroom. We had dance party breaks. We sang songs. We read so many stories! Lessons included movement, hypothesizing, discovery, play, modeling, practice, and lots of encouragement. She would kneel next to students when circulating to give them feedback at their eye level. I learned to celebrate taking risks and taught students to look for and use delectable "chocolate chip cookie words" that made your writing so vivid you could almost taste and smell them. Spelling didn't matter initially—writing is a process, and getting the ideas out was more important for step one! A decade and a half later, as I research nervous systems and learning, and contemplate what makes a safe environment, Mrs. Evans' classroom keeps coming to mind. Let's examine what can make that difference.

Nerd alert: Brain basics related to safety and survival

So, what's learning got to do with safety? The shortest answer? Everything! The long answer? Here goes!

Certain parts of our brain, like the brainstem and cerebellum, are fully developed at birth and are responsible for automatic things we don't need to think about unless there's a problem with one of them—like breathing, blood pressure, heartbeat, body temperature, and digestion. These brain structures work together with our *autonomic nervous system* to pick up information about the world around us and how we fit in with our surroundings. It's thanks to the autonomic nervous system that we somehow sense the immediacy of trust or danger when meeting a new person, or being in an unfamiliar school or classroom, without being conscious of how we came to think and feel that way. The brainstem houses a network of neurons—the *reticular activating system*—that scans for threats or rewards and helps us react quickly when it is alerted to danger, such as increasing or decreasing blood flow and heart rate to allow us to get out of there quickly, throw a punch, or my preferred survival mechanism: camouflaging into the wallpaper (Cozolino, 2013; Hammond, 2015). This is our in-the-moment act-react area of the brain, or Brown Brain (Shanker, 2020).

Our *limbic system* houses emotions, memories, and motivations and governs behaviors. This area of the brain reflects our ability to remember things, to learn from experiences, to bond with others, and connect existing knowledge to new knowledge. It's also where we regulate emotions. We have some specialized brain structures in this area like the *thalamus*, which takes in sensory information, and the *hippocampus*, which is related to memory and emotional regulation. The *amygdala* is the brain's fear center, able to react in less than a second to any perceived or suspected threat (Cozolino, 2013; Hammond, 2015). We can consider this the nonverbal Red Brain (Shanker, 2020).

We also have a *cerebral cortex*, comprising multiple areas which help to process our sensory experience of the world into ideas and mental representations. Visual processing, auditory processing, our awareness of our body in space, and language skills all reside here. The *prefrontal cortex* (or PFC) is an area I frequently discuss with students. This is the primary residence of our *executive functioning*, which is made up of all the skills that let us think things through, give our ideas language, and carry out goal-directed behaviors (Cozolino, 2013; Hammond, 2015). Think of this as the reflective and intentional Blue Brain (Shanker, 2020).

All of this of course is an oversimplification—our brains are complex and capable of great things. Many areas of the brain and our nervous system work together to think, feel, act, react, and understand. We've even evolved to the point where we can ruminate about the past and experience anticipatory anxiety (Cozolino, 2013)! While different areas do different things, the central mission of all of these coordinated efforts is to keep us safe.

Now, sometimes our brain gets it right, and other times... not so much! In the words of Stuart Shanker (2017), "there is a fundamental difference between being safe and feeling safe" (p.1). Have you ever been walking somewhere—maybe through a dilapidated and dimly lit area, and all of your senses were on overdrive? It is entirely possible you were physically safe but did not feel safe. As human beings, our nervous systems are constantly scanning, often below our level of consciousness, for signs of threat or safety. We orient more to novel objects and situations than to things we already recognize (Cozolino, 2013), presumably to notice anything out of place in that garage.

This is called *neuroception* (Porges, 2004; Shanker, 2020). Without thinking, our bodies are registering minute environmental signals that tell us we can relax, be vulnerable, take a chance, learn something new, and try to do something differently—or not. These nonverbal signals get interpreted by our amygdala (AMY). Whether a survival mechanism or a cosmic joke, our amygdala is mature at birth and ready to defend us. AMY is a tiny almond-shaped area of the limbic system that could be easy to overlook—except make no mistake, it is the giant red danger button of our brain. When pushed, AMY sends cortisol stress signals to our sympathetic nervous system to stop our cognitive processes and to let our irrational lizard brain take over. It bypasses any checks and balances or thoughtful debate, without our even being aware. Imagine an alarm system locking all the doors to the command center so no one can get in to the controllers. That's what happens in our brains when AMY goes on alert. We are left, locked in the stairwell, with only a few options: fight, flee, freeze, or fawn (essentially, to use every social tool at our disposal to gain approval and avoid any negative repercussions)!

Now, AMY is incredibly helpful when we are staring down a wild animal, but less helpful when we have a bill to pay or a work deadline. You see, some of us have more sensitive AMYs, which means we might experience more frequent amygdala hijacks. It makes me think of my father's car alarm, which is overly sensitive, blaring in staccato rhythm as a leaf wafts down onto the hood. While I'm using a lot of metaphors, what's really interesting is that when children who were in a rational Blue Brain (cerebral cortex) state were given electroencephalograms (EEG) measuring their brain's electrical activity, the test showed calm blue patterns in the PFC and very little activation in the Red Brain (limbic system). When they had more activity in the vigilant Red Brain, this was reflected in larger red waveforms in the limbic system and very little blue activity in the PFC. If the child were to go into full non-rational threat response or Brown Brain, the EEG spiked strongly in the left hemisphere (Shanker, 2020). This demonstrably proves that rational thought gets shut down when scanning for or responding to threat! (It's worth noting that adults experience this, too.)

When it comes to learning, a small degree of stress can be beneficial, stretching us just outside of what we already know and where we feel comfortable, helping us to learn new skills. If this rings a bell, it's because teacher training likely taught you about Vygotsky's Zone of Proximal Development (1986). Under these conditions, our brains actually produce neural growth hormones and make new neurons and connections in the brain. We have optimal *neuroplasticity* (our brain can change, grow, form new links, and so on).

Anxiety—long-term activation of the fight/flight/freeze part of the nervous system—takes a considerable toll on our body and brain. Anxiety is like encountering highwaymen right after paying at the toll bridge. First, we face an exorbitant energy cost as our brain focuses on survival. Second, it also dumps a huge dose of the stress hormone cortisol into the bloodstream. This necessitates the shutdown of our digestion and cellular repair. The presence of cortisol also dampens the immune system, making us more prone to illness (Shanker, 2020). It also ceases neuroplasticity and any brain growth, stalling the connections between neurons and the reorganization that happens as we learn. It impairs the functioning of the hippocampus, where we form the memories we need for learning (Cozolino, 2013). Brain cells die off in response to the higher metabolism needed.

I'm sure you can think of a few students—like those with activated attention systems—who react like that car alarm: hypervigilant scanners who detect threats more readily, with a greater margin of error, than their peers. They are on *neuroceptive overdrive* (Shanker, 2020)—hyper-vigilant, amped up on stress hormones, misreading situations, and react-ing to danger where there is none to be found. The threats they perceive aren't just physical ones. Our brains react in less than a second to any sign of social rejection as if experiencing danger (Hammond, 2015). I switched schools when I was 11 and was badly bullied. It is the one year of my childhood where I remember almost nothing about what I learned at school. Bear in mind that I have vivid memories of projects, lessons, and activities, all the way back to kindergarten. My nervous system was activated, and I wasn't able to form new memories. Like many students, I didn't outwardly show my distress. We might not detect high stress or anxiety in students, particularly the fast hand-raisers, perfect test scorers, and first volunteers to help. Not all anxiety shows up as yelling, ripping worksheets, or chronic stomach aches.

Children who experience chronic stress or who have experienced childhood trauma tend to have problems with attention, perception, creativity, problem-solving, and motivation (Hammond, 2015; Shan-ker, 2020). Multiple adverse experiences a child goes through have a compounding effect, though even a single early trauma, such as being born premature or undergoing invasive medical procedures, can result in hypervigilant nervous systems, despite the child not remember-ing those experiences (Delahooke, 2019). Learning difficulties due to chronic activation are mapped in the brain, like a smaller hippocampus (memory) and a larger amygdala (emotions) (Cozolino, 2013; Delahooke, 2019; Shanker, 2020). Children in survival mode have a lower tolerance for any stressors, and their responses are unconscious survival mech-anisms, hardwired into their biology. How does this manifest in the classroom? We see difficulties with learning and greater Brown Brain stress responses, which may be misinterpreted as willful misbehavior.

Fortunately, brains can be rewired. This is where you come in! With careful attention to the environment in our classroom, the types of challenges we present, and the relationships we build with students, between students, and between each student and themselves, we can help students to grow their brains and change their relationship to the world around them (Cozolino, 2013; Hammond, 2015). It may take months or years, but neuroplasticity is real and offers potential for everyone.

INSIDER'S PERSPECTIVE

Matthew Tinto, Teacher to students 9/10 years old (grade 4 in the US) and 11/12 years old (grade 6 in the US)

Fostering a safe and supportive classroom environment is critical in giving students the opportunity to feel safe and giving them the ability to take risks in their learning. An important component of building an effective classroom community is the use of class check-ins before or after lessons, which was particularly useful in helping students understand what they were feeling and why they might be feeling that way. We also regularly had class discussions on effective strategies that they could later use and keep in their "toolbox" to help self-regulate both in and outside of the classroom. This consolidation took place during individual and group conferencing, where students shared ideas and strategies they found most effective.

Expecting everyone

Planning for our classroom to be a safe haven for students begins before we've even met our students. We account for the variety of needs we anticipate that may show up in our classroom and put things into place proactively. A sense of safety comes hand in hand with predictability, so the better we've thought out the whys behind our classroom design and routines, the easier it is to reassure students and guide them toward self-management. Jo, a neurodivergent teacher, designs her classroom to build in the structure and support she and her students need.

INSIDER'S PERSPECTIVE

Joanna Maselli, Secondary School Drama, English,
and Special Education Teacher with ADHD and
parent to a neurodivergent kindergarten student

For environment, I think the biggest thing is that your classroom is your classroom, even if you share it with other teachers, and that you are welcoming students into a space. I always say, "I'm welcoming you into my home, not because I am the owner and I set the rules, but because I want to create a sense of hospitality." My students are guests in my home, which is my classroom, and I acknowledge early on that it's structured in a certain way, and will always be throughout the year, which allows me to function best as their teacher so that I can meet my responsibilities and do my job the way I need to do it. I make that explicit to my students, not in a domineering way, but in a way that is saying to them, "This is the rationale for why things are the way they are."

I invite them to share with me throughout, and I like to do this slowly. I don't like to do this too much all at once in the beginning because I don't think that that's very authentic, especially for teenagers, and especially for neurodivergent students, because trust really needs to be earned. These are students who by the time they reach high school may have had some really negative experiences with school, with judgment, with their social-emotional safety, or with their physical safety. So, slowly over time, I create opportunities for me to do two things: I collect information on them in the form of questions, surveys, and activities that are geared toward learning about their past experiences of school, with the subject matter, and their prior knowledge; and I give them tasks that allow me to observe them. Some tasks I would assume should be comfortable and familiar to most students at that point, but then I also throw in a few challenges that I know will be new things to see how they respond to challenge.

I also tailor my environment to make it more hospitable to them. I want them to be able to be comfortable with me in my space, even though it is my space, and it's my space for very good reasons. I think that when teachers are not domineering, but they are confident and in control, especially of the environment, that can also offer a lot of safety and comfort to our neurodivergent students who are not well attuned to environments that are more chaotic or unpredictable. I think being able to say, "This is the way my classroom functions, this is why I've structured it this way, here's how I want your input to make it more welcoming for you, but then here is how it is also going to be on a consistent basis." That can do a lot to soothe the student's nervous system.

I observed this a lot with my son as well. When there are things he doesn't like or doesn't agree with, if he gets a reason, even if he doesn't agree with the reason or he doesn't like the reason, he's more able to go along with it versus his anxiety taking over. And the other piece is, it's predictable. "Well, so-and-so is our teacher today, and their rules are X, Y, Z, and I don't really like those rules." He's capable of acknowledging, "This is the way it's going to be, I don't really like it, I wish it was different, but I know they have a reason." That is very different from what we used to get, which is the panicking and the school refusal when he didn't know what to expect.

Physical layout

INSIDER'S PERSPECTIVE

Evelyn (pseudonym), autistic High School Teacher with possible ADHD

I hate fluorescent lights. They're the worst. I'm used to putting up with discomfort, so it took me a really long time to realize how draining it is for me to spend a lot of time in institutional settings like a school. Whenever the classroom lights get turned off, there's an immediate sense of relief and calm and a lack of pain that feels almost indulgent, like a treat I'm not supposed to have. I'm glad there's more awareness of light sensitivity now;

teachers can turn off some of the lights (so students with vision problems can still see the board), or they can buy covers for lights to make them less bright.

How you design your room says a lot about your values as a teacher. The caveats here are that, unless you are the sole teacher in that space or you are blessed with an unlimited budget, you may not have much say in the furniture or equipment housed within your classroom. I'm not talking so much about having a Pinterest-worthy classroom. Unfortunately, or fortunately, educators are notoriously thrifty, scouring freebie groups, driving around the city to collect used chairs and bookshelves, and, though this shouldn't be an expectation, buying things out of pocket. I'm not suggesting you run out to the nearest chain store to refurbish the classroom singlehandedly, or even that you have to subsidize your classroom (you shouldn't have to). Non-fluorescent lighting, a humidifier, and fans are all great for traditional classrooms, but there are plenty of less burdensome ways to adapt your classrooms, organize, and prepare for the students on your class list. Here are a few principles to consider when setting up:

Space
Is there room for all learners to navigate between spaces and around the furniture? If you have a student who is a wheelchair user, with a bigger body, or using crutches or walking aid, will they find it easy to access what they need to? Are there tripping hazards or other barriers?

Desks and tables
What makes the most sense for your classroom space? How will you ask students to engage? Do you have groups of desks or large group tables because you emphasize collaboration? Desks laid out in a U because class discussions are central to your lessons? As you go through the year, you will discover who needs to be closest to the front to see the board or to you in order to attend more easily.

Taking into account positive or neutral peer relationships and seating students with at least one person they are comfortable with can go a long way toward building community. Survey your students privately. Watch the dynamics. Be mindful of the invisible labor you may be unintentionally assigning to quieter students when you place them strategically next to a student who might benefit more from proximity to you. I was often expected to keep peers in line. When I was 12 (grade 6 in the US), I was seated for a whole year next to my two biggest bullies. When I was 14 (grade 8 in the US), I was seated next to a student nobody liked, who wrote out his school hit list and designed bombs, and who had poor hygiene. The stigma for us both was terrible, and I wish the teacher had talked to him to find out what was going on and showcased his strengths to the group so we could come to better appreciate him.

Materials management

Which materials are to be freely accessed and shared by all? Are these items within easy reach of all students? I hope my classroom sends the message that students and I coexist and share space and that the daily materials belong to all of us. Pencils, pencil crayons, markers, glue sticks, paper, tissues, paper towel, and more are there to be used, no permission needed (within reason)! One incredible teacher I knew had students at collaborative tables, each with shared bins of materials and color-coded file organizers for all student work. No desks to contend with, and a place for everything!

INSIDER'S PERSPECTIVE

Dr. Andrea Liendo, Grade 1 Teacher for over 30 years

As a teacher of 6- to 7-year-olds [grade 1 in the US], I always felt it was important to set up my classroom with a variety of centers and independent opportunities for students to explore and learn. For example, my classroom had a sand center, a paint center, a drama center, an art table, the kitchen center, and a writing center that included scissors, glue, various forms of paper, markers, and colored pencils, in addition to a science touch table and any other center sparked by student or teacher interests. I also provided cars and trucks, Lego, building blocks, puzzles, and board games. Board games were frequently homemade by students or me, but commercial games such as Word Bingo and Guess Who were also included.

Free-access sensory tools

This may sound terrifying to you, but I have free-access sensory tools in my classroom. Rubik's cubes, fidget spinners, stretchy bands, squeeze balls, and more can be found in bins in the calm zone. These aren't free access from day one—rather, I teach mini-lessons on each tool, how it should be used if being used as a tool; how it would look if used as a toy instead (which would prompt me to ask, "Tool or toy?"); how to pick a good tool for the time (some tools are better for relaxation breaks, and some help us to focus; some we can use while keeping our gaze toward the front or the teacher, and others we can look at while still listening and looking up intermittently); and how the ultimate purpose of a fidget tool during a lesson is to help us share a thought bubble and be able to listen and think about the topic, and respond.

There is something amazing that happens when you use this approach: everyone wants to try the tools, but when the novelty quickly wears off, the students who really need the tools are the ones using them! If you see a squeeze ball being tossed in the air, you ask, "Tool or toy?" or ask whether there is a more helpful tool for their brain. This is an opportunity for students to learn more about themselves and how they listen and learn best. They may find some tools so absorbing that they are great for a break but aren't an effective tool for lessons. You can talk to students about specific engagement look-fors that help you both to identify when they're listening, even if they aren't making eye contact, which can interfere with processing for some neurodivergent students. For example, does doodling, coloring, or using a fidget tool help them keep their thoughts mostly on the lesson topic, so they can answer questions or participate in a demonstrable way? If not, it's likely not the best tool for this time.

A change of scenery

I love seeing classes with a variety of spaces to move between. It reminds me of my office days and being able to freely wander down to the kitchen for more coffee, pop my head in to say hi to a colleague or two, stop at the literal water cooler, and so on. Students sometimes need to get up for a movement break and a change of scenery, too. Do you have a variety of microspaces to move between, such as:

Calm zone

This could be a seat in an area with a few posters of breathing exercises, emotions words, or affirmations. It could be a bench with pillows and some mindfulness cards or a comfy chair next to a lava lamp. It could be a rocker in a reading nook. A colleague brought in some soft lamps to use instead of glaring fluorescents. My class has a small castle tent with a cool textured rug, a giant emotions pillow, and some weighted shoulder snakes. There are other zones around the room where students can look at a glitter jar, select a new kind of breathing strategy or mindfulness exercise listed on popsicle sticks, test out some yoga cubes, or access sensory tools. Sometimes, these spaces may be available outside of the room, but creating a microspace within may send the message that self-regulation and wellbeing is vital to our growth.

INSIDER'S PERSPECTIVE

Kai, 7-year-old, ADHD

Sometimes, when I get angry or the classroom is too loud, I go to the "calm down corner." Because it's in the corner of the room and the chair has a cover, I can sit and take deep breaths and calm down. I like it because it gives me somewhere to go whenever I need a moment when I'm sad or mad. My teacher lets me go whenever I want so I can listen to how I'm feeling and do something about it.

Workspace options

I am a believer in having multiple spaces where students may work, such as a quieter area with a desk carrel for privacy and reduced visual stimulation. Consider having a multipurpose large table that could be used for cooperative work, for station rotations to conference with the teacher, or to go to for any students who have questions or need more instructions after a lesson. In general, how students work doesn't bother me—if they want to stand perched over their desk or sit somewhere on the floor, or in any other area of the classroom, I'm open to it. Whatever works best for their brains.

Tech corner

Few classes these days have a desktop station available for student research or word processing needs, but this can be a helpful addition for work periods or station rotations. A positive outcome of the Covid-19 pandemic has been more equitable access to technology. Oh, to be so lucky as to have a class set of devices! If you do, you'll definitely want a designated cart to store and charge the devices.

Library

Do you have a comfortable and welcoming reading area? Is it organized by theme, by genre, alphabetically, etc.? Do the books represent a cross-section of societal diversity, including races, cultures, neurodiversity, disabilities, genders and sexualities, family structures, life experiences, and problems relevant to the age group in question? Do books come in many formats, such as picture books, graphic novels, novels, non-fiction, poetry books, short story compilations, or even an audiobook station? We are introducing students to what could be their gateway text into the world of reading or writing! Can students leave reviews or is there a section to have "recommended by," much like the employees at bookstores do? Are bookmarks available?

The walls

What message do you want the walls to convey? How can you display meaningful aids without visually overwhelming students? Be selective about what goes up and when, considering what is being taught. Are there places where students can display what is meaningful to them? A student art wall could allow students to see themselves and their influence on the room. You can rotate what is on display much like an art gallery does, with student involvement!

Be aware that some students can become overstimulated by too much clutter, too many posters or visuals, jarringly bright colors on the walls, etc. I've walked into a few classrooms and had no idea where to look, feeling my mind on overdrive trying to take it all in. I always make sure to have at least one bare wall area, and this is usually the one at the front so that students will have less competing for their attention in that direction.

INSIDER'S PERSPECTIVE

Megann Roberts, Special Education Resource Teacher, learning disability and ADHD

I find that maintaining a visually "clean" classroom is not only important for student achievement but also their wellbeing. When a classroom has competing visuals, my students find themselves overwhelmed. It makes it difficult for them to locate helpful information, which defeats the purpose of having visuals! By no means is our classroom boring or bland, but it definitely errs on the side of minimalist. Knowing that "attractive" is not easily defined, I engage students to ensure their voices are heard; I have my students walk around the school, peeking into classrooms, and when they find spaces they find helpful, they ask the educator for permission to take a photo. We then print the photos and work together as a class to establish norms for classroom decor. I've found that when students see their preferences and their own work on our walls, they take much more pride of ownership in their work and learning space.

Communication outlets

Everyone uses alternative communication sometimes! Low-tech and high-tech alternative communication options increase expression and access for everyone. Are there physical or visual ways to vote, indicate preference, and communicate ideas in other ways besides speech? These could be things like voting sticks painted different colors on both sides to indicate choice; printed or digital communication boards with options to be pointed to; alphabet magnets on baking sheets; whiteboards to give a visual answer; the ability to type answers on a device or input an idea in a virtual activity like Padlet or Mentimeter; and so on. Donaldson and colleagues (2023) recommend lanyards with small, printed letter boards for all staff to aid communication with any student encountered in the school or at recess. These would allow students to spell to communicate, as some students will find oral communication a barrier all or even just some of the time.

Other barriers

Can you anticipate any other problems or preoccupations that may come up for students and which you may be able to circumvent? Besides the obligatory first-aid items, do you have extra snacks or sanitary pads available?

The physical space is just the beginning. We are just as intentional in the atmosphere we create, and the relationships and community we foster.

Making things predictable

Predictability helps everyone. As an autistic person, I panic whenever I don't know what's expected. I google photos of places and where I can find parking before I head out somewhere new. My racing heart slows down just a little when I remove some of the guesswork.

This is true for students of all ages, too. Routines can help everyone navigate and understand some of those communal expectations. It's great to generate some of these together! I've loved hearing how other teachers, like Lincoln, balance novelty with familiar structures.

INSIDER'S PERSPECTIVE

Lincoln Smith, K–12 Inclusion and Accessibility Teacher and Teacher Educator, ADHD

I had the privilege of working with an English teacher and a math teacher that each used structures to their instructional planning that, by default, had multiple access points and processing opportunities. The English teacher did it by lesson (four parts to each lesson), and the math teacher did it by the week (each day of the week was a particular routine). Since working with them, I've adopted a combined approach.

Every lesson has a "calibration" activity, which is some kind of individual response to a prompt, or a review activity. Depending on the day, the response to a prompt might be written, drawn, or discussed aloud. If it's a review activity, it may be a pop-quiz, collaborative game, or a retrieval practice activity (e.g., group brain dump). We then have the "lesson," which can be a video, my own brief lecture, a guest, or sometimes even another student present-ing something to the class. We then have an engagement activity, which, again, varies depending on the day. Sometimes this is independent work, sometimes pair work, and sometimes group-work. I endeavor to cycle through these so that students have different ways of engaging and processing day to day. Finally, there's a "synthesis" activity. This is often a writing or drawing activity, where students summarize their main takeaways or questions. There is also a single line, four-point rubric that is the same every day on how the students feel like they engaged with class that day. They grade themselves, and then I give a grade. If there's a discrepancy, we talk about it before the end of the period. Sometimes, students want to make up for a class, and we figure out a way for them to do this before the next class.

Overall, the pattern of each lesson is similar, allowing for comfort in the routine, while the components change enough from day to day to provide novelty and to support different ways of accessing and processing the material. It's an approach that I and my students have loved!

While routines will vary depending on student age and what subject(s) you teach, here are some general considerations:

Arrival routines

How will you foster comfortable transitions, beyond introducing where to line up and where to store student belongings? Will you establish a quiet activity to transition everyone from whatever state they're enter-ing? A familiar task to ease into the day? A challenge, to grab those who seek novelty? Independent research or genius hour? My elementary students write or draw a success from the past week, and then have time to chat, read, or draw as they'd like, and my older students work on group challenges while I call students for individual conferencing. My university students have a flipped classroom model, where they have 30 minutes to peruse a reading for discussion. Consider this time a warm-up for the nervous system—not time to spring a test or quiz!

Handing things in

Students should know when and where to hand in forms and assignments. Is there a specific hand-in bin? Are things collected after the teacher prompts the whole class, or are students expected to remember deadlines and submit at any point on the day work is due? (The former tends to have higher success rates!) You may be fortunate enough to have digital submissions and reminders for students. I have worked with students who've felt that, in missing a deadline, all hope is lost, and they shouldn't hand it in late. Think about ways to build in both predictability of the where and how as well as flexibility around when they can hand things in, so dread does not overtake students and prevent their success. Some learners may take a little longer to conceptualize and digest particular tasks.

Getting help

How do you want students to seek clarification? I've had many students confused by what their teachers expected. Some teachers have rules around waiting, in a queue, around the teacher's desk. Some prefer a student to stay seated and raise their hand. Some will say to ask peers first. You could have a table where students go if they want more review or teach the class sign language or another visual signal so they can indicate the need for support nonverbally. What makes sense for your students?

Accessing materials

We all have a stake in keeping things in good condition. What are the routines you would like students to follow related to specific materials in the classroom? Teach when these are available and how they should be used as you introduce the materials. This is more pressing in elementary, where markers and glue sticks dry out after a capless night. You'll also want to remind students to use the sharpener in short bursts at non-lesson times! I've even had to tell a few students that, due to paper regulations at the school, they can't take half a pack of paper for their grand comic-making plans, but that they may take a few sheets each day. (This has sometimes led to illuminating conversations about what they have access to at home, and perhaps an errand to the dollar store to buy the student their very own sketchbook.)

Transitioning between subjects

If you teach multiple subjects, you may want to have a visual time countdown (as there are lots of digital ones available) along with verbal reminders of time left. Some students may find it difficult not to be able to finish a task in class, so reassuring them if there will be more time later can lessen their worries. If you have multiple grades in the same class, those routines are so important, so one cohort is settled and knows what is expected of them before you proceed with the small group lesson for the other section. What communication system might help students who transition in and out of the class for instruction in English or special education supports to adjust when they return to class? It can help students to know what's coming next and what's expected of them, so, in addition to the schedule, you could demonstrate what should be out on their desks by holding up the textbook and folder, or—better yet!—take photos of core materials at the beginning of the year and print out small versions to include next to your schedule. Students can see what they should have in front of them well in advance, so you aren't asked 30 times!

Breaks and bathroom

What are the expectations around leaving class? How will students communicate that they are taking a break or using the bathroom? Do you trust them to come and go? Do you need them to signal or ask you? Do you prefer they wait until a work period? Especially for more literally minded students, you may also want to let them know exceptions to any rules—as an autistic student might have an accident waiting for the work period, not realizing there is flexibility in emergencies! Some teachers will have a system where students write on the board or take a lanyard designated as a hall or washroom pass. I'm more of the ask-me-so-it-registers-that-you're-out-of-the-room kind of teacher.

When it comes to breaks, students can take mini-breaks easily in the classroom. This could be getting up to get water or a fidget tool, doodling, or using the calming castle. When they need a longer break, they can ask or signal to me so that I know if they are going to walk down the hall and back. We also have a class agreement that they can have a small snack upon arrival, in addition to the other two designated school snack times.

Technology

We love it, and we hate it! When can students access personal devices vs. school devices? What are the routines and expectations associated with this? Teenagers are expected to be better at managing technology, using computers to take notes and collaborate with peers. If they are misusing it to go on social media, I try to remember their brains and executive functioning are still developing into adulthood, so they may need guidance. When I've taught adults, we have a class talk around device use and review the research on splitting attention and learning (hint: we don't actually multitask as well as we think!), and students share the impact it can have on them when someone in their field of vision is on Instagram or TikTok. Then we make an agreement. Most groups decide to limit use to taking notes or virtual coloring, if it helped them to listen, while closing any other tabs or apps besides the readings or notes related to the course during lessons or activities. I promise a certain number of breaks where devices could be used and of course they are welcome to step out for anything pressing. One class wanted to work on being as present as possible and opted for no devices during any direct instruction or peer presentations and simply elected one note-taker for these times. It isn't something I ever want to police, and having a talk where students come up with the norms can help everyone think about the benefits and try to apply the terms of the agreement. Gentle reminders and check-ins about whether their environment is helping their learning can also work.

Younger students may require more structure and oversight, such as reminders when to get out and put away a computer. You might have a student in charge of collecting and charging the technology (if you're so lucky to have class devices). You may be open to students using a computer at any time, or you may pick select times (of course, never taking away a vital communication aid for students who need it to be understood). To help students discern, you might consider a symbol on the board or a computer visual on the visual schedule so the student can see which parts of the day devices are needed. You might make the explicit connection that devices are less likely to be available regularly and/or supervision increases when they are misused for games and social media instead of the assigned purpose, though you'd prefer not to have to police devices. Have a class talk about the barriers students encounter and how shifting attention and inhibiting impulses is really hard and come up with strategies as a class (Faith, Bush, & Dawson, 2022)—personal strategies as well as ways peers can support each other.

If you have a student who experiences stress when transitioning off of a device, have a bin for the student to place the device in. You can gesture to the bin or bring the bin to their area, and you won't need to verbally prompt as much. Give a lot of processing time to follow the instructions and indicate in advance that the period is coming to an end so they can save and shut the device. I don't know about you, but if someone came into my living room during *Grey's Anatomy* and told me they were turning it off, I'd struggle too. Never grab the device out of their hands, as it's not worth a power struggle. (See some ideas to collaboratively solve individual issues in Chapter 5.) With pre-teens, I get them to think about how their brains feel when disconnected from devices as opposed to after checking social media. What's most conducive to their learning? As an alternative, I play soundscapes and brown noise or allow headphones and music. During longer work periods I model how to use the Pomodoro Technique to work uninterrupted for a set period of time (15–25 minutes) followed by a mini-break (5 minutes).[1]

Work period choices

What options are available to students for where and how they produce work? Can they relocate to another area or workspace? Can they access snacks, gum, music with headphones, etc.? Older students may be able to go work in other locations of the school while younger students require more supervision. Can they access other spaces besides an assigned desk, such as a class reading area, an alternate table, or a desk carrel? Can they stand at their desk, move to the hallway, relocate near a friend, work cross-legged on the floor, etc.? I once handed a worksheet and a pencil to a student seated under their desk and told them cheerfully I'd be happy to help them if they had questions. Surprised by my response, they said nothing and got it done. If I'd started demanding them to get out from under the desk, I doubt we'd have had the same outcome.

Early finishers

Are there options available for early finishers? It's a balancing act because we don't want to penalize the fastest students by giving them more

---

1   I love https://pomodorokitty.com

work every time. Students have the right to enjoy breaks and reap the benefits that come from an unencumbered imagination. We also don't want them to be in a constant state of boredom (everyone is entitled to an appropriate level of challenge) or to always rush to finish. We want students to use time with us, so we are there to answer questions. Think of possible expectations, such as using the time to doublecheck; to work on other assignments; for silent reading, independent research, drawing; etc. If they are interested, you could have a student help other students, peer edit, or assist with something, but be mindful of the potential stigma of relying on their labor too often and the urge some students may have to please you. Let them know it's okay to say no if they want to do something else, without any repercussions. I've seen some incredible classrooms with ideas for fun challenges students can try, like different brain teasers, story starters, logic puzzles, or math problems. I'd be inclined to conference with those frequent early finishers to find a way to engage them over the long term. What would they like to learn about or do? Do you want them to report back to you what they're learning?

Missed classes

How would you like students to handle missed content—and who might need your support to follow up and catch up? From time to time, students may be absent without notice. Tell them how you'd like this to be handled. Older students may communicate with you through email or an online platform, while younger students may need more precise information, such as brainstorming with them when it is a good time of day to check in about any missed lessons. If they are very young— or any age but with forgetful tendencies!—reminders are appreciated. Students who miss—or are excused from—lessons with high frequency may have activated attention systems, finding the demands of school overwhelming or even threatening, especially those whose nervous systems are easily activated by external demands and who suffer from long-term stress. This may present as school refusal, shutdowns, or even as frequent somatic complaints, but can be misinterpreted as the student making excuses or being lazy or defiant. In fact, under the surface, their nervous systems are in constant alarm, making small tasks seem insurmountable. Work on fostering rapport and safety, incorporating student choice and ability to negotiate on what is being asked (e.g., scribing or orally assessing), increasing breaks proactively, breaking work down into manageable chunks, issuing indirect compliments (e.g., giving a thumbs-up or praise to students in the vicinity; writing on a post-it), and depersonalizing requests (e.g., "According to the schedule, it's time for language"), and collaborating with the student and their family.

Upcoming changes

What are upcoming changes that might be stressful for some students? Who would appreciate a heads-up? While some students may not bat an eye when you change the seating arrangements, it can be a lifesaver to others to have a heads-up of significant changes. Tell them what to expect in advance. If you will be away and know in advance, you can let them know what may stay the same and what may be different. I have known a few students who benefited from a sneak peek of a change in an upcoming unit. These students who notice and respond most to environmental changes will likely also need to know any alterations to the layout of the room, such as an impending desk change. To help with field trips, I talk the class through the itinerary, expectations for each component, and show pictures of field trip locations. Think and talk through how you can ease this transition and what strategies or supports students can access to cope.

Classroom cleanliness

What are the class norms around maintaining the class and individual spaces? What times of day or activities might need specific routines or time allotted? Do students know what tidy should look like? You might have formal roles students rotate through; friendly competitions comparing the cleanliness of each desk group; or even just a general standard of how the class should look, with everyone expected to contribute to the tidying. Tidying norms can be established for snack times, lunch times, art class, science, and end of the day. Speaking of...

End-of-day routines

Are there supports for students with slower processing, sensory sensitivities, anxiety, etc.? How can this transition be made easier? There can be a lot of hustle and bustle so a student may benefit from packing up a few minutes earlier than peers or bringing their backpack to their desk to pack. In high school, you could dismiss a student a few minutes earlier to avoid chaotic hallways. Another barrier can be recording any homework and deadlines. Some students may benefit from writing these in their agenda earlier in the day (like immediately after each subject, or once in the morning and once in the afternoon) or simply taking a photo of the homework board. You could recruit a student to upload a picture to a virtual classroom for all students. This is an example of assistive technology in action! It removes the frustration factor for those with fine motor or language difficulties who have already been working significantly harder than peers for whom writing is automatic. Ensure the class knows expectations around final dismissal. For very young children, it often involves directly handing off each child to their parent or approved guardian. Explain any safety rules and give them the reason why.

When you can, have conversations about how to cope with unpredictable changes, such as emergency drills, unexpected visitors throwing off the lesson, or changes in schedule like cancelling an outdoor event due to rain. Let them know you'll inform them as far in advance as possible, and when something is a surprise, you're there to support them through it. Brainstorm a list of self-regulation strategies that may help: deep breathing; affirmations ("I've got this"); self-talk ("I can line up and follow my classmates"); and remembering that anxiety feels uncomfortable but it passes.

There are plenty of other routines and group expectations that may become necessary to develop throughout the year. This is a great opportunity for democracy in action. What do students think would be a fair way to solve the issue? Commit to trying it out and coming back to the drawing board if necessary!

Welcoming everyone into a community

Positive rapport

We all remember that teacher—at least I hope so! The one you connected with. The one who looked happy to see you. Who greeted you by name. Who seemed to care about the events in your life. Some of us were lucky to have a few of these along the way. (Mr. Lee came to see me sing my first solo, two years after he taught me at a different school. Mrs. Morrison came to see me as Anne in *Anne of Green Gables*!). Philip reflects on his own experiences, as both a neurodivergent student and as a teacher, and that power of connection.

INSIDER'S PERSPECTIVE

Philip Dennis, ADHD/dysgraphic New Teacher

Growing up as a disabled and neurodivergent student, there were many occasions that I was not fully understood by teachers and not given the support I needed. When I was 11 and 12 years old [grades 5 and 6 in the US], I had the same teacher who really took me under his wing and tried to spend time to get to know me so he could help me better. This teacher took the time to understand me and was able to cultivate interest in school that lasted beyond a few months, as was typical. Because he tried to get to know me and actually connected with me, I became more interested in working with him, with my accommodations, and overall succeeded more in those two grades than my entire public-school career.

As a student teacher, I find there are obstacles for fostering a good relationship with students, but I also think it creates an opportunity. You are not quite at an unreachable level of power. When I was in practicum in a variety of grades, my knowledge of popular culture and local slang, along with my understanding of how people of different socioeconomic backgrounds interact, allowed me to connect with students. By connecting with both nondisabled students and disabled students through commonalities, I was able to foster both interest and excitement in work. The students were on task more often, would raise their hand and answer questions, and come to me asking for help when they needed it. I became trusted.

Surprising no one, it turns out we learn better from people we like (Boeltzig et al., 2023; Cozolino, 2013; Hammond, 2015; Shanker, 2020). As children, we learn how to cope with the rollercoaster of life through co-regulation, provided we have that supportive adult. Just one positive adult relationship—teacher, parent, or other—can be a protective factor against the mental and physical health impacts of trauma (Crouch et al., 2018). Relationships change the landscape of our brains (Delahooke, 2019). Neurodivergent students routinely tell me that they learn best when they feel liked and respected—which shouldn't come as a surprise. Don't we all? And these students are the first to pick up on the cues that an adult isn't enjoying them. (It must be those activated attention systems!) Automatically and unconsciously, before another person even says a word, we are reading those nonverbal messages that allow our limbic systems to attune—or not (Cozolino, 2013; Shanker, 2020). Unfortunately, neurodivergent students are often misunderstood by adults and shamed or penalized for their ways of being—such as processing by asking questions or not wrapping up a clarifying comment in nice social packaging. They may be punished for their stress behaviors that are triggered when the environment, the expectations, or adult responses are unsupportive. You know what they learn from these reactions? That adult, or that classroom, or that entire school is dangerous.

Learning requires relational safety. When we feel we are connected to our teacher and peers, our brains release positive neurotransmitters like oxytocin, which keeps our PFC functioning and prevents our AMY from hijacking us (Hammond, 2015) and also helps us to bond with one another. Our brains become ever more neuroplastic, able to adapt and learn. Conversely, when we don't feel supported by teachers, we are flooded with the stress hormones adrenaline and cortisol, which shuts down learning (Cozolino, 2013). The more often this happens, the more speedily and easily we slip into fight, flight, flee, or fawn mode. Anxiety is the nemesis of learning! (So too are stress, depression, overload, burnout, shutdown, and other dysregulated states, but that's too long to be a catchphrase!)

Think about the last time you had a rough day at school. If you have a friend or mentor on staff, talking it out with them can be reinvigorating, empowering you to solve the issue. Positive rapport protects us from stress (Shanker, 2020). When we feel safe to explore the unknown with someone, we can build our capacity. When we help someone else—a friend, colleague, or student—in the same way, we also get a little oxytocin boost for earning their trust (Hammond, 2015).

You have probably built rapport in a million ways. I don't pretend to know them all, but I'll share some general truths:

Curiosity

Students can recognize genuine interest or spot a phony a mile away. Genuinely start asking students—both in purposeful tasks soliciting their ideas and in passing conversation—about their interests, their lives, and their hopes. I've taught a budding artist or two who underestimated their talents. I began giving them very specific feedback about what I liked about their work ("Your use of color is very selective and incredibly powerful as a result!"). It's hard to brush off specific, observable feedback as someone "just being nice." I was responding to their work seriously and asking them questions about their process. Make a point to actively listen. Try to remember things students share, such as the extracurriculars they are involved in, wish them well, or ask them how that tournament went later. I often write things down so I remember to follow up! Amber, a neurodivergent teacher, talks about the value of curiosity in fostering relationships.

INSIDER'S PERSPECTIVE

Amber Borden, Secondary/High School Teacher, AuDHD

When I was in my practicum, for any type of get-to-know-you questionnaire, forum, or activity, I would always go through and create my own little profile of each student. This isn't in terms of *oh, they're good or bad*, but just in terms of what they know about themselves, what they are already advocating for or saying ("Hey, this is something that I could need or use a little bit of help with"). I make sure to have this big list of everybody in the class and anything that they're interested in, their hobby, or afterschool program, or even their future goal. This becomes my own little personal connection list. I try to find something, however small or big, that I have in common with every single student so that I have some sort of talking point with everybody.

Just by nature of being neurodivergent, that's how our brains work. We are always making connections, and we'll bond with people and show that we care by saying, "Oh, I have this similar experience." Even if it's not actually that similar, it's, "You know what? Your experience made me think of X, Y, and Z." It's that soliloquy kind of sharing or bonding. I will usually build that into lessons, and I use that as a starting point of chatting with students. If I'm talking to them about one particular interest of theirs, then usually that helps lead to more and more things. And you know what? If I have a student who inevitably doesn't put anything for an interest, I try my darndest to figure out what they like.

Humor

Sometimes I incorporate a funny story, sharing or imitating silly laughs as a class until we are all in stitches for the benefits of shared laughter. Shared humor releases dopamine and oxytocin. At the same time, it serves as a moment of levity, which decreases anxiety, increases self-regulation, and enhances memory of content. Compare this with the teacher using biting sarcasm or a derogatory remark, which can result in the opposite of positive engagement (Cozolino, 2013). Autistic students and other direct communicators may be more likely to take these literally or take longer to understand the joke; they may be laughed at by peers or adults as a result. One of my coping mechanisms with peers was laughing at everything, so that my occasional cluelessness would go unnoticed. You want to make sure you're laughing with students, not at them. No one wants to be humiliated, so please be the kind of teacher who helps build social connections rather than one who adds to the arsenal of bullies. You don't need to be a comedian, but a ready smile and evident enjoyment of interactions with students goes a long way. Having a sense of humor about yourself and your mistakes in the classroom can model how to handle things with grace too.

Greetings

Say hello to each student as they enter the room. Use their names if you can and a unique message: "It's nice to see you, Elise!" "How's it going, Dan?" "Good morning, Rowan." Turn your whole body to give your full presence.

Gratitudes

I am intentional in showing students that they are impacting me and my classroom. When I make a request, I often phrase it like, "Darryl, can you help me by turning off the lights?" I regularly tell the whole class and individual students the things I've noticed and appreciate about them. This also helps me to not get so caught up in the checklist of things to do that I neglect relationships. I always have something good to say when I get to speak to a parent.

Clean slate each day

As you develop an ethos in your classroom where mistakes are learning opportunities, make sure the students know that you don't hold grudges. A challenging moment will pass, the day can be turned around, and you will celebrate that a student takes a deep breath, asks for help, shares their feelings, reflects, gets back on track, or tells you later what support they need next time. Instead of focusing on the challenging moment—a small slice of pie out of an otherwise good pie chart day—the focus is on learning. (Yes, I have made that visual with students to show that a blip isn't the end of the world or a lasting memory for me.) Hopefully, students will allow you the same grace on your less-than-perfect days.

Inviting expertise and opinions

Ask students what they think. Do they like the idea of changing a lesson to address a more pressing concern or curiosity? Where might they like to go on field trips? Do they think they need more time? What do they want to play during gym (physical education)? Do they have an idea to make a lesson better? Do they have advice to give to next year's students on how to have an amazing year of learning?

Following through

The most important part about soliciting feedback is having students see their voices are important. It's adjusting a lesson based on what they said. It's remembering to turn on the closed captioning going forward. It's booking that trip they asked for, if you can, or explaining why if you can't. It's telling them you remembered that they loved when you played that review game, and that's why you're doing it again (Dymond, 2020). Say out loud in class: "I made this change because of you. I heard you, and I am learning too. Thank you for this great idea that will have an impact on others too."

Wellbeing first

I have found enormous personal benefits from letting go of rule polic-ing and refocusing on student wellbeing. This requires an awareness of your own triggers and a conscious responding after a breath or two in a way that models what you want students to learn to do. For instance, if one of my graduate students misses a class or a deadline, I manage my own emotional response and then reach out to see if they are okay and whether I can help them. They often react with surprise. "I'm an elementary teacher," I say, "I don't let anyone fall through the cracks!" As soon-to-be teachers, I hope they take note and remember how they felt in our interactions and how they too can demonstrate patience and support with their future students. Saying this also reminds me of my purpose.

Being predictable

Students need to know that if they approach you with a problem, you will react in predictable ways. My students know if I can listen right away, I will; and if not, I'll let them know when I'll be free. They know they're never in trouble with me, but we are going to talk through and come up with action plans together if it's a more serious problem. They won't be yelled at for struggling with something, even when I'm trig-gered myself. I take my job as a co-regulator seriously.

Sunshine calls

In primary classrooms, teachers may only call caregivers when a stu-dent does something wrong. Make a call or send an email or note to every student's parent each term about something wonderful you've noticed about their child. Think beyond academics. Validate soft skills, like showing empathy, asking group members for their opinions, and offering help. Keep an anecdotal log or checklist of example look-fors and train your brain to spot the exceptional.

Group identity and self-concept

We all want to be part of the group. Some of us pull away when we experience social rejection. Any environment where we feel invisible or excluded immediately activates distress signals and activates AMY (Hammond, 2015). There is an unfortunate link between how a student is treated by peers and their later mental health and wellbeing (Shanker, 2020). This link is more accurate in predicting future mental health issues than the students' academic performances and other achievements in school. In fact, the brain area that lights up for physical pain lights up for social rejection, threats, disrespect, and shame (Cozolino, 2013; Hammond, 2015). So, whether a student experiences full-fledged bullying or a more subtle exclusion where they are never invited to join, they have higher cortisol levels, impaired memory and learning systems, and are at greater risk for mood disorders, PTSD, and difficulties with sleep and emotional regulation (Cozolino, 2013).

Zaretta Hammond (2015) shares how racialized communities are more alert to threats based on history. I suspect the same may be true for neurodivergent students (especially racialized ones) who have been routinely ostracized, misinterpreted, and subjected to punitive approaches rather than supports for their emotional and sensory needs. Schools become sites of nervous system activation, rather than the safe havens they need to be if we want students to grow, learn, and connect with others.

Feeling supported in a community has enormous benefits to physical and mental health (Cozolino, 2013). I'm a big believer that, once students connect to us, it can be easier to connect them to others. I have taught several students who were more interested in chatting to me and, in time, as I challenged them to participate with peers, they stopped looking over their shoulder for my approval and started enjoying being a part of the group (Dymond, 2020). How can we as teachers connect a potentially disparate group of students from varied walks of life? Turns out, not only do we learn better from those we like, but also those whose beliefs and ideas we view as similar to ours (Boeltzig et al., 2023). This has implications for students who feel different from peers—whether or not peers share their perspective. As teachers, we have to intentionally create a group identity and respect for individual differences.

While connecting students to others, we are simultaneously helping students to build a relationship with themselves as a learner. So often, how students see themselves is in relation to others in the group. In working with many students, I've come to think that one of our driving forces as humans is to hide the shames and insecurities we have internalized. Unfortunately, this seems to start early, as some students come to believe they are less competent, less intelligent than peers, or unlikeable. They may go out of their way to hide or keep their head down, or conversely act as the class clown or get kicked out of class—all to avoid the embarrassment of someone seeing their struggles.

In a retrospective study of adolescents with ADHD or depression, McKeague and colleagues (2015) found that negative responses from others led to internalized negativity and self-stigma. One coping mechanism was to try to hide difficulties, which I hear all the time from my students. So, in a way, any student encountering a barrier or an area where the learning feels harder may internalize that as a personal failing, reinforcing an activated attention system during those subjects and activities. Undoing damage to a student's self-concept—ideas about their own competence, intelligence, and worth—takes a lot of time but is necessary work to get their brains back online for learning, and for community- and capacity-building. Changing the focus from performance outcomes to growth-through-process can support everyone in having a healthier relationship to learning.

Sometimes, when a student isn't achieving, they are given easier work (Hammond, 2015). They may miss out on the teaching and learning that highlight the relevance to their lives and which ignite curiosity. In my early days as a substitute teacher in one of the school boards, I was left with worksheets for teenage students with reading disabilities of the type that had a picture of a feline and a fill-in-the-blank C___T. Watering down work does not an enthusiastic learner make! It impacts their view of themselves and their capabilities (Baglierii & Lalvani, 2019). Furthermore, these students—whose activated attention systems and other learning variabilities get in the way—are not given the same opportunities to develop cognitive tools (such as critical thinking and problem-solving) that come with greater challenge and complexity of learning materials (Hammond, 2015).

On the flip side, students identified as gifted tend to have access to experiential learning, challenge, and choice. While they are enjoying interest-based inquiry projects and field trips, their classmates who would especially benefit from engaging opportunities to create new background knowledge miss out. Often, learners who disengage are subjected more heavily to punitive approaches, threats, and reward systems that tend to penalize them while rewarding the students for whom compliance and learning come more easily (Hammond, 2015). It doesn't sit right with me that school systems sometimes deny learning opportunities as a punishment for having difficulty learning the way schools teach!

Human brains have an exceptionally strong negativity bias, focusing 20 times more on negative experiences than positive ones (Hammond, 2015). Our mood also affects what—and whether!—we remember (Zheng & Gardner, 2020), since chronic stress can inhibit memory formation. Think of a difficult-to-connect-with student. How many positive memories do they have at school? The repeated stacking of negative educational experiences inevitably impacts how students feel about school, the future, and themselves as a learner. These beliefs become deeply rooted in their limbic system, making it that much harder for us as teachers to build the self-concept of a learner who already believes they can't learn. Unfortunately, sometimes educators come to believe that too.

Additionally, those of us who are neurodivergent may experience *rejection sensitive dysphoria* (RSD), which makes dealing with perceived criticism and failures even more emotionally charged. I am guilty of coping with my own RSD by masking my difficulties and developing a perfectionism that drains me. I once had a boss say I was like a machine as a worker, doing twice the work in half the time. This level of productivity was not sustainable in the long run and is the reason why I crashed throughout high school and beyond after getting home each day. Until I started taking ADHD medication, I would get home from teaching and immediately crash, lying in bed in the dark, preferably with a cat to pet, for at least 30 minutes before I could summon the energy to do anything else! Let this be a cautionary reminder not to overlook students who appear on track and highly motivated. Considering what's fueling their success can tell you a great deal about their internal state and needs. It is hard to feel like an accepted part of a community when your nervous system is on overdrive, trying to fit in.

All this to say, for students to share with us when they are struggling and persevere when something feels hard, we need to create a classroom culture where our students can manage their feelings, be comfortably vulnerable, and feel supported to take learning risks. Their fundamental need for safety must be met. They need to feel that each member of the class is invaluable to the overall community, rather than in competition. Everyone is working on different things and in possession of unique expertise and positive qualities. Students and teachers alike can give advice and encouragement. Asking for help must be positioned as a strength, rather than as a deficit. So, how do we build this kind of a community?

Community building

There are endless ways to promote classroom community, and variations for all ages and stages. I'll focus on general principles. If Anthropology 101 taught me anything in university, it's that the hallmarks of society have much in common with a classroom community.

Community meetings and democracy in action

I think often about how, if we want students to see the value in participating in democracy, we have to give them opportunities to see it in action. You can collectively generate classroom values, which act as agreed-upon expectations for how we want to interact and problem-solve issues and which apply to teacher and student alike. I feverishly type student ideas while projecting it for the group to approve and refine until we have a list. In virtual classes, students make suggestions in the chat, which I later compile. In both cases, we review the compilation of values and expectations in a future session to see if we have any edits or additions before posting. Sometimes, teachers will do this as a "Our classroom feels like/sounds like/looks like" group brainstorm, or a list of things we try to do. I prefer positive phrasing of what to strive toward rather than a long list of do-nots, which has never in the history of the world inspired anybody positively but sure has planted a few ideas of how to disrupt things. (Case in point: My aunt Cindy lived in an old schoolhouse which had a big red emergency shut off button by the toilet. Considering my neurodivergent cousin Max's propensity for curiosity, Cindy realized she'd have more success at avoiding plumbing disasters with a sign reading "Thank you for leaving the button as is" rather than "DO NOT PUSH THE RED BUTTON!")

Now, before you think students are going to suggest silly or chaotic ideas, remember that we all love predictability. Be prepared to logically point out any possible concerns, and allow students the opportunity to weigh in. "My concern is, having a snack at any time might be a distraction to people around you. Does anyone have any thoughts about this and what might be reasonable?" The class can then test out the class norm for a bit and bring it up for review at a later community meeting. You can seek input or troubleshoot issues as they arise by posing questions to the class, such as:

- Do you want to have a choice of groupwork or independent work for this next project?
- The transition after lunch is taking too long—what are some of the barriers? What suggestions do members of the group have?

Don't be afraid to ask, "What do you think?" When students realize their voices shape your classroom, they will take this level of trust seriously. The solutions students can generate, individually and collectively, are often far more effective than our own suggestions. Inviting students to raise concerns will also give you a window into their priorities and experiences.

Rituals

Communities connect and strengthen existing bonds through shared rituals, such as specific ways of greeting one another. Sometimes, rituals evolve as an outcome of community meetings. One year, we had a "talking Lego car" that was passed around when people wanted to have the floor to speak. Other years, we manage fine without. Voluntary gratitude sharing could close community meetings. Rituals also can bring in sensory, emotional, and spiritual experiences together (Hammond, 2015). This might include daily or weekly events, such as a set time of day for a mindfulness practice, music, reading poetry, or other multimodal elements; prayers in a religious school; or even using a rainstick, rhythm or music patterns, or call-and-response to get student attention. These engagement methods work especially well for students from collectivist cultures (80% of the world), who have developed strong neural pathways which most efficiently process and learn through familiar cultural learning practices (Cozolino, 2013; Hammond, 2015). You could even ask the class for ideas of new class rituals!

My students love suggesting videos for short brain breaks and songs connected to class content, which I preview before playing. They enjoy starting the day with a seemingly silly "Would you rather...?" question to debate and have started suggesting their own! The time needed is minimal, and the payoff to group rapport, critical thinking, and expressive language skills has been exponential.

Art wall

I have a bulletin board devoted to student artwork. Students can post what they want, so long as the content is age-appropriate and won't get us in trouble with the principal. When needed, students curate the display, deciding what comes down to make space for a new exhibition. It becomes a beautiful visual record of our year as a classroom community and also of students' evolving talents.

Emotional awareness

Whether in a read-aloud, community meeting, or established check-in ritual, developing an awareness of one's own and others' feelings helps everyone. That said, it can be easier said than done for some of us. Many neurodivergent people experience alexithymia, where it is difficult to pinpoint internal experiences and identify emotions. I often work backwards, such as when I recognize my heart is racing. Did I drink too much coffee? No? Perhaps I'm anxious about something? Labeling feelings has been shown on brain-imaging tests to reduce the emotional intensity and restore functioning to the PFC, our logical thinking command center (Hammond, 2015). I do daily emotions check-ins with young students and adult learners alike! Whether it's a slide of images or gifs to choose from (like "How do you feel on a scale of panda?"), a magnet board where students move their own names under a particular feeling, or a list of wellbeing activities and a prompt of "What do you need this week?", check-ins send a message that you care about the whole student. It also gives you an idea of who to follow up with later to find out if you can offer support or reassure them it's okay to let something slide.

There are immeasurable benefits to improving these abilities, and lots of ways to open up the experience beyond words. Students could select from several well-selected gifs or images or find their own to best represent their feelings. They could paint a picture or select a song. Some alternative communicators may benefit from a tablet or other device with feeling words or picture cards and the necessary processing time. One of my neurodivergent graduate students shared an alternative and augmentative communication app called Leeloo that they sometimes use when words fail—because even the most eloquent of autistic people can find themselves at a loss for words. You can teach students what happens when we experience an AMY hijack.[2] Developing a somatic awareness of changes that happen as we move from a calm state to a dysregulated state gives us our best clues of when to use a strategy like taking deep breaths, getting a drink of water, going for a walk down the hall, taking a brain break to think about Minecraft, or whatever relaxing pursuit may work. It takes 10 seconds for stress hormones to take over the PFC, shutting down learning for 20 minutes and staying in the body for up to three hours (Hammond, 2015). The better we all get at recognizing a trigger and implementing a personal strategy, the more we can prevent complete dysregulation!

Sometimes, it's hard to self-reflect on big feelings. There is nothing quite as effective as finding a relatable read-aloud, which provides emotional distance when talking about the character's experience. Another benefit of learning through stories is our brains synchronize with one another; and regardless of whether we are listening or telling a story, our brains activate as though we are the main character (Hammond, 2015). You can prompt students for what advice they'd give a character, how they'd support them if they were their friend, and other questions that help develop empathy, perspective, and problem-solving skills through depersonalized conversations.

Mindfulness and moments of pause

I teach a smorgasbord of stress-relieving exercises: guided meditations, visualizations, affirmations, breathing exercises, physical stretching, running on the spot, body scans, loving kindness, sensory awareness activities, drawing an imaginary safe place, shared laughter, and more. There are so many studies touting the effects of mindfulness, such as: improved wellbeing, psychological, and medical outcomes; reduced stress; and prevention of burnout (Delahooke, 2019; Murphy, 2019). Mini-breaks also help learners to subconsciously consolidate learning (Oakley et al., 2021). I build in different breaks throughout the day so students can identify what works for them and can eventually use these as personal strategies to independently self-regulate. Variety is import-ant because not every strategy works for every person or allows them

---

2   See www.karadymond.com/resources/amy-hijack for ideas.

to access a state of calm. Learners with aphantasia, for instance, will likely prefer body scans and external anchors like their breathing when approaching somatic work rather than visualizations. As I learned from my mentor, Dr. Shelley Murphy (2019), it's important never to demand students close their eyes for any of these mindful moments but rather to invite them to lower their gaze or close their eyes if comfortable doing so. Some of our learners with activated attention systems may find it more stressful to let their guard down completely, which would be counterproductive to your aims.

My students create cards with their preferred strategies and the context in which these might be useful (e.g., school, during math, at home). They collect these in large ziplock bags labeled as their "personal strategies bag." Now brimming with strategies, these serve as a visual reminder of all the tools students have at their disposal. This is a step toward individual self-regulation and autonomy, which follows from creating a classroom culture where everyone can ask for and access what they need.

Varied groupings

You likely already have your own great ways of mixing and mingling students. You might do this initially to have students find common ground, like discussing interests. Especially at the start of term, you want students finding similarities and beginning to form that group identity. Some of my favorite methods I learned in teachers' college, such as forming fruit salads, by labeling each student as a fruit type (e.g., banana, apple, orange). Students circulate until they have made a salad comprising one of each type. When I adapt this, I might link it to a curricular unit, such as finding different planets, civilizations, or structures. You might have students walk around and form groups of a certain number, such as calling out "Four!" and students form a group of that size as quickly as possible and then discuss a specific prompt for two minutes. This can be a good way of activating background knowledge on a topic before a lesson or task.

I've also given students a large sticky note with a math problem. They had to solve their math problem and then find other students with the same answer (different equation). To compare opinions, it can be revelatory to have them stand on a line, either closer to one wall or the other, positioning themselves according to the strength of their conviction. For example, I've had graduate students stand in a line from "Inclusion is the best placement for all students" to "Inclusion is not the best placement for all students," which generated many discussions when we folded the line to find a partner to speak to. (This also makes a great pre- and post-assessment to see whether those opinions change after a lesson or unit!)

Value in teamwork

I show students a video on YouTube that shows two strangers at a train station who play a piano together. Their combined efforts create something unexpected, beautiful, and better than what one person could have created on their own. When we learn how to effectively work in a group, tasks can be completed more efficiently and with better outcomes when multiple ideas come to the table. We break down steps to groupwork: share ideas; weigh in on ideas; agree on what to do; make a plan to divide the work; and review all the components together.

My autistic students used to hate groupwork. I would give them challenges such as a turn-based building of a Lego structure, wordlessly, without correcting another player's contribution, adding one piece at a time. They would have to adjust their ideas and adapt to one another, filtering some of those immediate negative thoughts we all want to blurt sometimes when someone's idea conflicts with our own. Recently, a group pitched new rollercoaster designs to me (pretending to be a theme park CEO), coming up with a theme, drawing the ride, and presenting additional persuasive elements such as accessibility, safety, and marketing ideas. Then, they built one rollercoaster and surrounding park out of Lego and other objects in the class.

Teamwork challenges may include puzzles, brainteasers, or building purposeful structures. Think about all the ways you might be able to nurture the intellectual curiosity and strengths of the group while also necessitating—and reaping the benefits of!—working together.

Given that groupwork can be stressful, it's important to use it as a tool, occasionally, and at times optionally. Many autistic students dread groupwork because of prior negative experiences and just not knowing how to navigate it. We may have a great idea but not know how to perfectly express it and may take over to try to show what we mean. Autistic ways of directly communicating may rub others the wrong way, who take feedback personally if it isn't wrapped up in nice social packaging. So, opting out at times can reduce stress. However, anything that is harder and which we want to improve at does take practice, so I encourage students to join a group occasionally, and I help to form groups, so no one is left out. This is every neurodivergent student's worst nightmare. Trust me!

For success, you can structure groupwork; outline what the group is to accomplish during the time period; and teach mini-lessons on challenges that may come up, such as how to divide the work or problem-solve when there are many ideas. We always talk through what good groupwork looks like before students get to work, so everyone keeps their eye on the prize. You could try assigning roles and missions—even secret missions!—like: "Your job is to make sure everyone shares an idea" or "Your job is to check to make sure everyone knows their role" or customize roles to showcase student strengths and needs. Before and after, have students reflect on challenging and easy parts of groupwork and set personal goals and strategies for next time.

Affirming identities

We signal how everyone is expected and welcome in the books in our library, the materials we choose, and the images and videos we show in lessons. Aim to showcase the heterogeneity of humankind: ethnicities, socioeconomic status, gender and sexual diversity, neurodiversity, body shapes, abilities, and disabilities. These shouldn't be relegated to one day or month. This is where we start, but affirming continues through our interactions with each student. One of the best personal ways to affirm an individual student is by talking to them about what makes them tick. What are they passionate about? What do they dream of? How do they like to spend their time? When students know they are important to you, they see the classroom as a place where they enjoy being—and everything else follows.

We teach something whether we respond or choose not to respond to a thoughtless or targeted remark that may harm someone in or out of the class. When I overheard pre-teen autistic students using "gay" as an insult or negative tease, I knew I had to address it. I asked them how they felt whenever they've heard "autistic" as an insult. How might it feel for someone who is gay, or has family members who are gay, to hear their friends or classmates use that identifier in that way? Will they feel safe around those people? Often, young students haven't considered the meaning of the words and the possible impacts. (It can be confusing when some identifiers are bandied within groups but are not acceptable if you are not from that group. You might explain the origins of words, the history of marginalization, and efforts to reclaim words—or simply point out, as I did, the impact of using people's lived experiences as slurs and brainstorm other ways of expressing themselves.)

Interdependence

As members of a community, we rely on and support one another. Look for ways to highlight these important dimensions. You can preface requests with "Can you help me by…" and then thank them later (Dymond, 2020). Let students know when they've had a positive impact on you: "When I got home, I kept thinking about what a great class discussion we had yesterday" or "You all really inspired me!" You can also encourage interdependence between students by having them explain concepts to each other, problem-solve together, develop a study guide, or identify unanswered questions they'd like to review as a whole class. You can have a class expertise wall, where students identify if they are comfortable being approached for help in a particular subject or topic area.

Students who don't easily identify personal strengths may need you to point out that they are an expert with tech or they are someone who is a good listener to their friends (which may be easier to absorb in a very private format, such as written down rather than said out loud in front of others). Some students who are not used to positive feedback may resist it. Keep at it. You might bring those defenses down more easily by asking for them to help with novel tasks like unlocking the classroom door or running something to the office, giving them the trust that few adults probably do and thanking them (Dymond, 2020), rather than compliments. I am a bit of a broken record saying how it's as much a strength to offer help to someone else as to ask for help!

Honor different ways of being and doing

When I think about identity-affirming classrooms, it's less about cultural food days and token nods to group differences, and more about connecting to each individual, in all their humanness. I know I didn't always do a great job of this in the beginning of my career. It was hard for me to understand life or learning experiences vastly different from my own. I, like many teachers, did well in school and usually enjoyed it. As I listen and learn from students, I've become more understanding and patient. I've realized the boon my exceptional memory has been to my schooling—an advantage not afforded to everyone. Now, I get curious about learning differences, engaging them in dialogue about what comes easily or harder to them. I try to approach this in a value-neutral way (Chapman, 2020), so that students don't come to feel less than or stigmatized when they admit some things feel harder. Some things are easier, some things are harder, and that's part of being human. From there, we can work together to find strategies and supports that help. These moments are invitations to look inward and ask: Are my expectations neurodivergent-friendly? Are they necessary, fair, and achievable by everyone—or is there room for any other possible way?

Dispel the myth of "normal"

As early as day one, I begin conversations about neurodiversity. We talk about how all brains are different, though sometimes we group brains under labels when they have more similarities, called *neurotypes*. We review various terms like (so-called) neurotypical, autistic, ADHD, gifted, anxious, dyslexic, dysgraphic, dyspraxic, and more. With younger students, I focus on strengths before expanding to developing areas and barriers. We talk about how each person's brain lights up in response to different topics and activities. The more time we spend learning or practicing, the stronger our neural pathways become. As our brains strengthen this wiring, it requires less effort to do those things, becoming automatic over time. Our hobbies and fascinations literally change the structures of our brains. You could say all brains are custom-made and specialized, regardless of neurotype!

Students then chart out brain strengths in a bar graph; cut and paste labels or pictures of their brain strengths onto pre-drawn brain reproducibles; or make models with strengths represented as various colors of clay. This year, we made 3-D representations using a jumble of pipe cleaners and a legend to show which color strands represented which areas of expertise! We create a wall to showcase our collective knowledge and talents. THERE IS NO NORMAL!

Appreciation for similarities and differences

To get students relating over interests, we do a whole lesson on interests as self-regulatory tools, where students ask each other what activities make them feel relaxed and happy, what could help them flip their mood if they were feeling upset, and similar prompts. We talk about how our brains are so powerful that even just thinking about our passions can have a similar effect to engaging in them.

What's harder for your brain?

Just like every brain has its own unique strengths, we all have things we are working on, or that are harder for us. Depending on the group, I might use an analogy. For video gamers or tabletop role-playing game students, it's a bit like leveling up a character. You make choices that strengthen your abilities in some areas, and other areas aren't as well developed. (You could go so far as to talk about how Dungeons & Dragons parties are successful based on having all sorts of brains and abilities, just like this classroom...) I'll share my own specific challenges, like being disorganized and losing my keys or glasses—even finding them in weird spots like the refrigerator. There are times I can be very forgetful. Strategies I use include making lists on my phone, so there's less to keep in mind, and asking students to remind me of something.

Then we brainstorm, and I write down some common difficulties that may happen in school, such as having a hard time understanding math, reading but not retaining the information, forgetting verbal instructions, having difficulty seeing the blackboard, or feeling abject terror at the thought of a class presentation. Beside these, we record tools that could help, such as: calculators and math manipulatives; using assistive technology to read text out loud; written lists or exemplars; glasses; pre-recording a presentation or presenting just to the teacher or a small group. We talk about how it's absolutely okay for students to access different tools, because we all have different needs. After we've discussed depersonalized examples and it has been made abundantly clear we all have things that are harder for us, students often volunteer sharing personal examples. (I never force whole-class participation and will have students let me know a couple of examples privately in a ticket out the door or journal.)

Culture of learners

Knowing the impact we teachers can have, it's important we use it to gently challenge learners to challenge themselves and take on greater independence in their learning. It's important for all students to know that learning something new can feel overwhelming or impossible at times. Zaretta Hammond (2015) recommends teaching students about "the learning pit"—the proverbial cliff we fall off when confronted by a difficult concept. Ultimately, we have to problem-solve our way out of it, until we emerge, emboldened by new knowledge and experiences. This pit is characterized by "productive struggle" and triggers an AMY hijack. We have to help them keep their cool, believing they can and will learn. Hammond suggests four core values that make up an academic mindset:

- I belong to this academic community.
- I can succeed at this.
- My ability and competence grow with my effort.
- This work has value to me.

As I say to my students, we are allowed to be learners. We are allowed to try and trip up. Our limbic brakes don't need to kick in when we encounter new information. As students develop their academic mindsets, they tend to take more chances, work harder, and persevere when something feels hard (Hammond, 2015). A lot of this modeling comes from you demonstrating that you are learning and growing all the time. We are all works in progress! I teach mini-lessons based on all of the brain information in this book, so learners understand what is going on for them.

Perfectionism

Perfectionism is a wild stallion, ready to buck off any attempts of taming it. It takes a long time to calm an activated nervous system, stallion or otherwise. Emphasizing learning as a process can help remove heightened emotions. Break down due dates and build in feedback checks as part of assignments. Think about how and when to use a flexible turn-in policy. Talk about how mistakes are learning opportunities. Top athletes learn more from analyzing how a play went wrong than from winning. We can improve if we use mistakes as feedback and come to understand where we went wrong. Get curious!

There can also be a creative value in mistakes. Better ideas can emerge, like masterly artworks that wouldn't have been possible without some cognitive flexibility. Your own response to making a mistake in front of the class can also help to set the tone. Laugh it off! Teach how we approach hard things and how these feelings come up in everyone—but we get to the other side. There is always more than one way of doing things! I like to tell students how something I was most afraid of trying ended up being one of the most rewarding. Once while I was traveling with a friend and her siblings in France, an opportunity to kayak for three and a half hours down a river presented itself. I'm pretty far from athletic and wasn't sure I'd be able to. In fact, I was downright certain. (I've had this feeling of limbic brakes kicking in many times before, even stopping riding a bike once my dad took off the training wheels. "Why would I put myself through that?!" 5-year-old me insisted!) This time, in adulthood, with some positive peer pressure, I grudgingly agreed. I survived—even if it left me popping ibuprofen for the rest of the week. It was glorious and gorgeous, looking up at sandy cliffs and gliding past picturesque villages. It has become a reference point to try other new experiences which trigger that initial buck and whinny.

Learning on display

You may want to designate a learning gallery wall or bulletin board where students post work they want on display. We also want to be intentional about honoring effort. Perhaps put up photos of class learning and shared experiences, especially when students are trying something new, on a field trip adventure, or deep in scientific inquiry. Have a Wonder Wall, where the group posts research questions and queries we can't answer—yet! You could assign student researchers or invite them to volunteer to bring answers to community meetings, if they so wish.

Show grace as they grow

Sometimes, assignments will be late. Homework will be incomplete. Executive functioning issues can get in the way and are usually a sign that the student is struggling with something. Students encounter different barriers with different tasks. What is easy for one may be dauntingly incomprehensible for another. Not everyone has the same memories, background knowledge, access to help at home, etc. I take a deep breath and remember they're still learning. I don't expect perfection (and hopefully they don't expect it of me). Help them break it down if the sum of its parts is too big a task. Manageable bites, and more frequent check-ins! A balance of accountability and flexibility sends the message that they are more important to you than homework, though of course you care and will need to problem-solve if the homework is never done. If you must have homework?

Accessibility tool of the day or week

A few years ago, I decided to teach various accessibility tools and encourage students to test them out and see what resonates. I taught the same tools at the elementary level as at the graduate level, in my courses for students studying to become teachers. Without fail, in every class, at least one student would thank me for teaching them about text-to-speech readers because they could better retain the information of a text when they heard it read and read along. This was a huge learning experience for me, as I realized how many people get by, passing grade to grade, without realizing why school feels hard for them and what can make it easier. You could say it inspired this book. Teaching accessibility tools to everyone helps each person discover new aspects of their learning. It normalizes that everyone can use the tools and strategies they need; whether to help them face challenges, self-regulate, or access content. Some tools:

- speech-to-text recorders
- text-to-speech readers
- Bionic Reading font
- brown noise (or other types of noise and soundtracks)
- the Pomodoro Technique
- coloring sheets or playdough during a lesson.

There are so many possible tools, and we are only limited by our creativity! We have ongoing candid conversations about what things help us and in what situations. I love those lightbulb moments when students realize something really works for their brain. These can often inspire new class norms. Is it fair to expect everyone to do this in the same way? Is there any other possible way? It presents the chance to explain differences that exist in needs and supports. I will never insist on eye contact or whole-body listening the way it was taught to me, now that I know that many neurodivergent folks find eye contact distressing and painful. Can I encourage them to look toward the front at the board or projection area? Absolutely. Can they advocate that they listen better while coloring? Absolutely. Everything evolves in conversation with students. As my wise friend and co-researcher in accessible education Dr. Kathy Broad says, "Students teach us how they need to be taught."

Student voice

As learners get in touch with their needs, it becomes easier to self-advocate. If our goal is to create independent but also interdependent learners who tell us when they encounter barriers and who ask for help when they need it, we have to give them that chance to give us feedback! We can invite our students—collectively in a community meeting, or individually—to suggest ideas to make our class more accessible. I try not to swoop in to solve a student's problem unless they are truly at a loss to generate solutions. I want them to feel their voices are important and are capable of making change. Working in partnership has the additional benefit of reducing our cognitive load, as students are the ones suggesting strategies or tools. I've learned so much about good teaching from what individual students have told me!

Student choice

Offer choices when you can. When I was in grade 8 (ages 13-14), my teacher used choice in powerful ways. When the class was reading *Animal Farm*, I was assigned *1984*. For both the book report and a math project, we rotated through stations and picked subtasks to complete. He had ranked tasks according to challenge, and we had to add up to a certain number. We could complete two Level 3 tasks, six Level 1 tasks, or a combination of tasks adding up to 6 points. Being able to choose what tasks you wanted to do meant we had a vested interest. The level of challenge felt right. He would also encourage students to sometimes pick a harder task and see how it goes. Choices in your classroom may include:

- what to read
- which prompt to respond to
- how to respond (oral, typed, written, art, video, etc.) in assigned work
- how to participate (orally, with a nonverbal cue, typing, using a whiteboard, writing down questions and thoughts to show you later, etc.)
- graphic organizer style
- format of assignment

- who to work with/sit with
- what to do when done work
- what to research (those of us with interest-based attentions do so much better with self-directed learning when we are interested!)
- how to present their knowledge (presentation, video, slides with audio; privately, whole class, or in a small group).

This level of flexibility may sound scary—and it's okay if it is. Just recognize that we tend to clamp down and control more in the classroom when our teacher nervous systems are activated (Cozolino, 2013; Faith et al., 2022). Like us, students feel greater safety and engagement when they have a modicum of control. From there, we can coach students to try something different and expand their comfort zone and skills in time. Studies on children with ADHD show they do so much better in classrooms where they are afforded a sense of agency and flexibility and have a teacher who is willing to adapt the environment for individual needs (Barkley, 2020; Gallichan & Curle, 2008). This approach also leads to greater self-concept. So, wherever possible, give kids a chance to make their own choices. Their lives are managed in so many ways.

Build in metacognition—for everyone

We want to get students reflecting. Studies show *metacognition* (thinking about our thinking) doesn't just happen and has to be deliberately activated (Fleming, 2014; Gardner et al., 2016). If giving them a choice, ask learners how it went, if that choice worked for them, and what they learned about their own learning. Have them set regular goals and provide you with feedback about where they are at. This is also an opportunity to teach them to show themselves grace and give themselves a break if they tend to be hard on themselves.

Everything is a learning opportunity, and students are your partners

I turn to students to help me solve problems, knowing that they will benefit far more from exercising the critical thinking, perspective-taking, communication, and flexibility skills required to work through a situation. Recently, half of the small group class I was teaching was unexpectedly absent—and on a day I was planning to introduce a new topic. I asked students what they wanted to learn, and we planned a new day together. Part of the time, they worked as a team to build a bridge out of blocks. They became engineers together, problem-solving as it didn't line up or support how they wished. The result was stunning!

Solicit feedback in various ways

Invite their opinions and questions, privately and in any way which works for them (written, typed, spoken, drawn, etc.). This could be an anonymous questions bag, a daily journal, or a ticket out the door with a thoughtful question or two. This is how you discover their goals, their worries, and their fascinations. You can ask them for feedback on how you're supporting their learning. You can ask fun prompts, like what rule they might create if they were in charge of the world. Always respond, because students of all ages like to know their ideas are being appreciated and engaged with. I use voice notes to respond to graduate students, which imbues my messages with my personality and allows it to feel more conversational. You can prompt general sharing, such as, "Is there anything you'd like me to know?" When students start to spontaneously share glimpses into their life, like they just got back into crocheting or they are celebrating their birthday over the weekend, you know a rapport is developing!

Make your classroom a place where their ideas have impact

What do they want to learn? What do they think would be fun to do as a class? What suggestions do they have for your classroom to run more smoothly and for lessons to be more enjoyable? We are modeling how to take and use feedback, too, which can also help with the per-fectionism piece! You could come back to the group and address the suggestions: "Okay, I heard you and adjusted..." When a suggestion is not feasible, you can explain why, which gives them your perspec-tive and also shows them that you listened in the first place, even if you made a different choice. When they see their feedback is valued, it reinforces that the classroom belongs to everyone, and everyone belongs in the classroom.

Reflect each day or week on your lessons

What worked? What didn't? Which of your expectations limited cer-tain students? What changes would you make for next time? What did you notice about certain students? You may want to keep notes of observations, gratitudes, and thoughts that occur to you throughout the day.

The goal is self-advocacy. Here are some fantastic practical examples from Megann Roberts of how to help students self-advocate in your classroom.

INSIDER'S PERSPECTIVE

Megann Roberts, Special Education Resource Teacher, learning disability and ADHD

I find that placing visuals to support student needs on all desks is an effective way to support every learner in my class. For example, I've co-created a table of behaviors (unexpected and expected) with some prompts to encourage self-advocacy at the bottom. The Unexpected column held ideas such as "farting" and "yelling during lessons," while the expected columns held ideas such as "asking for help" and "letting the teacher monitor other people's choices." The prompts at the bottom included "When you are _____ (e.g., humming), it's hard for me to _____ (e.g., focus on my work). Can you please _____ (e.g., stop or work a bit further away)?" I then taped the table to each student's learning space using book tape, to encourage continued growth in self-advocacy between students.

To encourage self-advocacy for students and educators, I worked with my students to create posters with a self-portrait at the top, and three columns below the portrait. The sections "I...," "So...," and "Then..." were filled with jot notes about themselves and how educators (me, their French teacher, etc.) can best meet their learning needs. The "I..." column was populated with details of their learning style (e.g., learn by watching videos and people showing me; learn by having opportunities to do hands-on activities). The "So..." column detailed how they can set themselves up for success (e.g., need to sit near the front of the room so I can easily see what the educator is showing on the document camera; it's helpful to wear headphones so I can hear the video clearly; having 10 minutes of "exploration" time helps me get used to the hands-on materials). The "Then..." column provided helpful information, with tips on how educators could best support their achievement (e.g., remind the class to check out the video linked in our online classroom; point out the new poster on the chart stand; set a visual timer so I don't lose track of time).

Good prompts at the beginning of the year

- "How are you most comfortable participating in class? How do you like to 'show what you know'?"
- "How are you most comfortable communicating with me if you need my help? (Reminder: Everyone needs help and asking for feedback is a strength!)"
- "What does good listening look like for you? What helps you to learn your best?"
- "What do you want to get better at this year? What do you hope we will learn about?"
- "What types of lessons grab your attention? What types of lessons do you find boring or more of a challenge?"
- "What are your favorite topics to think and learn about?"
- "Can you remember any lessons or activities in your past that got you really excited? What was it that excited you?"
- "What strategies help you when you are feeling upset at school? What do you need from me at these times?"
- "Is there anything you would like me to do differently? How can I best support your learning?"
- "Is there anything you would like to share with me?"

Conclusion

So, there you have it—you've just read a chapter brimming with everything you didn't realize you needed to know or think about to support students to feel a part of things and to build physical, emotional, and relational safety. This is fundamental to teaching, and where we must start.

CHAPTER 1 HIGHLIGHTS

✓ The interconnectedness of safety and learning and the impact of stress on the brain and body.

✓ With careful attention to the environment in our classroom, the types of challenges we present, and the relationships we build with students, between students, and between each student and themselves, we can help students to grow their brains and change their relationship to the world around them.

✓ Considerations for physical layout.

✓ Tips for creating predictable routines—and which routines to create.

✓ We learn better from people we like. Ways to foster positive rapport and relational safety.

✓ How to dispel the idea of "normal," build appreciation of similar and different strengths and weaknesses, and normalize accessing help and supports for everyone.

✓ Metacognition ("thinking about thinking") has to be activated in students and is the first step to self-advocacy. Make sure you are using your own metacognition too.

Questions for the reader:

✓ In what ways do you foster a neurodiversity-affirming environment?

✓ What is one addition you may incorporate to what you already do well? (Don't overwhelm yourself—allow change to be gradual.)

✓ What is one practice you might discard or adapt?

✓ What do your students value about you and your classroom?

How We Absorb Information

Input, Communication, and Processing

Maybe it's telling, but when I think of my own primary and secondary education, desk rows and a teacher modeling grammar or a math problem at the blackboard comes to mind. This kind of learning relies on our declarative memory system, which transfers facts and event-based knowledge from our working memory to our hippocampus, to eventually—hopefully!—our long-term memory (Oakley et al., 2021). Although this is not the only way we learn, the conscious channels most often required at school are what we delve into in this chapter.

At its simplest, information processing is how we make sense of and remember information we take in via our senses. School tends to emphasize learning by listening, reading, and seeing, which works all right for processors who easily take in information delivered via those mediums. This chapter will give an overview of information processing and then focus on the input and communication preferences of various learners so we as teachers can enhance how we communicate, while the next chapter will go more in-depth on working and long-term memory, attention, and cognitive load in the classroom—and how to help learners learn more effectively.

As learners, we have preferences for how we process information, which may vary based on the topic or activity. For instance, if you were to sit down with some friends to play a new and complicated board game, you might be the person who needs to read all the rules through from start to finish before anyone even thinks of touching the board.

Or you might prefer that someone explains the rules to you. Maybe you repeat those instructions out loud to get them to stick. Perhaps you're the kind of person who just wants to play the game and be told information as you need to know it, since it's too overwhelming to keep all the game mechanics in your head.

Since I started teaching, students have shared many insights into how they best process information, and it's helped me to make easy adaptations that are now second nature to my classroom instruction. Take, for instance, small access points I've built into the seemingly simple task of playing a short video for the class. Amidst the hundreds of students I've taught, a few had diagnosed hearing impairments that necessitated certain adaptations for playing videos. I always made a conscious effort to play captions when they were in my class, but I generally neglected this strategy when there wasn't an obvious need. That was a serious oversight, I came to learn. Maybe a decade ago, a highly chatty student who was active in all our discussion-based learning explained they have difficulty understanding videos without captions (likely an undiagnosed auditory-processing difference). I was gobsmacked, as I'd never picked up on any needs in this area! (Students themselves may be unaware of their own needs, given how inaccessible assessments can be.) It was a good reminder that you can't always tell who needs what; so, I now ensure all videos have captions enabled, because you just never know who might benefit.

Now, because teaching is complicated, you may have other students who feel a bit distracted by the movement and brightness of captions. There is some research that having identical text to auditory narration, along with another visual source, like animation, may create extra cognitive load because there are three sources to process. Two visual streams may cancel each other out, so the person splits attention trying to process both text and images, and each overwrites the other, so the person doesn't remember as well in general. Similarly, when auditory information is identical to visually presented information, it can take more effort to process the same information twice (as explained in Zheng & Gardner, 2020). I've found changing the color to a grey or more muted shade is less jarring for other students, and, more importantly, everyone can access what we're learning.

Another intentional strategy I use when showing videos came out of learning about different attention systems (which we'll get to in greater detail in the next chapter). To guide attention to what's relevant, it's helpful to prime students before watching a video. We might tap into existing background knowledge with a pre-discussion on the themes of the video. We might hypothesize what we'll see in the video, based on the title, the cover, or what we've been learning about. Before I hit play, I give students a cognitive framework for their attention by letting them know a question or two we will discuss after the video. I also display the question and review it orally, so they can process the information through multiple channels and so there is no need to take up precious working memory by storing the question. Clipboards are available to students to access as they wish if they want to write down or draw their thoughts, so they don't forget what they want to say. After the video, I'll repeat the first question and give processing time—at least 30 seconds—before asking for an answer. I let them know how everyone processes at different speeds, so I don't just take the fastest raised hand; rather, I want to hear from everyone in the room and give them what they need to be able to participate. Sometimes, students will discuss the question first in partnerships or groups.

Just as I get curious about students' learning, I am often introspective about how my own brain works best. I now use captions for personal use, after recognizing my own auditory-processing differences in loud, noisy, or chaotic environments. Suffice to say, it really does benefit more than just the people who need it, as I am no longer completely in the dark and annoying my partner for clarification every 30 seconds when watching highly complex shows with lots of characters, fast-paced action shots and scene changes, and entire universes of unfamiliar place names. (I'm talking about you, *Game of Thrones!*) I invite you to interrogate your own learning throughout this book, which may inspire some candid conversations in your classroom with students around how your brain works, too.

As a teacher, I don't necessarily need to know the ins and outs of all the processing differences present in my classroom, but knowing some common experiences can help me meet needs from the outset, even without knowing who specifically needs what! Still, it is helpful to have some rudimentary insights into how learners generally learn, just as it's helpful to glean some insights into potential processing differences. This chapter will aim to illuminate the most significant aspects for teachers to understand about information processing.

Nerd alert: Brain basics related to information processing

Information processing is made of many complex processes. Since I am not a neuroscientist (and I suspect you are not, either), I'll present a rudimentary explanation of how information processing works: when you are exposed to new information, your brain makes very quick decisions about whether this is important information. If you don't need it, you forget it. If you need it very briefly, you might rehearse it or try to memorize it, and you'll forget it shortly later. If you need to remember it, you'll have to do some work to make meaning out of it and call it to mind over time for it to really stick.

Psychologists consider there to be various sensory memory inputs, the most studied of which are visual sensory memory, which processes things like movement, color, and orientation, and auditory sensory memory, which processes sounds (Zheng & Gardner, 2020). According to Zheng and Gardner, memory of sensory input that is not being consciously held in mind fades away quickly—a quarter of a second for visual input, and at least eight times longer for auditory input. Think of this as all the sights that pass you by on your drive home. If there is no reason to attend to it, and your nervous system isn't on alert, you likely won't take note of the order of stores, the faces of people walking by, the color and make of all the cars you pass.

Now, if your engine starts to make an unexpected noise, you'll take note. My car is making a sound—is there a problem? This is akin to using *short-term memory*, which is when you have to briefly think about the information. You may then begin to question the sound (it sounds like a garbage disposal!), and you begin to try to make some meaning out of the sensory input. You decide to follow up with a mechanic tomorrow and aim to form a description of the sound, when it occurs, and any other relevant factors. Here, you are utilizing *working memory*. Working memory kicks in whenever we are holding information in mind and trying to use it in some way.

Not everything that we hold in our working memory sticks around forever. Let's say you decide to pull over. You look out the window and, lo and behold, the telephone pole right next to you advertises the phone number for a local mechanic. You decide to call them, but you don't intend to memorize their digits (unless you're intent on becoming their best customer). You have to use your working memory to take that phone number (visual input) on a sign and type it into your phone (not to mention, remembering why you're calling in the first place!). What strategies do you use? Interestingly, studies have shown that people often convert that visual input to auditory input by repeating it out loud or in their head, if they're able to imagine sounds. Similarly, if we're trying to retain information relayed to us orally, folks who can visualize in their imaginations may convert the information to visuals in order to remember better or write it down so it's also processed as a visual (Zheng & Gardner, 2020).

What if it's information we want to remember for longer? On a brain-based level, when we think, electrical and neurochemical signals are sent between neurons (through the empty space called synapses). Your brain encodes the neurons used to communicate that thought or action. The neurons activated begin to connect, via spiny finger-like appendages called dendrites which reach out to connect to axons of other neurons, the thin fibers that transmit electrical impulses, almost as if hungry for knowledge. The more we think about or practice something newly learned, the stronger the connection between those neurons becomes. If you want that new learning to stick, you have to revisit that information. It stays in your short-term memory for up to 10 seconds, whereas if you are actively engaging with this information, your working memory holds this for up to 20 minutes (Hammond, 2015), depending on age and how you are working with this information. (We will talk a bit more about this in the classroom context in the next chapter.)

Maybe you still remember your childhood phone number, or the phone number of your grandparents or childhood bestie because of calling them so often and having to keep the digits in mind to dial them. In the age of cell phones, we rarely remember phone numbers since we skip the working memory step! If we want to deeply learn and remember information in *long-term memory*, we have to practice or actively engage with it (especially within the first 24 to 48 hours), link it to what we already know, and repeatedly retrieve our increasing understanding until we've formed a strong neural pathway that makes it accessible to us whenever we think of the concept (Hammond, 2015; Oakley et al., 2021). Through intentional practice and retrieval, those connected neurons develop a fatty coating, myelin, that makes their communication even more efficient, strengthening the neural pathway.

Depending on the complexity of the learned information, deep learning may build a superhighway between different areas of the brain! Essentially, the more you practice riding that bike or doing long division, the easier those tasks become and the less you have to think about them. In fact, when we really know our stuff, it's entirely automatic and doesn't take much cognitive effort! However, if you're like me and you gave up trying to learn to ride a bike when your dad took off the training wheels, or you simply never mastered long division, these actions are not automatic, and attempts would take considerable cognitive effort. I'd be an overthinking mess, struggling to coordinate the sequence of steps because any of those new dendrites formed in the initial learning stages as a child were pruned as a result of avoiding bikes and math for 30-odd years. Good news for me: If I want to learn those things, it's never too late, at least in theory. As far as anyone can tell, our learning capacity is virtually endless, and relearning something is easier and faster that second time around (Hammond, 2015; Oakley et al., 2021; Zheng & Gardner, 2020).

One of the most interesting things to me about how we process—and what we remember—is how we conceptualize what we've learned. How does your mind think? We all vary in our minds' abilities to spontaneously call up visual, auditory, or other sensory information, either from memory or when imagining some new scenario. I've learned from many curious conversations that not everyone "sees" images in their minds as they read. Not everyone hears *Bohemian Rhapsody* in their head when they hear someone say, "poor boy" or "Galileo." (If you're like me, I don't apologize for planting that earworm—it's a brilliant song!) Not everyone can imagine how adding a spice to a dish will change the taste. And I cannot effortlessly imagine what an apartment will look like with different furniture or colors. So, why is this important to know? We are so limited by our own experiences. It is easy to assume that how our mind works is how everyone's mind works, but it is simply not the case.

Processing needs of various learners

Activated attention systems
If you think about it, so much of our earliest learning is unconscious and automatic, building our neural connections as we watch others. When we watch someone doing something purposeful, whether it's tying their shoes or reading us a story, mirror neurons activate areas

in our brains in a similar pattern to the other person's brain activation (Hammond, 2015). We yawn when they yawn; our tongues activate, listening to them speak; and we attune our emotions to theirs (Cozolino, 2013). Evolutionarily speaking, we are biologically primed to watch and learn, and our earliest cultural learnings reflect this.

Some of us have a harder time attending to the actions and ideas that convey cultural meaning. We may need to be directly told where to look or why something is meaningful. Communicating effectively with learners begins with getting their attention. Some students may find it easy to direct their attention where you want, while others may be focused elsewhere. Some students may be distracted by their own thoughts or imaginations, especially if they have *hyperphantasia* and experience thoughts as lifelike sensory imagery, while others may be distracted by external stimuli. Learners who have experienced *trauma*, who have *anxiety*, or who have *sensory-processing differences* may be rapid scanners, noticing all the stimuli everyone else seems to be able to tune out like white noise. It can be extremely difficult to focus where a teacher wants when you're highly sensitive and observant, noticing every sound, smell, lighting flicker, breeze, temperature change, visual distraction, the overwhelming colors on the bulletin boards, and more. It's important to note that these learners can be incredible out-of-the-box thinkers, noticing patterns and details others don't. Most of us have experienced temporary upward surges of anxiety at various times—trying to get back to sleep in the middle of the night, or in a large examination hall, when we're about to give a speech on stage—where we suddenly notice every sound, internal sensation, sideways glance, ticking clock, or you name it. For some students, overburdened processing is their usual state, significantly diminishing their cognitive capacity to focus on your lesson. As we learned in the last chapter, they may need support to calm their nervous systems before anything else.

If you do grab their attention, your students' ability to keep thoughts on the topic are also variable. Learners with *executive functioning difficulties* (which may come along with learning disabilities, ADHD, autism, traumatic brain injuries, trauma, long Covid, and more) may have reduced working memory capacity, making it hard to sustain attention and get the gist of what's important (to you). They may find it easier to do more challenging work in the mornings, so if you have control over your schedule, consider building these subjects or tasks in earlier in the day.

It may also seem counterintuitive, but some of us need an extra channel of information to process if you want us to focus (Barkley, 2020). In meetings and presentations, I am a pen-clicking leg jiggler, which helps my body stay activated enough to listen. I can't seem to ever get through a podcast without falling asleep or zoning out, unless I'm driving or cooking. I'm less prone to being distracted in these motor tasks when I also have something to listen to. In dividing my attention between the words and the actions, I seem to be able to tune out all the bits which other people's minds filter automatically, which normally jump out at me. I don't get thrown by the bird flying by, the sensation of the wind, the billboards and bus advertisements—or by all the other tasks I see needing to be done in the kitchen (I'm talking about you, dishes!).

Conversely, there are times I may need to cut out channels of information, depending on the amounts of stimuli I need to process. Recently, I was driving at night, and it started to thunder and rain so heavily it sounded like banging on the roof of the car. The wipers were going back and forth, the water obscuring my vision for a fleeting moment between wipes. The headlights from other cars were like shocks to my brain, compounded by the reflection of lines painted over and repainted, which made it more difficult to discern where my lane began and ended. To focus, I had to turn off the radio and air conditioning and ask my passenger (politely) to be quiet. There was only so much I could process! Fortunately, I know my cues of when I'm overstimulated and I'm able to make choices to support my information processing. Often, our students don't know theirs yet. This is where teaching the use and experimentation of a variety of listening tools such as coloring sheets, fidget tools, and purposeful movement in your classroom may come into play (see Chapter 1 for some suggestions in implementation). A creative and intuitive teacher, Amy, shares a window into information processing in her classroom.

INSIDER'S PERSPECTIVE

Amy Craze, Elementary (Primary) School Teacher

I believe that to support information processing in our most neurodivergent learners, it is vital that we see the whole student. We need to be keen observers who are in tune with the strengths and needs of each student and, more importantly, what drives and ignites a spark of curiosity within them. Only upon doing this will we have the tools to provide a hook for their learning and carve out their individual next steps. I have found that some of my most interesting and neurodivergent learners have restricted interests and that it is challenging to maintain their attention unless the tasks they are given directly pertains to them. When these interests are awakened, however, I have seen a hyperfocus that can emerge, attention and retention of details I never thought possible. As educators, why are we not using these vested interests to push each student to meet new learning goals?

I am reminded about one incredible student I worked with years ago who is an autistic ADHDer. Teachers had warned me that this student spent the majority of the day wrapped in their own thoughts and refused to participate in group lessons or produce work. Throughout that first month, I ensured I embedded time in my program each day for free exploration, inquiry, and play. I watched, listened, and waited for my opportunity to find an in with this student, and one day the opportunity presented itself. During our inquiry period, this student came up to me and boldly stated that they would like to go on a field trip to Colombia because they'd heard they had buried treasure there. I knew then I had found my hook.

During our inquiry period over the next few months, I collaborated closely with the student on planning an imaginary journey to Colombia. Together, we engaged in procedural writing to draft permission forms and compile a comprehensive checklist for our departure. We applied number sense by meticulously budgeting for our trip, tackling various challenges, such as equitable treasure distribution. Exploring time zones and journey durations, we plotted our route and printed maps, while delving into geometry and simple machines through the design and construction of a 3-D model of our transportation vehicle. As we worked, they internalized and shared every detail of our planning and research with the other students. Their working memory was supported because it was relevant to them. This experience highlighted for me how important it is not to try to fit a student into a curriculum but rather to wrap the curriculum around their interests. We can support information processing for all students if we draw from their curiosity and carefully craft their next steps in a way that is meaningful to them.

Students with ADHD or who are autistic often have interest-based attention systems, easily activating when the topic is appealing and struggling to switch, painfully even, when the topic is not. This is called *monotropism*, a theory developed by Murray, Lesser, and Lawson (2005) to explain the neurodivergent ability to become fully absorbed for extended periods of time by the things that fascinate us, which can be to the exclusion of noticing anything else—needing to eat, drink, go to the bathroom, or get up and move. When we enter this kind of flow state, the things that would normally distract us can seem to vanish. I won't always hear someone talking to me when I'm hyperfocused, while at other times these interruptions stop me being able to focus. It all depends on how absorbed I am! While other people's brains can transition easily even when a topic isn't of interest, it can become distressing to shift away from what I'm finally excited about. Some lucky monotropists have interests that align with school, so they may never appear to struggle or be identified as having any brain variation or needs.

Even our culture and upbringing shape how our attention and processing function. Hammond (2015) describes how brains of children from collectivist cultures are primed to understand new learning much more efficiently when it is relayed through storytelling, call-and-response, song and dance, rhythmic clapping, and so on.

Students whose brains are wired in these ways won't find it as easy to open their books and pay attention for rote, sage-on-the-stage kinds of delivery (though I think we're all coming to realize this form of instruction doesn't work too well for most). Given that 80% of world cultures are considered collectivist (Hammond, 2015), this suggests we can significantly increase classroom engagement when we consciously plan to use some of these culturally responsive techniques! Here are some of the best strategies to employ to help these learners:

- play to learners' strengths
- tap into interests
- add novelty
- provide a challenge or puzzle to solve
- appeal to emotions
- highlight relevance and what's important
- introduce exercise breaks
- practice mindfulness to develop sustained attention and calm activated nervous systems
- allow fidget tools
- use information-processing pathways already well established in their brains to cue attention.

You'll want to provide both sensory-reduced spaces and selectively use the excitement-inducing factors of video, color, cool fonts, dramatic lesson hooks, gestures and whole-class movement, and anything else you might think of to get those neurons excited!

Alternative communicators

There are a variety of reasons students may communicate differently. In the alternative communicator category, you may encounter students who are nonspeakers, or those who occasionally find spoken communication to be a barrier and who express themselves in other ways besides mouth words. Many autistic people who appear to communicate verbally with ease have times when they are unable to speak, especially when overwhelmed. Other neurodivergent factors to consider will be discussed below. Even without a specific diagnosis, students may have a preference to express themselves through gesture, text, image selection, artistic responses, and more.

Apraxia is a condition that makes it difficult to coordinate on demand, to speak, or perform motor tasks. This can occur in both autistic and non-autistic people and with or without an intellectual disability. There is a wonderful documentary called *Spellers* that gives a glimpse into the lives and hopes of nonspeakers with apraxia.[1]

Anxiety and additional stressors can influence how comfortable a

---

1   www.youtube.com/watch?v=8h1rcLyznKo

person feels speaking. Some folks may speak at some times but not others.

Other students may experience *expressive language difficulties*, finding it hard to express what they know and translate a tangle of complex ideas to be able to say and respond to someone else. They may find it hard to organize their thoughts to express them and feel the pressure of everyone else being able to communicate more speedily. Whole-class mindfulness, breaks, sensory tools, and access to alternative communication means (like being able to type or write questions, using a letterboard or device to point to or spell out phrases, and using gestures or sign language) can help a person feel included and able to participate. What could work in your classroom?

Deaf or *hard of hearing* students may need more patience to communicate with you. Some may use mouth words, sign language, or both. Welcoming responses in formats besides speech may allow them to express their ideas to the fullest. Discuss with them what helps them express themselves. You could develop a visual cue if they're shy to ask for help in front of the class or even better—teach the whole class an ASL or BSL symbol (depending on where you are in the world) to use when anyone in the room needs clarification. There's no shame in needing something repeated!

All alternative communicators benefit from more processing time when we talk and when we solicit answers, agreeing on alternative ways of getting teacher attention, use of visuals to support lessons, and written instructions they can reference as needed. Then again, doesn't everybody?

Note: Since we're talking about processing, there is a saying in the autism community: *Presume competence*. Some autistic people may not speak, but this doesn't mean they don't understand. When we assume someone doesn't understand, we also have the tendency to make the work easier—and if we don't provide the appropriate level of challenge, the person may zone out (seeming to confirm our hypothesis that they don't understand, when really, they could just be bored).

Specialized processors

I use the term *specialized processors* to refer to learners who encode and retrieve information in a way that is less common than the majority and who may require teachers to understand the need to adjust their communication. Let's unpack who might fall into this category.

Processing speed

We tend to assume others process information the same way we do. We want students to get to the conclusion we're pointing to as quickly as we do. I can't tell you how many classrooms I've observed where teachers ask a question and immediately take the fastest hand-raiser. A student will tell me they never get chosen to speak—and they are right. We as teachers are so nervous about things not flowing that we get that little wave of gratitude to the students who help us move along. We have to be careful not to privilege the speediest processors, who jump to conclusions before we've even finished asking the question (this is a characteristic of some *gifted* learners).

Oakley et al. (2021) recommend teaching children the strengths and drawbacks of faster and slower processors and highlighting the story of the slow deliberating Santiago Ramón y Cajal, who won a Nobel Prize and is thought of as the father of neuroscience. A rapid processor is much more likely to assume they are right and miss evidence to the contrary, finding it harder to shift perspective. In contrast, students who process more slowly may have more nuanced, reasoned thinking and more easily correct for errors if given time to do so. Our processing speed can also be variable, enabling our mind to race in subjects we deeply understand while facing speed bumps in others.

Some students may be overwhelmed by too many instructions or repeating the same question to them while they're still processing from the first time. Students with any learning difficulty in the subject where their difficulty comes up tend to put in greater cognitive effort, which may affect how much new information is retained.

Increasing your wait time after asking a question and soliciting answers can equalize access and open up your classroom discussions to many more participants than the usual suspects. Calling directly on a student may elicit a freeze response, so for some students, you may need to talk to them to find out how to encourage participation in a way that works for them. Do you want to let them know a question in advance or have a signal when they feel confident to answer something and be called upon? Will you build in a chance to speak to a partner first, so that ideas are percolating and organized enough to speak out loud? Will you honor alternative communication, such as showing answers on a whiteboard, giving a thumbs up/middle/down, other gestural forms of participation, or reflective journals as participation in retrospect? Have a conversation with the class about why you sometimes wait before selecting students and teach your class how processing speed is not an indicator of success or smarts, but just a thinking difference that brings different strengths to the classroom. Posing a question in advance, writing it down, and building in opportunities to write down ideas or discuss with peers before you ask for student responses in a whole-class discussion can increase the likelihood that you'll get more answers from learners who process your questions at different speeds.

Mental imagery

If you are someone who reads and calls to mind vivid mental imagery of what you're reading, you are a visualizer. Mental visualization, scent memory, sound recall, and the ability to imagine the activation of other senses all seem to come on a spectrum. I've worked with students who seem to be 4-D processors, whose visualization abilities allow them to walk around in internal worlds so rich in detail it's like being in a video game with full special effects. This may be considered *hyperphantasia*. Their brains think very differently from their classmates with *aphantasia*, who think without generating imaginative memory aids. (People can fall anywhere between these two extremes—for instance, I can visualize fairly well when I read, but often faces are blurry and lack detail. When I think of an apple, if I focus hard enough, I can "see" something apple-ish sitting on a counter for as long as I sustain the effort. A friend of mine can smell, taste, and rotate a perfect bright red apple in her head, with seemingly no effort at all.) I first learned about aphantasia about five years ago, and since then I've surveyed each of my classes. I've had at least one student every year who identifies as an aphant. It's thought that aphants make up 1–4% of the population (Cherry, 2024; Kendle, 2017) and hypervisualizers make up about 2.5% (NeuroQ, 2022).

In teaching about mental imagery differences, I explain that some people think in pictures, and some people don't. Some people can strongly imagine, some people can imagine a little, and some people tend to learn better by doing than by imagining. There's no wrong or right way to remember or process information, but it's really good to know what type of processor you are because you will use different strategies for reading comprehension, studying, mindfulness, and more.

As an interactive activity, I ask students to imagine an object—usually a food—in their minds that they are likely familiar with. They can show me by raised hand whether or not they can "see" it. I sometimes ask if they can imagine the smell or taste of the object, if it is a food. Then, I ask them to transform it in some novel way they likely haven't ever seen, like putting an orange in a wig and a cape. Some students who can visualize the orange on its own can't transform it. That's okay, it's just important for teachers to know we may need to show more visuals as aids, rather than assuming students can just figure out how something works which they've never seen before, or that they can remember a visual after we've put it away!

Auditory processing

Auditory processing may also work more efficiently in some students than in others. If I'm in a setting with a lot of background noise and chatter, I can't filter out any of it to focus on the person next to me talking. Despite my best intentions and my will to lip read, I get lost. Students have told me the same thing: they can't focus in the classroom because they hear every conversation, every pencil scratch, every dropped water bottle—and sometimes those loud unexpected noises reverberate in their brains long afterwards. Sometimes, those of us with slower auditory processing will ask for clarification and figure out what you'd said previously part way through your answer. If you've ever learned a second language, you might relate: as a beginner when you listen or read, you grasp the initial subject and verb but as people speak to you more quickly and with increasing linguistic complexity, you process words in isolation and gradually make sense of it, usually well after. It just takes longer for the meaning to land.

Deaf or hard of hearing students really need you to communicate differently with them, and benefit from frequency modulation systems, which act as a microphone with amplification that is heard only by the student in their hearing devices, clear articulation, proximity to you, reduced background noise, closed captions on videos, and the ability to clarify easily when they miss something.

In general, learners with auditory-processing differences will benefit from increased processing time to figure out what was said, reduced or controlled background noise, visuals to support meaning, and text to read along. Unfortunately, not within my control at a boisterous pub on an evening out, but mostly within your control in a classroom!

Detail-oriented processing

Some brains process more information at one time. Autistic brains, for instance, may attend to more sensory input. ADHD brains are also more responsive to environments. According to Peter Vermeulen (2018, 2023), autistic brains end up processing more information than others. So-called neurotypical brains tend to reduce the amount of work they need to do by making a subconscious prediction of what they expect in the world around them. They then only need to process information that is different from their predictive schema. It's kind of a rapid generalized processing. In contrast, the autistic brain expends energy and processing power on all information, not just the salient details—the most relevant prediction errors.

For us autistics, when something doesn't compute, we have to make sense of it and adjust our understanding of the world. Our nervous systems are always taking note. This means we weigh all prediction errors equally, even ones that others readily dismiss as inconsequential and not worth further energy or attention. Our schemas are at risk of becoming even narrower, which can mean we make more prediction errors. Logic and cognition are the only tools we have to help us make sense of a chaotic and unpredictable world! We have more of an overactive, detail-oriented processing, which has implications for working memory and cognitive load—the more you try to do or think about at one time, the less you can remember.

Autistic brains also sometimes struggle to process visual and auditory information at the same time. Many autistic people report that making eye contact is stressful or even painful. They end up focusing on the forced eyeball gazing and can't process information from both channels at once. I know I have definitely lost track of what someone was saying as I wondered in my own head if I'd been staring for too long, if I'd looked away for the requisite few seconds often enough, and whether or not they were experiencing my gaze as unusual. Worse still, I've done the double return-the-question while focusing too intensely on the social niceties that I forget to listen:

"Hello, how are you?"

"Fine, thanks, how are you?"

"I'm good, thanks; how are you?" Followed by wishing the ground would open up and swallow me whole. You can guarantee I heard nothing else they said. It's amazing how much embarrassment clogs your ears! Here is another example from an autistic student about how this phenomenon relates to when people speak to her.

INSIDER'S PERSPECTIVE

Rozarina Md Yusof Howton, Graduate
Student, AuDHD and physical disability

My ear is really fine-tuned. To give you an idea, I can often tell who is playing the violin, by the style and the characteristic of the instrument. In some cases, I can tell who the conductor of an orchestra is, and even which music hall it was recorded in, purely from the style and the acoustics.

But when I talk to people I've never spoken to or met before, I really cannot make out what they are saying for the first 10 or 20 minutes because I haven't "generalized" their speech in my processing. Imagine speaking in English to someone from Taiwan with a very heavy accent or even speaking English to someone from the Scottish Highlands with their singsong tonality. You are both speaking English, but you cannot 100% understand each other. You will have to focus really hard to make sense of what the person said. This is what speaking to a new person feels like to me. So yeah, I am verbal, I can speak, but it takes a heck of a lot of energy to process all that. When I get mentally tired, I cannot form words anymore, even in my brain. So, no wonder crowds and noise burn me out.

Increasing predictability is going to help you to support detail-oriented processors. Try using a document camera while talking out loud, modeling tasks before expecting students to try on their own, showing exemplars, giving instructions one by one orally and providing a step-by-step list, providing audio instructions or videos they can play back later, not giving too much information at once or demanding eye contact, and—surprise, surprise—extending processing time. As we talked about in the last chapter, make sure you've established an environment where students can listen in the way they learn best!

Distinct decoders

We also ask students to process information as they read. *Distinct decoders* is my term for learners who encounter different barriers and access points when decoding and understanding written language. I use this category when I plan to consider how learners may be experiencing any text I've incorporated into the classroom.

We all sometimes encounter a reading that is so dry, we have to re-read, with conscious effort, at least one more time. We may read out loud or, if we can, "read" with a voice in our heads to focus on what is being communicated. Many readers need to put in that heightened effort all the time. There are assessments that can help to determine who decodes how, and there is a range of language-processing differences beyond the ones I'll mention here. My biggest tip is to break down reading difficulties to their component part—what is it exactly that they are struggling with? If a student doesn't like reading, I'll often ask them what part is hard. If they have no problem sounding out words and reading out loud, I'll ask them if they think they can remember the gist of what they've read. I might also probe whether they are able to visualize as they read or, if not, do they have the appropriate background knowledge to make meaning as they go? We might experiment with whether the meaning of the text would be more memorable if they heard it read out loud.

I've shared accessibility text-to-speech tools or Bionic Reading font (more on this later) with my classes, and a handful report back each year that they retain information so much better after using these tools. Some students might benefit by taking notes while reading—the act of writing out the important points, either with pen and paper, or to a lesser degree, on a Word document/notepad app helps with the sense making and extracting the important points of a text that has been given to them. Others might not have the working memory capacity to keep what is being read in mind and convert it to written or typed language easily as they go.

This isn't so easy for everyone, however. *Dyslexic* students have difficulty making meaning from what they see and hear. Dyslexia rates are much higher in English-speaking countries where pronunciations are inconsistent and not always sound-out-able (Smith-Spark & Gordon, 2022). There are many theories about the core of these differences: difficulties with the phonological processing, which is the ability to connect sounds to symbols (Hudson et al., 2011; Williams, 2022); slower visual processing (Manning et al., 2022); slower adaptation to sensory input (Perrachione et al., 2016); and trouble with executive functioning (Smith-Spark & Gordon, 2022), which is a common co-occurrence with all learning disabilities.

Dyscalculic students experience processing differences related to numeric symbols and math concepts. Dyscalculia means they'll have a hard time keeping concepts in their head (working memory) to perform calculations, following rows of numbers, writing, and so on—so following you whizzing through fraction conversions on the blackboard may be a challenge, and looking at a worksheet full of math questions certainly triggers fight or flight in me!

Some students are excellent decoders, even to the point of being hyperlexic readers who easily identify sounds of language and appear to have advanced reading skills, but you have to also make sure they are making meaning and not speed reading through vocabulary they don't understand. Hand me Victor Hugo's *Les Misérables* and I can fake my way through with a fairly decent accent (except for those more guttural r sounds!), but do I know what I'm saying? Not for the most part!

Which brings me to multi-language speakers! I'm in awe of people who speak and think in more than one language. They likely process text differently, depending on their familiarity with the language. If they are learning the language of instruction, they'll tend to make meaning on a word-by-word basis as they develop fluency, and hopefully become more comfortable making meaning in longer chunks of text as they learn and gain vocabulary.

It's worth mentioning that some studies suggest some autistic learners, no matter their perceived cognitive level, may also process each word as they come (Vermeulen, 2012). I have had a few instances of misconstruing meaning of headlines, before I cued into greater context. I had an embarrassing moment interpreting a social media post that read, "Long-haired cat people, what do you do about butt hair?" As a long-haired cat person, it took me longer than I'd care to admit to realize that the long hair referred to the cat and the problem was probably matting fur in sensitive areas.

Autistic folks often presume their strongest associated meaning with a term, even when they know a word has multiple meanings, and tend to interpret literally (Vermeulen, 2012). This can slow down auditory or visual processing considerably. I once had a student who could identify when people were likely using figurative language but was of an age where she didn't want to ask for clarification if she wasn't familiar with an expression. She struggled to remember sayings until she got home after school and could google them. Imagine how many opportunities for learning and social engagement she would miss right after the phrase in question, in trying to interpret meaning on the fly (an example of figurative language!)? Often, folks who process language differently are doing considerably more work and can only take in so much. This can also have an upside, as they may notice things differently, finding humor or additional insights that others miss when they process quickly.

Other autistic learners may be gestalt language processors. Rather than learning a word at a time, they combine and process larger units of speech or sounds, which can mean it takes much longer to generalize the associated meanings or to recognize words on their own. They may use echolalia, a way of repeating auditory information to process information, express feelings, soothe the nervous system, or indicate they are making an association, even if it is misunderstood by others. Here is an account of gestalt and echolalic processing.

INSIDER'S PERSPECTIVE

Rozarina Md Yusof Howton, Graduate
Student, AuDHD and physical disability

Having echolalia helps a lot, especially if one is a gestalt learner. How it sounds triggers an emotion. And that can help memorizing, learning, or just for fun, like a verbal fidget spinner. "Front Left Pocket" is one of them. I use my echolalia to process a piece of information to get the meaning, too. Let it sink in. I repeat the fact to myself enough times it sticks. Sometimes, when I have trouble "forming coherent sentences in words" I switch to musicality of the words. I have handed in some high-level physics homework with the text body for an equation explanation consisting of limerick-style prose. Or rhyming poetry. It seems to get over the "barrier of writing" in my head.

I don't learn word by word... That comes later. Before human words, I echolalia-ed my animals (cats, kittens, rooster), referring to them by their specific meow sounds. Bob's cat name was "EEwooooreaowrrrr." My first word was *cat*. This was because I liked cats, though I didn't realize this term meant the broad label of animal because it sounds different when one person says it compared to another. I thought it was a different concept, and it took me some time for it to finally click that the word means any of the furballs. I don't generalize well even now.

When it comes to processing text, distinct decoders benefit from explicit instruction in reading components that are harder for them, slowing down while we go through text or math problems, talking about reading strategies and promoting metacognition, highlighting what's important to notice in text, explaining figures of speech, using visuals, teaching how to use context clues, allowing text-to-speech readers, reading buddies, discussions related to reading passages, verbal instructions paired with written instructions (I record audio instructions on virtual classroom platforms), less text on a page, and more visible fonts. Hyperlexic decoders or speed readers may benefit from a particular font called Bionic Reading,[2] which bolds the first phoneme or two of text and causes the brain to track more accurately, a bit like this:

I love **th**is **f**ont and **f**ind **I** can **r**ead **ev**en **f**aster **wh**ile **ret**aining **mo**re **mea**ning, **b**ut **it** **m**ight **c**ause **explo**sions **in** **y**our **b**rain!

Measured movers
When we move, our brains benefit from increased oxygen and glucose (Reeves et al., 2016) and form more dendrites to help us connect our

---

2   https://bionic-reading.com

learning. This is true for everyone, but not all of your students will jump for joy when it's time for daily physical activity. I, for one, dreaded having my clumsiness in the spotlight.

Measured movers are my category for students we need to consider who have any difficulties with fine- or gross-motor coordination, such as dyspraxia and apraxia, or have visual processing disorders. They will find it hard to process information in order to imitate it or enact it. Dysgraphia—a fine-motor difference—can manifest as messy writing that doesn't fit in the boxes or stay straight on or between the lines. Learners may experience pain when trying to write or grasp a pencil. I was frustrated all the time in early elementary school when I had to use scissors and glue things together, usually mis-cutting and ending up with dried glue shedding like snakeskin all the way up my elbows! Sometimes, students with visual processing difficulties may be misdiagnosed as dyslexic or as having ADHD because they may appear to struggle with decoding texts and with variable attention, when their difficulties lie in how they process what they see. This may include distinguishing symbols and shapes, planning and sequencing, visual memory, tracking text, spatial awareness, and fine-motor and hand-eye coordination.

This doesn't mean we bench the students who find these things difficult in gym class. Studies show integrating movement into our teaching improves attention, memory, and the academic performance of students (as cited in Reeves et al., 2016). I certainly loved being part of musical theater as a teen, but I needed to practice routines at home because I could never pick them up with ease. I just couldn't hold the steps in mind and translate the idea into a bodily expression. If you gave me a video to follow on my own (removing the potential for embarrassment), I could pick up in a week of practice what my peers could pick up in a few minutes.

In our classrooms, we consider measured movers by pairing auditory instructions with pictures or videos of steps (especially ones they can reference later on when trying on their own), breaking things down to their component physical parts, pairing routines and steps with songs or rhymes so they're easier to remember, breaks to allow for consolidation in the background, creating more spacious test and worksheet layouts, increasing the line spacing, and more time to practice skills requiring motor coordination.

Procedural and declarative learning systems

There is also a slower but very powerful system of learning that flies under the radar. Our procedural memory system works below our consciousness, eventually enabling us to automate habits and actions. It uses a completely different entry point—basal ganglia—into our long-term memory (Oakley et al., 2021). Riding a bike, walking downstairs, driving a car, solving a Rubik's cube, speaking your first language, playing a sport or an instrument, brushing your teeth, and tying your shoes are just a few examples of things we can eventually do, automatically and efficiently (Cozolino, 2013; Oakley et al., 2021). We can access this information instantly, without thinking about the mechanics, which also enables us to daydream or think of other things—something the declarative memory system would certainly envy, if it was self-aware!

Some students may have a clear preference for one system of learning over another. Oakley and colleagues (2021) suggest that dyslexic learners encounter more difficulty with automaticity (automation of skill, in this case, reading) and instead may have impressive declarative skills (memorizable, fact-based knowledge). This may also be true of other learning disabilities. Personally, as a measured mover, my physical coordination takes much more time and practice (and may never be fluid or intuitive); and as an ADHDer, I struggle to automate habits, and so significant brainpower goes into tricking myself to do dishes, bribing myself to brush my teeth, and otherwise brain hacking my way through all the unpleasant but important day-to-day tasks!

Anecdotally, based on reports from the few aphants I know personally, I suspect non-visualizers may learn better through their procedural system, though research is needed to confirm this. Often, depending on the subject, your students may prefer processing via one, the other, or a mix of both. What are your preferences? My declarative system is my usual go-to, especially for subjects like history or a second language, where instead of learning via immersion, I take a cognitive approach, studying grammar and reading up on the proper placement of vowels, so that my practice is grounded in the facts I learn about the language. In drama, science, or when playing board games, I relish the hands-on, dive in, and learning by doing. Both types of learning support one another, so whenever we can, giving explicit instruction and hands-on practice will enhance students' initial processing.

Communicating for different processors

It's a given today that we adjust how we communicate for many learners—we wouldn't expect a student with a visual impairment to follow instructions written on the blackboard, or a Deaf student to have to process auditory instructions. Invisible disabilities like autism, ADHD, dyslexia, dyscalculia, and other learning disabilities are not as recognizable to the onlooker. However, we should follow the same principle: building in access and support for all needs is necessary and just.

For example, reading a book to your class is experienced by the learners in front of us in so many ways! The hypervisualizer or ADHD student might get distracted in their imaginings and tune out what you are saying. They may benefit from being taught how they can picture the read-aloud like a movie in their minds while you read (Dymond, 2020). The student sitting next to them may need to get up and act out the story, because their brains don't think in images so they can't use visualization as a strategy. Another student may be so eager for you to turn the page that they call out predictions. Maybe they can help you read the story or use a clipboard to write down their predictions.

Rather than writing these students off as lazy, willfully disengaged, or disruptive, we also have to make some adjustments to how we communicate for learners whose brains process and think differently. This is where *double empathy* comes in!

Double empathy problem

Damian Milton, an autistic researcher, came up with the idea of the double empathy problem (Milton, 2012). If a conversation breaks down in some way between an autistic person and a non-autistic person, the autistic person is most often blamed for communication breakdown. The non-autistic is less used to experiencing miscommunications; whereas the autistic person, by virtue of living in a world with many more non-autistics, has come to expect this and internalizes this blame as well. The result of this kind of thinking is that no accommodations are made, and the source of the problem is placed solely on one party. However, at the heart of double empathy is the notion that, in any social communication, it takes (at least) two to tango.

In a fascinating study, Crompton and colleagues (2020) examined this effect in action. They studied three groups—one fully autistic, one fully non-autistic, and one mixed group. Like a game of broken tele-phone, they had to tell a story from one person to another down a chain. Both the fully autistic and fully non-autistic groups had simi-lar outcomes. What may surprise you is that the mixed group, which included both non-autistics and autistics, completely fell apart. They remembered fewer details by the end of the chain and reported lower in-group rapport. Ultimately, researchers demonstrated that autistic people can successfully communicate but tend to do so when com-municating with other autistic individuals. I've witnessed the ease and comfort with which young autistic students communicate once they get to know one another in my special education program. I've had students tell me they don't feel autistic in our classroom (which breaks my heart—they are associating not fitting in with being autistic!), when what they really mean is that they feel understood and don't struggle to talk with people who think, and express themselves, like them.

I share this study and the concept of double empathy as an invalu-able reminder that, when misunderstandings occur, we shouldn't attri-bute it to an inherent autistic inability to communicate but rather to a mismatch in communication styles. If you'll allow me to extend this problem to include other types of processors, it's a good reminder that it falls to us to get the message down the chain to everyone.

Mitigating processing differences

So, how do we, as educators, mitigate processing differences and support as many learners as possible? We can aid students tremendously with very small tweaks. It isn't always intuitive, as there are many needs in any given class. You can wait to get to know students, a few months in, but why wait? One of the reasons I say labels aren't the be all and end all is that I assume I will have learners with every label in my class. I plan choices, alternatives, and supports for those activated attention systems, those measured movers, those distinct decoders, and so on—before they've even set foot in the room. To further refine what I do, I ask students questions about their processing styles right from the beginning of the school year. It benefits everyone to help learners to identify how they process and what they need. The sooner we open up reflective conversations with students, the sooner we can target our instruction and build student self-regulation.

Processing-enhancing strategies

This section contains a range of strategies that may work better with younger or older students or may be easy to adapt to the ages and needs of whomever you teach. Many ideas are presented so you can hopefully find one or two to incorporate in your existing programming. I frequently reassure teacher candidates that no one is expected to do all of them, all of the time. We change how we differentiate and open up access points depending on the activity, subject, time of day, and the learners in front of us. I hope these suggestions spark some ideas of your own!

Lesson design

It is important to design your lessons with consideration for the many types of processors you will encounter. Here are some ways to aid processing:

- Consider how lessons affect various learners.
- Consider your entry hook to activate attentions, such as:
  - adding challenge, like a brainteaser or sudoku puzzle
  - posing a question
  - using call-and-response, music, rhythm
  - getting their attention in a novel way, like a roleplay, funny video, meme, a picture to analyze what's happening, a newspaper headline to think about and respond to, etc.
  - telling a story, using poetry or motivational quotations to access emotional connection.
- Connect to background knowledge, such as by:
  - priming background knowledge with visuals, video clips, etc.
  - before you watch a video or read a story, showing and saying out loud some questions you will ask afterwards
  - asking whether they can make connections to previous units, other subjects, or things they know from daily life
  - relating new concepts to student interests and strengths.
- Build in opportunities to do/explore hands-on (procedural learning) as well as direct instruction (declarative learning).
- Chunk information delivery and build in consolidation breaks to process new information, such as by:
  - building in a short pause to think before you solicit answers

- giving time to talk to nearby peers about what they just learned and questions they still have
- giving time to write down an idea or questions before discussing as a class
- incorporating mindfulness, exercise, and stretch breaks.
• Use alternative communication, such as:
- encouraging participation by soliciting responses on whiteboards (e.g., as words or emojis in response to parts of the lesson)
- incorporating communication devices, class volunteer translators for nonspeaking students or students who are learning the language, or apps to read ideas out loud (one time when I lost my voice, I used an app that made me sound like a robot to get students' attention. Whatever I typed, it read out loud. I swear, students listened more to Robot Miss Dymond!)
- using gestures (e.g., thumbs up, down, or in the middle) to indicate agreement or how well something is understood
- using sign language call-and-response (similar to Simon Says, but nonverbally) to grab attention, and seeing if you can get the whole class eventually following along
- teaching and using sign language cues to check for understanding or so students can indicate the need for help.

Environment

The environment in which we learn can have a big impact on how much we are able to process and recall. Growing up, Maja found her own ways to manage the chaotic classroom environment:

INSIDER'S PERSPECTIVE

Maja Toudal, autistic/ADD Psychologist

The classroom environment is so overwhelming for someone like me, who will notice the fluorescent lights flickering, the sound of a tapping shoe, the teacher's perfume, the patterns on everyone's clothing, and the traffic noise from outside. To actually absorb the subject being taught, I would have to position myself very carefully in the room—not too close to the door, not too surrounded by other students, not near a dysfunctional lamp, but certainly never at a wobbly table or chair. I also often did much better at focusing if I had a secondary task, such as drawing. In later school years, I took to coloring my notes, but as a small child I would often draw animals in my notebooks.

As teachers, we are in constant competition with the many sensory stimuli in our classrooms. Even the place where a student is in the classroom can have ramifications for learning. Below are some tips to try to bring more calm into the learning environment:

- Reduce extraneous stimulation.
- Allow students to listen how they do best, with fidget tools, coloring sheets, etc., so long as they can answer questions or show they are retaining in some way.
- Consider stations to process content in different ways—hands-on, direct instruction, small group discussions, procedural, declarative learning—related to the subject. You can strategically allow students more time at stations if they need longer to process information delivered a certain way.
- Consider buddies or groupings where individuals can support and access the strengths of others.
- Utilize the benefits of learning outside of the classroom and in meaningful contexts (experiential learning).

Communicating for all processors

Different processors will have different needs to best aid them in absorbing and remembering information. So, how can we as educators adapt our communication for everyone?

- Speak clearly and directly.
- Use a functional modulation system or proximity for learners who need to hear you better.
- Use closed captioning on videos.
- Use visuals in your teaching. We process pictures twice as quickly

as we do words (Hammond, 2015), most of the time—in times of visual overwhelm, we may find it easier just to listen.

- Model processes and talk out loud.
- Use a document camera.
- Incorporate songs, rhymes, or mnemonic devices to help communicate steps or related concepts.
- Strategically increase your wait time so more students can process information.
- Write down questions and instructions, and always pair with auditory instructions.
- Post pictures or videos of steps.
- Post audio instructions along with written instructions.
- Show exemplars of final product.
- Reduce clutter in texts and use interesting fonts for headings but aim for readability overall. For instance, dyslexic students may benefit from letters which are more spaced out, such as in the fonts Arial or OpenDyslexic.

Direct instruction in access points

Teach students what they need to improve their access to material and to process information more easily. Here are some tips:

- Explicitly teach strategies as you expect students to use them in class, such as:
  - using context cues as a reader and critical thinker
  - visualization (for those who can) during read-alouds
  - alternatives to visualization for non-visualizers; for example, externalizing information on written lists/graphic organizers; acting things out; or using an external anchor during mindfulness like one's own breathing.
- Remember to highlight relevance: tell them why they're learning and what's important to focus on.
- Explain idioms and other figures of speech.
- As you learn which components of a task are hard, you can provide some explicit instruction in those skills for those who need it.
- Teach a Tool of the Day or Week, so students have exposure to assistive technology or strategies that may help their processing. Some examples:

- text-to-speech apps that read text out loud (Google Read & Write, Speechify, etc.), which encourage multimodal processing. I've taught students of all ages to use text readers for improved reading comprehension. Hearing text and reading along helps to remember details, especially for younger students and those distinct decoders (Singh & Alexander, 2022). Fun fact: Listening to audiobooks activates the same brain areas as reading (Deniz et al., 2019)!
- Bionic Reading font
- mindfulness, which extensive research shows both calms us down and can extend our ability to sustain attention (Hammond, 2015; Murphy, 2019)
- a variety of fidget tools (not toys!) and how/when to use them, as outlined in Chapter 1.

Encourage metacognitive talks

Get students thinking and sharing about their processing and communication needs so you can better understand and support their learning. Here are some ideas:

- Have whole-class and individual talks about what is easy or hard about a subject, topic, or task—to help you to understand and to promote student metacognition.
- Teach students about various aspects of processing in a value-neutral way (none is better than another!) and get them thinking about and articulating their own processing experiences. Some core concepts to include:
  - *Processing speeds*: Explain how we all need variable amounts of processing time, which is why you sometimes build in time to think before coming together as a class, and how different thinking speeds are okay. Review the story of Santiago Ramón y Cajal (Oakley et al., 2021) or René Descartes (Shanker, 2020), who described themselves as slower processors.
  - *Procedural vs. declarative learning systems*: Survey them about their learning preferences. Explain that, as a teacher, you try to build in opportunities for all learning preferences, so it helps to know who gravitates more to what.
  - *Degrees of visualization*: Ask students if they can visualize—and

to what degree, as described earlier. Explain visualization isn't the only way. For those who don't visualize, there are other strategies to help you learn and remember information. As a teacher, knowing who visualizes and who doesn't helps you to include different access points—and it empowers students to figure out what works best for them, too.

• Incorporate *metacognitive prompts* into lessons as group brainstorms or after activities as tickets-out-the-door or exit tickets.

Metacognitive prompts

Metacognitive prompts are questions that inspire students to self-reflect about their thinking and learning. You can start using metacognitive prompts by moving from general prompts at the beginning of the year to more specific. Explain to students that, as you and they make discoveries about their own brains, they can become stronger learners, as they determine what works best for their brains. You can print out written prompts or write several options on the board. For students who find it difficult to write, you could have options available such as checklists, or multiple choices to check off rather than short answer responses, a digital version, or by doing it orally.

For students who have more difficulty identifying their own learning needs, especially when getting them to think about and identify which parts of a task are hard, you can create different access points. Depending on the student, you may be able to narrow down to potential difficulties with component parts to figure out where they struggle. For instance, a reluctant reader may be able to answer yes or no questions orally or with a thumbs up or down in a private conference to illuminate what strategies may be helpful: "Can you read it out loud?" "Can you understand what you read, as you are reading?" "Can you understand when I read it out loud to you?" "After reading, can you remember what the passage is about, or does it slide out of your brain?" Sometimes, oral questions demand more working memory or processing. Externalize it via a written list, asking the student to underline or highlight the statements that are true for them. Google Forms and other survey options can be helpful and can be offered digitally to those who prefer to type! Prompts may include:

• "How do you learn best? (e.g., listening to a teacher, watching something done, doing something, reading about it, etc.)" You may also get ideas from the worksheet templates on my website with ideas for student self-advocacy.[3]

- "When is listening easy? When is it hard?"
- "What things help you to listen? (e.g., visuals, not having to look at the teacher, coloring, doodling, taking notes, specific fidget tools.)"
- "What things absolutely do *not* help your ability to listen?"
- "How do you think? (e.g., pictures, words, concepts, feelings, etc.) How do you remember?"
- "How do you prefer to be given instructions? What makes it harder to understand instructions?"
- "How do you experience reading? What kind of reading do you enjoy? (e.g., picture books, graphic novels, audiobooks, novels, fiction, non-fiction) Is reading ever easy? Is it ever hard? What parts are hard?"
- "Would you use the Tool of the Week? Why or why not?"
- "What did you learn about how you process information this week? What strategies or tools helped you?"
- "What can I do differently in my lessons to help you to better understand information? How can I communicate more clearly?" (Feel free to make this subject-specific. Anonymous surveys can also be set up on Google Forms or other survey software.)

Conclusion

We all want to be the kind of teacher whose words and lessons reso-nate with students for years to come. Some learners will learn easily the way we teach, and some will need us to communicate more clearly and to create different access points to help them to understand and process new knowledge. I hope this chapter reminds you of all the ways you are already communicating effectively—and gives you an idea or two to try!

---

3   www.karadymond.com/resources/selfadvocacy-templates

CHAPTER 2 HIGHLIGHTS

✓ An overview of information processing—how we make sense of and remember information we take in via our senses.

✓ Activating attentions by moving from the "sage on the stage" format to using techniques from collectivist cultures.

✓ Making adjustments to how we communicate for learners whose brains process and think differently, just as we would for students with a more visible disability.

✓ Increasing your expected response time to help students who respond more slowly and to encourage fast responders to consider their answers more deeply.

✓ Specific tips to support activated attention systems, alternative communicators, specialized processors, distinct decoders, and measured movers to maximize their processing and participation.

✓ Thoughtful ideas to engage students in metacognition so you can learn more about their processing profile.

Questions for the reader:

✓ In what ways do you already support various processing needs?

✓ What is one new strategy you might bring into your classroom? (It takes time to trial and test new things so give yourself the space and grace to do so.)

✓ What will you replace or remove from your pedagogy?

✓ What do students say makes the difference?

How We Grapple with Ideas to Deeply Learn

I used to work in theater. My passions were playwriting and acting, but I was a jack-of-all-trades. I was a great stage manager, responsible for remembering all the director's decisions, communicating any new director whims to the designers and crew, sharing the schedules and script changes with all relevant parties, setting up the stage and back-stage, tracking each prop and set piece, doing the laundry and laying out the costumes, knowing all of the stage directions, crew cues, and actor placements, signaling every lighting and sound cue, and being the general wrangler of all. In one production of *Julius Caesar*, I knew every person's fight choreography so well that I could have filled in for a missing cast member at any rehearsal. There really was no aspect of a show that I was fuzzy on. Sound like a lot to keep in mind? You have no idea! Stage managing is truly executive functioning at its finest. Executive functions (EFs) are a cluster of skills that help us to engage in goal-oriented behavior.

Compare this with my executive functioning yesterday: I was rushing to get home for a Zoom interview after work. On the way, I needed to stop to get a cake, as that evening I had plans to host a friend for dinner. I also needed to tidy, prep the meal, and go and pick them up at the train station. There were a few things that threw off my plans: it was raining, and I was running late. When I got home, I discovered the dishwasher seal had broken (it was only a matter of time, as the machine was going on 20 years old). Dishes are my least favorite chore, so I felt compelled to research and order a new one immediately. I also had to put on some laundry, clean the washrooms and any areas of the house we'd be hanging out in. Managing okay so far. Putting my google thumb to good use,

I emailed a local appliance shop to ask about availability. They phoned me back as I was folding the dry clothes I'd forgotten in the dryer the weekend before, which I discovered when transferring over the wash. Ding dong! The doorbell chimed, and it was a door-to-door salesman with an offer on an internet deal for the neighborhood. As I struggled to keep my cat from escaping through the front door and politely tried to extricate myself from the conversation, I remembered the meatloaf I'd planned to make would take an hour in the oven—and I had to pick up my friend in about 15 minutes, and it was a 10-minute drive away. The frenzied prep of the main course began so I could get it in the oven. In the end, I was 25 minutes late to the train station (the prep always takes longer than the recipes state!) and I entirely forgot about the Zoom meeting until I received an email about it today.

I have no idea how I was so good at stage management, because I can't organize my own life or remember what's in my fridge's crisper drawer of doom where all the veggies go to die! Maybe it was the pressure of a deadline, which is ever-present in theater. Perhaps it was the flow state I could easily access, which for me is not activated by chores, as Marie Kondo I am not. Herein lies the grand mystery of neurodivergence and executive functions: sometimes they work flawlessly and sometimes they don't. In this chapter, we're going to look at a few of the EFs we most rely on when we're first learning and practicing new concepts. Ready to put the fun back into EFs?

Nerd alert: Brain basics related to executive functions

Right behind your forehead is your prefrontal cortex, an essential brain region which houses human beings' abilities to plan, organize, and get things done by regulating our emotions, attention, and actions. This part of our brain operates a bit like a slow talker, reacting less quickly as it formulates its hypotheses and conclusions than our Flash Gordon-speed nervous systems (Hammond, 2015). We can best access this part of our brain—and our executive functioning skills—when we feel safe, calm, and not in a state of burnout. (Once burnt out, it can be close to impossible to access executive functioning skills. We can recover these only when given sufficient time and support to heal and rest. (Toudal

& Attwood, 2024)) Each student's unique executive functioning profile is a strong predictor of future academic success and can explain more than 50% of variance in school performance (Visu-Petra et al., 2011).

Experts debate exactly which cognitive processes make up our EFs (Barkley, 2012; Faith et al., 2022). A list I turn to, time and again, comes from Faith and colleagues: working memory, sustained attention, organization, cognitive flexibility, response inhibition, time management, planning and prioritizing, goal-oriented persistence, metacognition, and emotional control. In other words, all attributes that help us to begin, work through, and finish a task over time. In this chapter, we'll look at the executive functioning skills required for learning, recalling what has been learned, and studying. In essence, we'll examine the EFs we use for building mental schemas so we can reliably remember concepts at will.

Executive functions, adult assumptions, and automaticity

Our full range of EF can take up to three decades to develop, and neurodivergent folks may take even longer. Folks with ADHD may take 30–50% more time to mature their EFs (Barkley, 2020). When you think of it that way, that 12-year-old student may have the organizational and emotional coping skills of a 7-year-old. Imagine how often they get frowned at, spoken harshly to, guilted, or punished for not yet having the brain wiring of their peers? This is important to remember as adults, because sometimes we can assume children and teens have certain abilities just because we wish it to be so. There's a phenomenon that happens when toddlers begin to speak. Parents may assume challenging moments are caused by willful misbehavior—rather than the same types of frustrations and stressors that parents were more understanding about before their children could express themselves in words (Shanker, 2020). Similarly, a large study found that almost 60% of parents thought children under the age of 3 would have the response inhibition to not do something forbidden; and almost 40% thought children under 2 years of age had this level of willpower and insight. Do you know when these abilities actually develop? At the very earliest, around 3.5–4 years old! The same study found that more than 40% of parents also believed that, before age 2, their child could take turns and share, skills which generally develop around 3 or 4 years of age (as cited in Delahooke, 2019).

We may make a similar but opposite assumption that a child or adult not speaking in words lacks understanding and the ability to communicate. We may leave them to their own devices, rather than engaging in purposeful, connection-building ways and unlocking what two-way communication we can.

Both scenarios break my heart, because I think of the damage to the adult–child relationship and to child self-esteem, and I imagine a plethora of missed opportunities to develop problem-solving and communication skills together through co-regulation when a student is assumed to be more able than they are—seen as defiant rather than struggling with something they can't yet do—or when they are seen as less able than they are. It can be hard to face our own mistakes, but when I feel that tension where I could easily get locked into a power struggle with a student who isn't meeting my expectations, I now try to turn inward to reflect: Is this expectation reasonable for this student at this time? What is getting in the way, and how can I be more supportive? What can we both learn from this for next time? I try to get curious, rather than attributing blame or assuming some moral failing.

EFs have been shown to develop more slowly in those of us who have auditory-processing, math, or language-learning disabilities (Barkley, 2020; Magimairaj & Nagaraj, 2018; Smith-Spark & Gordon, 2022). Similarly, activated attention systems or specialized processors who have sensory processing difficulties may experience greater executive functioning challenges, as one study of autistic students with sensory sensitivities found (Pastor-Cerezuela et al., 2020). Any learning difficulty can make it harder to process and hold information in mind or to develop automaticity, which helps us to do things easily, without having to think about it. A good example of this is the first time you learned how to drive. How many things did you need to keep track of? How easy or difficult was it for you to check the sideview mirrors, rear mirror, blind spot, and shift gears without looking down? I learned on an automatic transmission, and I still remember feeling completely overwhelmed by the sheer number of things I was expected to do. Now, driving is almost second nature. It's become automatic, and so I've clustered skills together and no longer need to expend so much cognitive effort to do them. They don't use as much working memory because I'm tapping into stores of long-term and procedurally learned information.

Distinct decoders, alternative communicators, or measured movers who haven't yet automatized initial skills may be focusing all their efforts on an area that is harder for them—such as spelling in dyslexia or the mechanics of writing in dysgraphia or dyspraxia. These efforts mean they are missing out on the increasing complex coordination of skills and brain regions that their peers are practicing as they move on to creating lengthier sentences and experimentation with writing conventions. If writing or typing skills aren't automatized, more of a student's mental effort has to go toward these physical acts, so less brain power can be devoted to the actual learning task or question being posed. They will likely use less sophisticated language, even if they might add those details orally. If they're trying to take notes, it'll take longer and they'll lose track of what you said, eventually giving up altogether. Even for students without a recognized disability, a significant weakness in any area can use up more working memory capacity and make understanding and retaining what's being taught much harder. This can be internalized as a personal failure, which might have a ripple effect for years to come.

INSIDER'S PERSPECTIVE

Lindsay Ryan, Registered Psychotherapist,
39 late-diagnosed ADHD

When I was in grade 7 [Year 8 in the UK] and was introduced to integers for the first time, I struggled. No one could see how much I was struggling to understand the concept because I still did well on tests. But I relied on tricks, like using a ruler to understand adding and subtracting negative numbers instead of really integrating the concept. It wasn't until I was in grade 11 [Year 12], working as a cashier, that my understanding of integers was connected to money and the concept clicked. I was relieved to finally understand, but I also felt a sense of shame those four years because of how hard it was for me to learn.

When I reflect, there were a lot of reasons this concept was difficult for me but most importantly for the first time, I was integrating knowledge when I had very little initial knowledge to rely on. My brain was struggling and that felt different and scary.

I didn't know it was okay to struggle. And so, anxiety, shame, and avoidance started to travel with me when I encountered difficult concepts. I dropped out of grade 13 algebra when I hit a mental barrier with the concept of torque—shirking any subject that didn't come easily to me. And that anxiety followed me to my first attempt at university and was a companion during my statistics class for my Masters. Luckily by the time I was doing my Masters, I knew that learning was a process and struggling was okay, so I took the time I needed and found additional resources that worked with my brain to understand those difficult concepts. But it does make me wonder about what I may have accomplished if I had understood that earlier in life. And it makes me grateful I did not come against a learning barrier earlier on that would have dampened my enjoyment of learning.

Executive functions in action

Why some information sticks—and some does not

In the 2nd grade (Year 3 in the UK), my class was shown a video about microscopic organisms in carpets. In my brain, that dusty mauve tight looped fiber weave we all sat on and the horrifying magnified image of a creepy-crawly and its family with giant mouth pincers and too many legs are paired, forever.

I have often wondered why that stuck with me. Was it the relevance of the information, given I was seated on a carpet at that very moment? Perhaps it was the strong visual evoking an emotional response and sustaining my attention. Maybe it was the many times I revisited it in my mind, ruminator that I am, that made it stick. But it brings to mind some other questions. Why on earth do I remember that, but not the chore my partner asked me to do while I was thinking about the bills I need to pay? Why do I always remember exactly where he leaves his wallet and never remember where my keys are? Why do some things stick around as memories and others vanish?

Memories can be highly variable. My dad once bought a book on improving his memory in 30 days, and got home to my mother chastising him, "Honey, you already have that book!"

As an autistic person, my memory of events and conversations can be exceptional—with a few exceptions. If I am anxious or meeting someone new, I cannot for the life of me remember their name and face. If I'm preoccupied, I won't have the foggiest idea of what our exchange was. However, if I'm in a relaxed state of being and really listening, I'll remember our conversation for decades to come. I'm often surprised how little other people remember the outcomes of meetings, the decisions agreed upon, who shared that great idea in the meeting, where everyone was sitting—all things I can recall as vividly as if it were happening again, like déjà vu!

How do we form long-term memories, learn something well, or develop new abilities? First, we rely on three interrelated aspects of our executive functioning (Faith et al., 2022):

- sustained attention
- response inhibition
- working memory.

Our *sustained attention* helps us direct our focus, ideally toward what is deemed important in the situation so that we can make meaning out of it. Our *response inhibition* keeps us from getting up or shifting our attention to something else because we're bored, or a whim occurs to us. Our *working memory* keeps information in mind for the short term and allows us to use it, like when we do mental math or try to recall steps in a recipe. This is essential because, in order to learn, we have to do something with the new concept, or our brain discards it.

So, what we pay attention to fundamentally sets the course of our learning. Some brains, like those activated attention systems, notice different details—maybe not the ones you hope they'll latch onto. People with ADHD tend to react more to events around them, and then are more likely to forget what they were doing or return to their work (Barkley, 2020). According to Hammond (2015), the brain quickly decides if new information is worth keeping around. If it's not, it's forgotten in 5–20 seconds. So, those first few minutes of a lesson are make-or-break! But how do we apply this to lessons?

It is more likely to ignite interest when information:

- is relevant
- evokes a sense of curiosity or an emotional response
- has a powerful visual and/or auditory component
- incorporates a challenge.

If it hooks a person, that information may get into working memory, which can operate for 5–20 minutes (Hammond, 2015). This stage is aided by repetition, rhythm, music, movement, a sense of novelty, stories, and metaphors, which help us to identify patterns and placements for the information amongst information we already know.

According to Hammond (2015), we also have to do something with the new knowledge if we want those neural pathways to cement, and ideally within the first 24 hours. Within 20 minutes, we've lost 40% of what we were taught on average. Within 24 hours, if we don't give it a second thought, we've lost 70%. However, if we review or apply that information using either our procedural memory (unconscious, experiential body learning), or our declarative memory (facts and figures, what is consciously known) within 24 hours, we actually remember 80% of what was initially learned. Using both declarative and procedural systems in our classrooms to help students understand a concept helps more powerfully form long-term memories!

The importance of working memory

Around the age of 7 and up until 11, our working memory improves, along with sustained attention and verbal rehearsing (Magimairaj & Nagaraj, 2018). There may also be some improvements in adolescence (Shanker, 2020) as the whole kit and kaboodle of EFs develop and become more automatic. Most people can only keep an average of four items in their working memory—though, with variable processors, some people may have more or less expansive capacities (Oakley et al., 2021).

We are using working memory when we watch a teacher do a problem, when we work through a problem, and when we try to remember the lesson later. If we sustain attention and practice or think about a newly learned fact, the little dendritic spines of our neurons reach out for parts of other neurons, forming a network. Our thought skips across the gap in between the neurons, and this network is strengthened, becoming faster and easier to access as we practice and make connections between what we know already and explore how it applies to different contexts (Oakley et al., 2021; Hammond, 2015). If we already have background knowledge, we use less of our working memory to process this new learning (Zheng & Gardner, 2020).

When something exceeds our working memory capacity, our brains tire out and it slips out of mind. Students who might experience working memory challenges may forget all but the first (or last!) instruction given and be unable to take notes and understand at the same time. They will be more reliant on teacher-led approaches than students with larger working memory and faster processing (Kirschner & Hendrick, 2020; Oakley et al., 2021). A characteristic of their writing may be leaving out words or repeatedly writing the same word as they try to hold all the ideas in their mind (Oakley et al., 2021). Students with working memory challenges tend to struggle with mathematics, which is also true of students with ADHD (Barkley, 2020). Trying to distinguish what a teacher is saying in a noisy classroom takes up working memory capacity, as we are splitting our attention between sustaining attention and filtering out what is unnecessary (as cited in Magimairaj & Nagaraj, 2018). For folks with sensory-processing differences, this filtering can be next to impossible. Students are also using up their working memory trying to remember observations of a teacher modeling steps of a task they have to do (Oakley et al., 2021). This is why so many students look stunned or ask what to do immediately after the demonstration. As they grow older, students with smaller working memory capacities may find their own workarounds to compensate.

INSIDER'S PERSPECTIVE

Rozarina Md Yusof Howton, Graduate Student, AuDHD and physical disability

I need the physical input of writing out the important bits when reading, especially hard-to-digest text like publications and textbook material, even when I was a kid. A Huge Wall of Text in papers, documents, and textbooks is informationally and visually overwhelming for me! It tires me out. Making brief notes as I read difficult text helps me connect the disparate parts of the material with less cognitive strain due to my small working memory. That's also why a lot of physicists and mathematicians like to work with pen and paper, blackboard and chalk... writing out the problems helps us "intuit" the answers that our small working memory cannot immediately see.

If we're stressed out or tired, our working memory capacity may also be temporarily diminished. The week I left my car running in a school parking lot, I was listing my apartment for sale, writing report cards, and running around to almost 20 schools over four days for multiple meetings and observations, all requiring follow-ups. Even my muscle memory to take the keys out of the ignition wasn't strong enough against the to-do list I was running through!

When we hit a figurative wall

There is a moment—a measurable, visceral moment—when a person hits a wall, where there is no reward high enough for the level of cognitive or physical effort being demanded. Your brakes might kick in for cognitive, physical, social, or emotional reasons. It may be when you're asked to interpret a spreadsheet of numbers, or if you have to sing in front of 200 people. For another person, it may be telling them to climb a rope in gym class or to use a photocopier for the first time without any instructions. We can't gauge the experience of someone else's effort. Effort is a carefully calculated, uniquely personal formula that takes into account working memory, background knowledge, requisite skills, and processing demands.

Shanker (2020) describes a study where the researcher could tell when students would give up on a difficult task by watching for pupil dilation and heart-rate escalation. Interestingly, too much of either physical or mental effort can have this same result. Shanker calls this "limbic braking," an unconscious autonomic response signaling an intolerable peak of stress and a shutdown of effort. At this moment, a student's heart rate, blood pressure, and breathing rate skyrocket. Cortisol streams through their system, they sweat, and their blood glucose plummets. Their hypothalamus responds by conserving energy and stopping them in their tracks. It's not a matter of will or not trying hard enough. Limbic brakes are a sign of too much stress.

This happens frequently to students when they exceed their working memory capacity. Teachers may respond to this in several ways. They may coax or compel students to override their limbic brakes. If students do, their nervous systems remember and go into neuroceptive overdrive, encountering a fight or flight state every time they anticipate this difficult task (Shanker, 2020). It takes a high toll, mentally and physically. It's been shown in students with math anxiety that simply thinking about doing a difficult math problem lights up the brain in the same way physical pain would (Shanker, 2020). And when they are pre-emptively anxious, it takes up even more of their attention and working memory—making learning that much harder as they fight against their own fears and negative self-talk (Shanker, 2020). It is hard to get to that point of automaticity, which is linked to lower anxiety, visceral tension, and working memory load.

Adults might try to reduce some of the strain by reducing the complexity of the work, but that may be jeopardizing a student's chance to learn in more complex ways and develop their cognitive processes. Hammond (2015) reminds us that more strategic thinking and processing abilities are born out of challenge—new problems, puzzles, and inquiry. Oh, the balancing act that is teaching! Learners need chances to engage in critical thinking and complex tasks to get their brains communicating across areas and hemispheres (Cozolino, 2013). So, how can we help reduce load while still offering challenge? Instead of making a task easier, think about how to make it more accessible.

What helps with working memory?

Now, before you go down a rabbit hole—or try, like my dad did (twice!), to buy a book promising to improve your or your students' working memory, there is no evidence that we can improve the amount of information we can hold in mind at one time. It's part of human variation. However, we can circumvent the demand for working memory. There are a number of ways to do this which will each be discussed further below but include:

- accessibility tools that externalize information so we don't have to keep the minutiae of details in mind and are effective techniques to reduce working memory load, such as:

- digital to-do lists
- calendars
- visual instructions (think Ikea)
- reminder alarms for deadlines
- external memory aids that help us reference information we need as we work, such as:
  - charts, checklists, etc.
  - study guides
  - formula sheets
  - lists of steps
  - essential notes students should know (e.g., the important points which you could direct students to write down or simply provide).

You may notice bullet points help with your retention. They also help students! Design opportunities to make external memory aids in meaningful ways together, which may stick better, since simply copying or underlining or highlighting what we're told isn't deep processing (Kirschner & Hendrick, 2020). You may have your own creative ways to aid students' working memory, like Megann, who teaches special education.

INSIDER'S PERSPECTIVE

Megann Roberts, Special Education Resource Teacher, learning disability and ADHD

When working on units where information needs to be easily recalled, I work with my students to create Reference Rings! For example, when my Student Support Center students were learning to convert between units of measurements, students created small, key-sized visuals to help them remember how to convert "up" and "down" between metric units. They had a "key" for converting units of capacity, a key for units of mass, and a key for units of distance. I laminated the keys and hole-punched a corner so they could be stored on a ring. My students kept the ring in their pencil cases or looped into a binder (or, for one kiddo, just stuffed into their desk). Because students had created each key (their printing, their coloring, etc.), they were proud to use them. I encouraged my students to use their keys when working on assigned tasks, and they were encouraged to use their keys during assessment. This promoted the use of tools to support achievement; adults in professional fields regularly access manuals or guides, so we should be encouraging students to do the same!

Breaks also help reduce load! (I took a chocolate break right after writing that.) We can only actively think about something for 12–20 minutes, depending on age, and then need 5–10 minutes where our attentions wander before we can activate again (Sousa, 2001, as cited in Hammond, 2015). When we are at our working memory capacity, our brain will take a break, whether we like it or not. We can build pauses into our lessons so that student brains can cycle down for a moment (Oakley et al., 2021). This could look like asking students to:

- think of an answer
- draw their predictions
- talk about the concept with a neighbor
- write about what they are trying to understand.

It even counts as a break when you fumble with technology for a moment. Any of these pauses gives students' brains time to do a bit of consolidation unconsciously in the background. Breaks can be a reprieve from overwhelm, as Jo points out.

INSIDER'S PERSPECTIVE

Joanna Maselli, Secondary School Drama, English, and Special Education Teacher with ADHD and parent to a neurodivergent kindergarten student

When I think about how overwhelming the school day can be for me as a teacher and was for me as a student, that's been the starting place throughout probably my whole career when it comes to trying to develop and teach strategies for students to use to help break down their day into manageable pieces.

For those of us whose brains are wired to make connections—sometimes quicker than we realize or sometimes we're not even conscious of some of these connections—we can go into this overstimulated mode where we either shut down or melt down so quickly. This is because we are taking in a lot and it's happening very fast and our brains are trying to connect and make sense of everything, faster than we can even process the raw information itself. So, I feel like anything that you can introduce as an intervention to slow down that process, is going to help a number of neurodivergent students.

Mastery-based learning is really helpful in a lot of ways, as long as the definition of mastery is fairly flexible. What I am always trying to do is to make things digestible and to slow things down. It's a general approach that is very neurodiversity-affirming in the sense that we're giving students lots of opportunity to revisit the same sets of knowledge or information or the same skillsets and the same competencies over and over and over again, but from different perspectives or with different entry points or on different topics. And so, we can build in opportunities for students to practice applying things immediately upon learning them in more limited ways, and then developing that into complexity, whatever is required for the subject or the grade level later on down the line, and it's not just to build comfort. It's actually just to honor, in a neurodiversity-affirmative way, the fact that they want to engage with the material right away.

Sleep also allows our brain to take consolidation breaks—which is why sleeping on it sometimes yields positive results and we wake up with the precise solution to that short story ending or presentation sequence we've been scratching our heads over in all our waking hours.

The real fun fact is that, when we know something really well, we aren't constrained by working memory! Have you ever had a forgetful student with an incredible memory for their passion area? Our long-term memory (LTM) has infinite capacity, in theory, so when we link new information to what we already know, we can more easily remember and access the newer stuff. For example, squirreled away in my brother's long-term memory is every single Nintendo release date and game-related statistic, which he can tell you in a heartbeat. Ask him something he doesn't understand, and he walks away in confusion, blanking entirely on the question. This response is because his limbic brakes kick in and he can't rely on his LTM strengths. The question slid off the "slanted shelf" of working memory (Oakley et al., 2021). This is why interests are so important to bring into lessons and projects! Bringing Mario and Luigi into math problems helped my brother to conceptualize the math problems without as much working memory load so he could work through with a lesser degree of stress in learning.

Expertise enables us to think differently, spot similarities and differences, and handle greater challenge with more speed and ease (Kirschner & Hendrick, 2020). Some theorize this is because we have a schema—a cognitive framework for understanding the concept that is organized and contains related information and skills (Kirschner & Hendrick, 2020), which we can access rather than holding information temporarily in working memory. Similarly, when we practice something enough, we no longer have to consciously keep it in mind, like our first language or playing an instrument (Oakley et al., 2021). We learn differently when we are experts in something than when we are novices. A. D. de Groot's seminal study (1978) on the memories of chess masters and novice players found that grandmasters didn't necessarily have a larger working memory capacity or advanced cognitive skills, but they had stored more chess moves in their long-term memory. This enabled them to more easily and speedily flip through a mental rolodex of possible solutions, without cognitive strain (Kirschner & Hendrick, 2020). This is important as a rallying cry—"You can do it!"—but also as a cautionary tale because experts can learn in different ways than novices.

Would you be able to face off with a grandmaster? Students with expert background knowledge are able to learn through inquiry and experiential, student-led learning and won't encounter limbic braking. If students don't have the prior knowledge, just giving them discovery time and some manipulatives won't give them the cognitive framework to think about this new concept (Kirschner & Hendrick, 2020; Oakley et al., 2021). Inquiry-based instruction and searching for an answer to a problem use up reserves of working memory, so that it is not available to mentally connect concepts and learn (Kirschner & Hendrick, 2020). A student without this knowledge will likely sit there, uncertain of what to do.

It's also worth pointing out that all students benefit from learning "the why." For young children, "But why?" is a common refrain, helping them to make sense of the world. This tends to be a trait of many neurodivergent students, including those who are autistic and who have ADHD. Dyslexic students will generally do better when you focus on big ideas and connect to background knowledge than when expected to learn by rote (Shaywitz, 2005). Students with less content knowledge benefit from direct instruction and teachers prompting ways of thinking and connecting information, modeling, and being guided in their exploration and practice before they are expected to do it on their own (Hammond, 2015; Oakley et al., 2021).

Working on students' overall declarative (factual) knowledge about a concept as well as their procedural (embodied practice) knowledge is necessary before we can get them to think more strategically and metacognitively, expressing how they know what they know, what patterns they see, and so on (Kirschner & Hendrick, 2020). This is especially important for learners with working memory challenges, as without supported practice at school, how will they be able to keep it all in mind to catch up at home?

Getting things into long-term memory

Oakley and colleagues (2021) assert that the most important factor for strengthening concepts in LTM is revisiting the information through *retrieval*. We can't just re-read or follow along with a text or a process, which only uses our working memory. We have to test what we remember as we go. We can also tap into embodied knowledge through practice—again, so long as we are trying to solve without looking at an answer sheet or trying to remember the steps to the dance before we doublecheck. The more we do this, the more those new neural pathways get coated with myelin, which makes those pathways faster to access and more efficient.

There are many ways to use retrieval in class and at home. At various points in the lesson, you can have students write down or say to a partner what they think they just learned, in their own words. You could ask your class what the three most important points of the lessons in Social Studies were this week. You can teach them to make flashcards, to mentally work through a problem, to quiz themselves before they flip a page on what they think they just read, or to use mnemonic devices, such as how I learned the names of all the Great Lakes (HOMES—Huron, Ontario, Michigan, Erie, and Superior) by reducing the amount I needed to remember to one word with strong associations (Oakley et al., 2021). Challenge them to draw what they remember about the water cycle before reviewing it together. You can also teach them other memory strategies to aid retrieval, such as songs, rhymes, and mnemonic devices. I learned the names and orders of the planets while my teacher repeated the phrase My Very Easy Method Just Set Up Nine Planets and pointed to each planet on a 3-D model while we echoed, call-and-response style, each planet name (this was back when Pluto had full planet status!).

Notetaking

Students also benefit from being taught mental organization, like how to take notes and create cognitive frameworks to help them ascertain what is important and to make associations, such as how to find similarities and differences, identify patterns and relationships, evaluate most important to least important, and so on (Hammond, 2015). Students don't automatically know how to organize their thoughts and may need prompting at first to think in new ways. Teachers sometimes assume students will have these skills already and forget to explicitly teach them. When I ask teacher candidates how they learned to take notes or prioritize main ideas, the majority had to intuit how to do it themselves.

INSIDER'S PERSPECTIVE

Amber Borden, Secondary/High School Teacher, AuDHD

A practice that would have really helped me and other kids is to teach kids good notetaking skills much earlier on. We tend to only focus on teaching notetaking in school in the final year or two because we're assuming students are going off to university soon and will have to take lots of notes. We're never taught very well how to actually take notes, and, especially if you're a kid trying to take everything in and learn, you don't want to be sitting there thinking, "Okay, I have to fill out everything" and then writing out a note and relying on your own handwriting. Whether it's actually handwritten or you're able to have something recorded or being able to type something out, learning how to take notes is really, really helpful earlier on.

When I realized how to take notes, I just stumbled upon this method that worked really well for me using color-coding and different pens and highlighters. That was only in first year university. I was in Psychology, and so I kind of already had a good idea of how my own brain was working, so I was able to tailor my notetaking style to how my brain worked, but just think of all the things that we could actually get out of learning how to take notes properly for your own brain when you're a kid! Most kids will say, "Oh my gosh, now I have to study!" and then they burn themselves out for any quiz or test—and this pressure is from grade 3 [ages 8–9] onward all the way through high school. If they knew how to take notes, they wouldn't have to worry that there's a quiz or a test or feel like they've got to, like, burn themselves out in the process just trying to cram all the knowledge in there. Being able to access your own notes, learn how you think, and building in the metacognitive practices much earlier on would be incredibly beneficial.

Many students—particularly those with activated attentions or who are specialized processors—may take in different information and encode it in ways you might not expect. We can help draw their attention to relevant features, so the information is easier to retrieve and has more access points in their brains (Hammond, 2015). Talk out loud about your thinking process and what you pay attention to as a learner when reading, solving math equations, or during any other subjects. Graphic organizers can be great for cuing students to look for relevant information. We can also teach them to do this in more sophisticated ways with age.

I developed a notetaking system which helps draw students' attentions to what's important and makes it easier to develop study guides (Dymond, 2020).[1] Essentially, they leave a margin at the side and add a

---

1   Available on my website www.karadymond.com/resources/history-hacks

code with a legend in the margin for any important information, such as P for person, E for event, D for definition, etc. Encourage students to use short-forms, paraphrase, and utilize symbols, arrows, and equal signs to show associations, to capture meaning, and to help them encode information (Kirschner & Hendrick, 2020). Students can code their notes afterward if they struggle to do this as they go, adding colored highlighting or other ways of differentiating concepts and ideas. They can add emojis in the margins to capture how people felt in history at the events being discussed, which is drawing attention to the relevance of history; how do feelings inform decision-making, movements, and other human activities?

Students with working memory or motor challenges may need to concentrate on listening, making notetaking a barrier. When possible, have options. Some students need reduced-writing aids like organizers, fill-in-the-blank notes, and other alternatives to help them direct their attention to what's important. Allotting time to summarize the main ideas will help activate that retrieval *and* get students practicing prioritizing.

Building in varied techniques that get students thinking about information in different ways and revisiting concepts later increases the likelihood of main ideas being learned and remembered (Kirschner & Hendrick, 2020). When we consider access, we think about whether we can share notes, record lessons, give students the opportunity to record their own ideas in pictures, words, or audio formats, or some other brilliant idea you or your students may have. Ask them what might help them! Below, Lincoln reflects on his own experiences figuring out how to take notes and why it is useful to learn these skills early on.

INSIDER'S PERSPECTIVE

Lincoln Smith, K-12 Inclusion and Accessibility Teacher and Teacher Educator, ADHD

I didn't realize until I was in my Masters degree how I needed to take notes to pay attention. I learned then that I do best with notebooks that have completely blank pages so I can vary the size and location of different ideas based on importance and relationships and can freely draw images and diagrams to supplement.

Furthermore, I figured out how to use symbols in my notes and learned that I always have to be doing something (e.g., even doodling) during lectures if I have any hope of mentally staying on topic. Once I'd figured this out, I made a point to tell my professors at the beginning of the semester that I'd be doodling when they were talking, but that that was a sign I was listening, not not listening! They were all, of course, fine with this, but I do wonder (a) how I might have learned this about myself earlier and (b) what it would be like to not feel like I have to explain myself and pre-empt a misconception.

Notetaking can be done as a class, too, to help everyone understand what pieces of information are noteworthy—and why. Older students can crowdsource notes in a shared Google document, with different students responsible for collecting different pieces of information (the Dates Detective, the Biographer, the Event Recorder, the Definer, etc.). We can also teach them strategies such as color-coding—or in the case of individuals who can't discriminate easily between colors, using attributes like underlining with straight or squiggly lines, boxing key words, highlighting, etc. Teach several different brainstorming strategies, such as brain dumping, by writing all of their ideas down without editing, stream of consciousness style, before sorting them into themes or mind mapping on the same ideas. Some people benefit from sorting ideas in a more tangible way with post-its, so they can visually see the results of grouping one way or another. I teach students different ways of organizing ideas such as Venn diagrams, T-charts, and concept maps. We also talk about how some students benefit from talking it out with a peer or using speech-to-text before using a brainstorming method of their choice.

Studying and directing attention

In a similar way, we want to be as clear about what and how to study as we are about how to take notes. Teach them how retrieval works and why it's essential for deep learning and get them thinking about how they can use it in their daily life. If students need to demonstrate learning on tests, teach them the skills they need. Crowdsource a study guide.

Discuss the format of the test. What did students think was important from this chapter? What kinds of questions would they put on the test? Put them in groups to make flashcards and quiz one another. Ultimately, you want to explain the format and scope of the test. Some students will be able to infer this on their own, but many will not pick up on the fact that you spent four more periods reviewing figurative devices than you did on grammar. Telling them what is on the test helps ensure they don't get overwhelmed studying the whole textbook and directs their attention so studying becomes more manageable.

On tests and worksheets, reduce visual clutter. Maximize space, which will benefit activated attentions, specialized processors, distinct decoders, and measured movers. Some learners may benefit from wider lines when responding.

Although attentional supports help everyone, I have to include a shoutout to my people with ADHD. Renowned psychiatrist Dr. Russell Barkley (2020) points out that people with ADHD have trouble distinguishing between relevant and unimportant details. The same has been said about autistic folks (Vermeulen, 2012), and it may also be true of other folks with sensory-processing differences. Cuing can help with attention, but we still seem to turn away more frequently than others. We can find it harder to remember how to solve problems or to follow spoken instructions. We are more successful when you give us the information visually, and we thrive in classrooms that have flexibility and choice.

Tip! This isn't limited to learning. Writing down your praise for students (especially those with ADHD, who can be very hard on themselves) is a great way to ensure that it is remembered. Spoken praise is easier to forget. Out of sight, out of mind.

Strategies for attention and memory

These interrelated strategies can support attention, working memory, and deeper learning. They're equally important to know as a teacher and as a learner. We can plan these things into our lessons AND we can teach students how to make the most of their learning. Here are some of the difference makers for all kinds of minds:

Working memory supports

- Consider what parts of your lessons rely on working memory and where you may be able to reduce load.
- Teach processes you expect students to use, such as:
  - how to take notes
  - how to study.
- Get students connecting to prior knowledge and experiences. Helping students to see the relevance or to identify how a pattern is similar to another process they've already learned mobilizes the strength of information they already have. Each connection gives them more chances to remember information later.
- Build in supportive practice where students can access modeling and advice, as needed (kind of like an escape room, where some may be fine muddling through on their own, and some may ask for hints or need a little more guidance to determine what is relevant). Some learners may prefer learning through doing and repeated practice. This procedural learning can take longer than memorizing all of the facts and information (declarative learning) but tends to lead to automaticity. A blend of both approaches provides even more chances to establish neural pathways.
- Tap into interests to take advantage of long-term memory to learn new concepts and skills (and also benefit students by improving their expressive language and reading comprehension, by recognition of personhood, and by showcasing their strengths, building inclusion, and increasing comfort and engagement).
- Brains need breaks! Plan for mini-breaks and chances to chat, process, and think about what they just learned.
- Use memory aids—rhyme, music, call-and-response, mnemonics with new content to help create multiple neural pathways and access points which can cue remembering. I had a biology teacher who rewrote pop songs to help us learn concepts.
- Plan your lesson opening and closing carefully, as we tend to remember the first or last part of a lesson the most, which is known as primacy and recency effects (Hammond, 2015).
- Revisit ideas repeatedly, spaced out over time.
- Use interleaving—rather than solving all the questions of one type before moving on to another type of question, intersperse

different types of questions so students have to recognize when to apply the correct strategy (Kirschner & Hendrick, 2020).

- Use images and words to illustrate concepts, and ideally close together so students don't have to try to keep them in mind. For instance, flipping the page to find a legend and then referring back to an image on a previous page uses a lot of working memory (Kirschner & Hendrick, 2020; Zheng & Gardner, 2020).
- Continue to nurture a safe, comfortable environment as studies have shown that positive emotions may increase attempts and learning outcomes of students; and people with a happier outlook recall happy memories more easily than sad people, whose brains are primed to more strongly recall sad memories (as cited in Zheng & Gardner, 2020). This speaks to another power of a calm, supportive environment. It'll help things stick!
- Change the context sometimes and move outside for walk and talks on a topic with a partner.
- Clear clutter (both on the page and in the room). Try to assign fewer questions per page for less visual demand on working memory.
- Chunk questions/tasks rather than reducing complexity for students who need to tackle things in bite-sized amounts.
- Instead of making everyone write down all the deadlines in agendas at the end of the day, take a photo of the homework board and post it. This reduces working memory load and the frustration of one more transition. If students must write in an agenda, teach them to write in code (M for Math, L for Language, etc.) to reduce demands. Though in this day and age, posting any deadlines on a digital platform saves everyone a lot of headaches!
- Let students with smaller working memory capacities use other people's notes so they can focus more on listening (Oakley et al., 2021).
- When possible, reduce background noise and distractions.
- Make other access points available for students, such as related videos, extension questions to research, books, and more.
- Externalize some information with charts and posters for the whole class or lists for individual students.
- Teach and practice routines for independence so that students no longer have to think about the steps or what's expected.

- Keep repeating the big ideas to enhance memory and mental organization (Barkley, 2020).
- Play memory games to activate retrieval in class.

Let's hear how these kinds of adaptations have worked for a real-life student who had difficulty with spelling tests.

INSIDER'S PERSPECTIVE

Merryn, 10-year-old Student with dyslexia and ADHD

I hate spelling tests. I just don't understand why they are important. I know my brain, and they don't help it. One year I had so many words that I had to memorize and they just wouldn't stick in my brain. What helped me learn some of them was when I made up a story for each word. I remembered how to spell the word "five" when I pictured "five interesting vultures evolving." In grade 2 [Year 3 in the UK], my teacher showed me how learning one spelling rule at a time would help me with my spelling. She would only give me five words at a time to remember. I asked my mom if she would pay me for every word on the test I got right, and this helped me focus because I really like buying things. In grade 3 [Year 4] I liked when my teacher let me skip spelling tests altogether. Instead of spelling time, I got to have quiet reading time in the halls. The hall was so quiet and I didn't feel rushed to read my words fast. I could do it at my pace and take my time without anyone watching.

Attentional supports

- Cue and direct attention to aid information processing. This could be by use of color, arrows, and other symbols (visually), through gesture, or through cognitive scaffolds, such as itemized lists (e.g., "Write down 'Five main causes of WWII' as a heading and the numbers 1 through 5 below it...").
- Color-coding can speed up processing and can help with memory of relationships, order of operations, categories, and more.

If someone can't distinguish colors easily, use other attributes to distinguish these attributes, such as underlining with different types and thicknesses of lines, capital letters, circled or boxed terms, etc. Make sure students understand why the information is displayed a certain way—or challenge them to come up with their own systems of meaning making.

- Ask students to compare how they organized information with others. What did they notice that was dissimilar? How did their concept map look? What did they find that went in the center of the Venn diagram?
- Crowdsource notes and study guides.
- Give processing time before students need to provide an answer.
- Have students use technology to make memory games, flashcards, etc.
- Regularly re-establish attention. Remember minds naturally wander as we learn in brief intervals.
- List instructions in point-form so they are easier to understand and to see what is important to do. Many learners will feel overwhelmed by a paragraph with the steps embedded as a block of text and not know where to start.
- Be specific and clear about your expectations and what you are asking students to do.
- Show them examples and model processes, while talking about your thinking out loud.

In one study surprising no primary teacher ever, recess was found to improve focus and engagement of students, especially those who had ADHD (Jarrett et al., 1998, as cited in Reeves et al., 2016). Multiple studies have also found that incorporating movement into teaching, learning activities, or assessments can improve student learning and outcomes as well as their interest and attention during these times (Lindt & Miller, 2017). This could be associating content with specific movements, such as raising a hand any time they hear or see an adjective, or hopping when they step count and hit any number divisible by 5 (Lindt & Miller, 2017). This may be difficult for some learners' working memory, especially if only using auditory cues, so add in visuals, if you can, and slow it down if you have learners who are measured movers and whose reaction times may not be as fast as others. Use dance, roleplay, groupings that move to position themselves in a specific way to show their thinking, etc. During read-alouds, try to engage participation by creating a sound-scape; adding sound effects at specific moments to capture feelings; raising a hand when they hear one of the vocabulary words; or clapping to signify when they think there is a period at the end of a sentence (Lindt & Miller, 2017).

Direct instruction in access points

Environmental cues

Teach students to pay attention to sensory memories when they recall information. Many of my memories have encoded sensory details from the original context (I'm thinking about you, carpet beetles!). Where were we? What was I wearing? What were we doing? Interestingly, the environment in which we learned something can act as a cue to retrieve stored information. Studies have shown that students perform better on exams in the location wherein they initially learned the test material (as cited in Zheng & Gardner, 2020). My very cool biology teacher used to prompt us to think about where we first learned a new term.

Mental associations

Explain how connecting new information to something they already know makes meaning and gives those neurons something to connect to. Calling to mind related concepts we've associated with new information in our minds is a strong memory aid.

Context

Have students practice new skills in the way/place they will be expected to use it, rather than in isolation.

Multimodal remembering

If I gave you a pincode to remember, you might use a strategy such as speaking it out loud or visualizing it until you are able to write it down. Teach students to use verbal rehearsal (especially students with ADHD or dyslexia, who may not use this strategy on their own: Barkley, 2020; Smith-Spark & Gordon, 2022) or visualization, if they are able to.

Roman Room (aka Method of Loci) visualization

Another visualizer hack when trying to remember disconnected pieces of information is to make up a story about them and pair it with a familiar visual. For instance, imagine walking through your house and each room houses an item related to what you need to remember. You use the long-term memory to trigger the random facts (Barkley, 2020; Mind Tools, 2024).

Interests

Think of a way your interests connect to the topic.

Externalizing

Teach how to make lists or jot thoughts down to help reduce working memory load.

Retrieval

Arguably the best strategy to teach students is to try to recall information from memory rather than simply re-reading information. Strategies (Oakley et al., 2021; Faith et al., 2022) include:

- Say the thing you're trying to remember out loud.
- Visualize what you are hearing (for those who can) like a movie in your mind.
- Make charts or diagrams, or draw what you remember from memory before doublechecking.
- Make flashcards and quiz yourself or have a friend/family member quiz you (there are digital flashcard apps, too!).
- Test your recall as you read by stopping at intervals (e.g., paragraph, page) and thinking about the gist of what you just read.
- See if you can define a key word or concept or work through a problem without referring back to the textbook or notes.
- Take a moment to write down, draw, or discuss what you think you just learned.
- Test your memory for what you learned in a particular subject outside of school times, such as at the end of the day/week/ month.
- Explain what you learned to someone else from memory (even

to a pet, as the act of explaining is what helps it to stick, not the understanding of the other party!).
- Try to answer questions first without referencing the type of problem and the solutions in the text.

Tool of the Day or Week

Teach tools such as:

- text readers—Have students experiment to see if they attend and remember better when they hear a text read vs. reading alone. Research supports listening along with visualization as a powerful strategy that reduces cognitive load, even more so than reading and simultaneously imagining it, which both use visual channels (Zheng & Gardner, 2020)
- reading out loud to oneself as a strategy
- pacing and talking out loud (at home) while brainstorming
- spelling and grammar tools so learners can focus on getting ideas out and go back later to focus on the other details (reducing cognitive load)
- adding audio to aid recall—If memorizing definitions, record them being read slowly and listen to them when you go for a walk or on the bus. Try and say the definition in your head or out loud faster than the audio. (I used to memorize scripts this way!)

Encourage metacognitive talks

- Have whole-class and individual talks about executive functioning skills. Faith and colleagues (2022) recommend teaching these explicitly as well as in natural situations by pointing out when your own executive functioning skills are being used or not working as well as you would like, normalizing variability and vulnerability; and pointing out executive functioning successes when you see them. Some of the mini-lessons I give include:
  - *Working memory*—Explain how our capacities vary person to person and even task to task, depending on how automatic a skill is. Discuss various supports people use when it's hard to keep information in mind. What strategies do you and students already use?

- *Sustained attention*—Show that classic video where the gorilla walks through the basketball game and most students don't notice because they've been cued to count the number of passes. Our brains can be very selective and miss things. Part of developing as a learner is gaining awareness about what is relevant. Talk about when sustained attention is easy and when it is not, and what gets in the way. Is it internal distractions like imagination, or external distractions like the fluorescent lights and busy walls? What could help next time they need to sustain attention?

- *Brainstorming*—Consider which cognitive frameworks you want students to experiment with and give mini-lessons on how and why we use that type of tool. What sorts of attributes does it capture? When can we use it? What tools help students to get ready to write or organize their ideas before they are asked to express them in written or spoken word or in images/art?

- *Difference-makers to learning*—What are some things that strengthen capacity to learn? Exercise, sleep, food, and hydration all impact your brain's health and ability to form dendrites.

• Incorporate metacognitive prompts throughout the day, such as:

- "What helps you remember new information? For example, writing it out, drawing it, making a silly song or rhyme, watching videos about it, trying to visualize it, or practicing it."

- "What helps you pay attention in lessons? For example, doodling, taking notes, using a fidget tool, listening and getting notes from someone later, drawing what you're learning about, or your own great idea."

- "What helped you most in remembering information for today's test?"

- "Which retrieval strategies work best for your brain?"

- "When is [e.g., remembering/sustaining attention/organizing ideas] easier for you? When is it harder? What helps when it's hard?"

- "What strategy would you recommend to a classmate who was having difficulty with [e.g., remembering/sustaining attention/organizing ideas]?"

- "Which executive functioning skill do you want to better develop? Which tasks/classes use that executive functioning skill?"
- "What executive functioning skills did you use to beat that video game? Get to the soccer tournament?"
- "When do you notice your teacher's executive functioning strengths? When do you notice that your teacher struggles with EFs?"
- "What strategies do you see others using to support their EFs?"
- "Which executive functioning skill might be a challenge for you during today's scheduled activities? How can we make that less challenging? Where might you shine?"
- "What's one barrier you might experience in today's work period? What might help you through/over/around that barrier?"
- "How did that go for you today? What worked? Any unanticipated barriers? What might work better next time?"
- "What have you learned about yourself as a learner this week?"

Conclusion

This chapter speaks to the difference-makers that aid students in deeply learning new information. For teachers, knowing brain-based ways to help direct attention and support working memory while strengthening long-term memory formation is a game changer for how we teach. We can empower students, too, to meaningfully reflect and develop cognitive frameworks to guide their own thinking and studying.

CHAPTER 3 HIGHLIGHTS

✓ Executive functions (EFs) are a cluster of skills that help us to engage in goal-oriented behavior. This chapter discusses sustained attention, working memory, response inhibition, and mental organization.

✓ Neurodivergent EFs take longer to develop into maturity.

✓ If a lesson hooks a person (e.g., is relevant, evokes curiosity, is accompanied by powerful visual or aural elements, or is challenging), that information may get into working memory, which can operate for 5–20 minutes.

✓ Working memory capacities vary and impact how learners experience learning as well as what tasks may or may not be feasible. There are capacity limits and supports to be aware of.

✓ Limbic braking, or cognitive overload, is a sign students have hit a wall. Reducing demands is better than pushing them to override their autonomic nervous system, later working to build capacity another way.

✓ To learn, we have to *do* something with the new concept, or our brain discards it. Retrieval strategies, connections to background knowledge, and using both declarative and procedural systems in our classrooms help students retain concepts for the long term.

Questions for the reader:

✓ How do you get students thinking, remembering, and moving through the learning process?

✓ What is one new way of doing things you could test out?

✓ What could you stop, in order to make room for something more supportive?

✓ What sparks of curiosity and insight have you inspired already in your students? How did you do that?

How We Get Things Done

*Universal Design, Scaffolding, and
Helping Students Complete Tasks*

Brian has fine-motor difficulties. He is assigned a geography project which includes presenting a map for a fictitious island and a tourism pamphlet. He is excited by this project and works for hours after school for an entire week. He doesn't want his parents to help him, and they're impressed with his drive. He usually gives up when cutting and pasting is involved or anything requiring writing or drawing. He doublechecks that his parent put the project in the car on the morning when it's due. He's so excited to share his great ideas for Brilandia! A week later, he returns home, defeated. The teacher assigned a grade and included a note: "Brian should put in more effort. I expected more from him."

Patrice is autistic, chatty, and cerebral. She is given a social studies assignment to write a diary from the perspective of a pilgrim on the *Mayflower*. She puts off the assignment, as she is blocked when she tries to write from a first-person perspective. She doesn't get the assignment in, despite having lots of ideas for a short story from third person, which she is able to narrate to her mother when asked what she thinks life would be like, what someone might feel on the ship ride, etc. She doesn't think her teacher would be open to a different way of demonstrating perspective-taking, so she doesn't ask or explain her difficulties. Her teacher reminds her a few times and she says she forgot it at home. She gets a zero.

Santana has more than 20 outstanding assignments and assessments listed on Google Classroom. She appears disengaged in class unless it's groupwork. When she has any independent work, she gets up out of her seat, asks to go to the washroom, or chats with friends. She hates reading and can never answer questions after reading a text. When she does any writing at all, it is brief and does not match the depth of insights she gives orally after watching videos or dramatic performances of peers. She misses deadlines and says she doesn't care. She doesn't tell anyone, but when it comes to getting words on a page, or doing mental math, or remembering what instructions she just read, her mind goes blank. She has no idea what to do. With so many things outstanding, she feels she'll never be able to catch up.

Do any of these sound familiar? (They are composites of various students I've taught.) It's overwhelming as a teacher to think of all the needs in our classrooms. It's an unpleasant truth that, as much as we want students to produce graphic-designer quality work and be responsible for all deadlines, our willing it to be so is not enough if they don't yet have the skills. We also have to remember that effort has a history capable of weighing down students' ability to learn (Shanker, 2020). Brian no doubt worked harder than many of his peers, putting in the additional effort required to work through his motor challenges without limbic braking. He persevered. He worked through the hard parts. The teacher's assessment was crushing. What will happen on the next task, now that he has received the message that his efforts were insufficient? Will the effort vs. reward be enough, or might his limbic brakes take over?

If you read Chapter 3, you'll recall students' limbic brakes kick in any time they unconsciously or consciously feel a task is too energy-consuming or difficult or will not provide a sufficient reward. Some students' limbic brakes kick in more regularly. It isn't a matter of effort, but an autonomic biological response that goes off without the student's awareness or intention. If you asked me to figure skate for a million dollars, my limbic brakes would kick in. I'm like a baby giraffe on skates and the idea terrifies me. If you asked someone who had been skating all their lives, they'd probably be thrilled!

The behaviors we're seeing in these three students are indicators of the stress and internal struggles with which each is grappling (Greene, 2008; Delahooke, 2019; Shanker, 2020)—it's a signpost to look a little earlier down the road, to see where the roadblock occurred.

No one wants to make mistakes. It is easier for students like Santana to give up when they see an overwhelming mountain of outstanding work. Appearing not to care is preferable to either feeling or being perceived by others as incapable. No one wants their weaknesses to be on display.

This is where we go wrong sometimes when we teach our classes about growth mindset. The implication is that a person who is not seen as making progress is making a choice not to improve. This is a significant and erroneous value judgment. All humans have an innate need to do well. I always go back to the philosophy of psychologist Dr. Ross Greene (2008), which is essentially "Kids do well if they *can*, not if they *want* to."

This is why we need to think critically about how we perceive effort. We aren't accounting for how each student's amygdala aims to protect them and so easily trigger those limbic brakes. Because all learners have different strengths and challenges, they will experience tasks and activities in the classroom in different ways. What I fly through, you might get stuck on and take twice as long. What is a breeze for you, I may give up on altogether.

The more we learn about learner variability, the more we can plan pre-emptively and then responsively to learners. Imagine if we created a community where each student had a say in how they showed what they knew without non-essential assessment criteria getting in the way. If each student realized everyone, including teachers, encountered barriers. If they learned it was beneficial to talk about parts of learning that feel hard, and reaped the rewards of collaborative problem-solving and skill-building as a result. Imagine how easily we could help Patrice solve her problem, just by listening to her barrier and explaining what it is we need to see in the assignment. If we view learners who get stuck or who don't do as well as we expect as those encountering barriers, we might be better able to design options and supports that allow all the Brians, Patrices, and Santanas of the world to express their knowledge in ways that benefit them.

In this chapter, we'll tackle planning before we know learners' specific needs, more EFs that help learners get things done, how to identify barriers—and ways to help students find the leg up they need to overcome them.

Planning for everyone

Unit planning

Expecting learner variability means teachers can build in different access points, choices, supports, instructions, and executive functioning mini-lessons, right from the outset. Backward planning—where we consider learning goals over time and work backwards from the culminating assessment to consider the curriculum unit as a whole and the skills we must teach, lesson sequence, and design—helps us to think how we are framing learning as a process and scaffolding new or developing skills students will need along the way. This is planning on a macro scale. Here are the questions I ask myself:

What are the overall learning goals?

- By the end of the unit, what do I want students to know and show?

What am I really assessing in each task?

- From this vantage point, identify the barebone minimum requirements. Then, deconstruct tasks and look for all the other requirements built into the task. All of the extra bits can be adjusted for the learner. For instance, if what I really want to assess is understanding of new vocabulary, I could allow demonstration of understanding through:
  - oral expression
  - written expression
  - digital quizzes
  - matching definitions to concepts with post-its or cue cards
  - matching definitions on a worksheet
  - a drawing of the concept
  - a combination.

Do students have the prior knowledge and practice of requisite skills? Have I built capacity?

- Map out any skills students are assumed to already have, or which are needed for aspects of the task.
- Identify executive functioning skills embedded into the expectations.
- Look for opportunities to teach mini-lessons on skills and to "think out loud" to develop that skill.

What might be barriers for particular learners?

- Consider what might be uncomfortable for or unreasonable to ask of particular students.
- Identify challenges across the five domains (activated attention systems, alternative communicators, specialized processors, distinct decoders, measured movers).
- Brainstorm other possible ways of doing things.
- Ask the students what they think.

Lesson planning

On a micro scale, we also plan lessons as we go and look for ways to incorporate Universal Design for Learning and differentiated instruction. If you don't remember the specifics of those principles from teachers' college, simply think in terms of access, agency, and wellbeing. Let's say I'm planning a grade 2 structures lesson. My goal for students is to be able to sort objects by characteristics—rigid or flexible. Here are some guided questions I might consider (which are highly adaptable to any age or topic):

How do I engage students in ways that make them excited and comfortable to participate?

- Have I included a *hook*—like a challenge, call-and-response, rhythm and music, or a video?
- Have I *welcomed* students to join, rather than chastised those who need more transition time?
- Is my *general demeanor* enthusiastic? Can I tell a few jokes about the subject, even if students groan affectionately?
- Have I taught them the *habits*, *routines*, or *skills* they need later on in the lesson, such as defining "flexible" and "rigid" and classifying objects?
- Have I gotten them to think using *cognitive frameworks*, such as similarities/differences/commonalities? In this case, have we thought of objects in each category or that may have characteristics of both, such as bridges, and asked them to hypothesize why something that is designed to be solid might be considered stronger because it is flexible?

- Can I *phrase questions* in ways that invite more than one possible and plausible answer?
- If I use a graphic organizer to help direct attention and sort objects according to characteristics, have I taken a minute to *show how it is used*? (The next year I teach the lesson, I might challenge myself to develop a less scaffolded graphic organizer so students can pick what option works best for their brain.)
- Do I have a *document camera* or *projector* so I can model comparisons like a Venn diagram effectively for students? (While a regular old chalkboard can also provide this, some learners with smaller working memories may not be able to hold "talking out loud" in their heads and your body may block their ability to process what you are doing in the moment.)
- Can I make the lesson *interactive*—such as using an interactive whiteboard and inviting students to write or sort information on the screen; designing a low stakes class quiz game on an app like Kahoot or Quizlet; or inviting student volunteers to come up and do an I-spy game looking at objects for their classmates?
- Have I built in opportunities for students to make and share their own *connections*?
- Can I *gradually build capacity, comfort, and responsibility*, such as moving from teacher modeling, whole-class problem-solving, group or partner tasks to individual work?

How do I allow students to participate and show their knowledge in different ways?

- Could I create opportunities for students to show me what they know with a *nonverbal cue*, like a gesture we assign to each of the characteristics? (Many students will have no problem demonstrating their understanding orally or in writing. Others may be less inclined—or unable—to participate in these ways.)
- Could I use *physical materials for students to showcase knowledge visibly*, such as voting sticks with "Flexible" or "Rigid" on each side, or give the class whiteboards and have them record "R" or "F" as I show pictures of spaghetti, popsicle sticks, and other objects?
- Could I give students an *independent choice of performance task*

so they can pick a way of showing what they know? After I do a few of the whole-class options to practice identifying these traits in objects, I could give them magazines to cut out pictures of objects and sort them or provide physical cards to categorize with structure names on them. I could have students make posters and draw things that are rigid or things that are flexible. I can have students write riddles, so we guess what the object is: "I am sturdy and solid. You might call me rigid, but I do quite a lot. One of my important jobs is to hold up meals on my back. I support you during homework sessions. People sometimes sit around me and talk and talk."

- Could I utilize the power of many brains with an *inquiry project in small groups*? Students could design a bridge between two chairs made of popsicle sticks and one out of rolled up newspaper and compare which can carry more textbooks. (I haven't tested both of these, so make sure you do a trial run!)
- Have I built in some form of *reflection on learning*, to strengthen consolidation of concepts and student metacognition? For instance, students could draw or circle an emoji to reflect on how well they feel they understand the two new concepts we learned today.

How do I help various processors?

- If I show a video, can I use *closed captioning*?
- Can I show *visuals* to support comprehension?
- Can I speak at a *comfortable pace and volume*?
- Can I *define vocabulary* and externalize information by posting new terms?
- Can I *model* what I expect them to do, and show exemplars?
- Can I give *processing time* after I ask a question so that more students have time to collect their thoughts and potentially share an answer?
- Can I build in *thinking opportunities* to write down or share thoughts with a partner before inviting answers?
- Have I given *instructions orally, visually, and step-by-step*?
- Are there *several examples* I can show, so students know there are different models of success?

How do I adjust for learners with distinct decoding needs?

- Have I *defined* all of the words and used *visuals*?
- Are my instructions *clear, brief, and step-by-step*?
- Can instructions include *pictures* of steps?
- Can *students work in partners* and noodle out together what to do next?
- Can I *record audio instructions* on Google Classroom, or have I taught students how to use a *speech reader* when they encounter text they don't understand?
- Do they have access to *translation tools* if the language in which I teach is not their first language?
- Have I let them know *how to access help* in our classroom? Are there ways to do so nonverbally, like a signal or sign?

Have I included options for learners who need movement-based adjustments?

- Have I made available *larger manipulatives* or items of various textures if doing a sorting task to help learners with fine-motor difficulties or tactile needs?
- Have I considered supports like magnets on a baking sheet to hold things in place to *help students keep things where they want* in space?
- Have I considered the frustration factor and *adjusted fine-motor tasks*, offering alternatives such as pre-cut images to sort prepared in advance?
- Have I considered *alternatives to writing*, such as speech-text, point form, true-or-false statements, or fill-in-the-blank organizers?
- Have I ensured there is adequate *space to navigate around the room*, making sure that aisles are clear if doing groupwork or tasks that have students moving about?
- Are *materials within reach* of everyone? Have I ensured the placement of materials will not result in any accidental spills or bumps?
- Are there *kinesthetic* ways to teach this concept, adaptable for a range of movement abilities?

Let's hear from an educator (that's not me!) about the benefits they have seen through using Universal Design for Learning.

INSIDER'S PERSPECTIVE

Matthew Tinto, Teacher to students 9/10 years old (grade 4 in the US) and 11/12 years old (grade 6 in the US)

Incorporating Universal Design for Learning and what was essential for some really was effective for all students. Some of the supports for executive functioning that my students found particularly useful in my classroom were posting a daily schedule, the use of a class timer (so that students could see how much time they had to spend on a subject or lesson), and posting the school calendar so that students could keep track of important school events and due dates. Virtually all students listed these three as practices they found most helpful in my classroom. Regular social emotional lessons and understanding were also fundamental in incorporating "Thinking Classroom" math activities, where students have the opportunity to work in random groups to tackle authentic math tasks together on nonstandard whiteboards placed on the walls of the classroom. This allows students to get away from their desks, engage with each other, teach, and work through problems together authentically. Students get to work in random groups and teach other students what they know and learn.

During these tasks, students choose the problem they would like to solve as a group from a choice board and then answer the questions on whiteboards displayed on walls around the classroom. The students could use pictures, words, numbers, or diagrams to show and prove their answer was correct. While the students were working on the problem, I would check in with the groups to see how each group tackled each problem differently. Instead of answering questions or giving answers to groups while working through the problem, I would often ask questions and point out what I found interesting about what they had written so far. This helped to foster metacognition, self-advocacy, and resilience, as students worked in achieving the task as a group through the realization of effective cooperation. Once students had completed the task, pictures would be taken of each group's whiteboard and as a class we would discuss the different strategies each group used to show their understanding and which ones they found to be most effective. This would help consolidate their learning and make them excited for future opportunities to work together.

Planning across the day and week

Variety is the spice of life! Think of it this way: we don't want to force the Brians of our class to always need to show what he knows through writing. With his fine-motor challenges, we don't want to do his true knowledge a disservice. So, we are not privileging writing skills as the sole way to demonstrate learning. We can do this by zooming out for a broader view when planning our day and week and incorporate:

- a range of activities
- expression options (e.g., voice-to text, speech, drawing, written, gestural response)
- access points (e.g., hands-on, visuals, videos, text, critical thinking question).

So, if I have one lesson that is heavy on writing, I make sure other lessons are more discussion-based, hands-on, or incorporate roleplay or movement. This is an important lens shift, because like most teachers, I used to privilege how I like to learn best. I'm happiest loading my schedule with drama, discussion, and roleplay. I'm less comfortable with art projects, with my fine-motor and sensory difficulties. I've had to challenge myself over the years to learn from colleagues and get a little messy! I see the benefits it has for my students who don't love to learn the same ways that I do.

Variety can help students briefly interact with modalities and activities they are less comfortable with—a toe in the water, so to speak. They may build capacity or interest; and if they don't, you and they both learn something about their preferences. They also can take comfort knowing they will have other activities to look forward to in other lesson blocks.

Some of the questions I ask myself when looking across my day or week:

- Have I *balanced needs*?
- Have I ensured that the tasks students are asked to engage in throughout the day access *different modalities*?
- Have I built in *breaks* in many ways throughout the day?
- Will there be *enjoyable parts* for everyone?
- Is there a *throughline* to some of the concepts, such as linking a read-aloud in the afternoon to what we learned about in the morning's science lesson?
- How will I solicit *feedback* from students in multiple ways—such as casual conversation, lesson discussions, communication journals, tickets out the door, privately conferencing with a few students each day, and so on?
- How can I *weave learning across subjects* throughout the day or week?

Teacher candidates often wonder how to accomplish everything. As they settle into the profession, they'll learn how to integrate subjects for powerful learning that goes off the charts, like Andrea illustrates.

DR. ANDREA LIENDO, GRADE 1 (AGES 6–7) TEACHER FOR OVER 30 YEARS

One year, my colleagues and I all rented incubators and hatched duck and chick eggs in the classroom. None of my students, including me, had ever experienced a live creature being born that we were responsible to care for. This shared experience guided my classroom teaching for months to come. Student interest and initiative had been ignited. I provided the support, materials, and space for my students to learn and let student learning blossom. Students were engaged with purposeful daily mathematics, science, art, literacy, and writing activities, all revolving around birds and mammals. With teacher assistance, students discussed the similarities and differences between duck-lings and chicks and, with support, recorded the information on a large Venn diagram. Students would then be able to create a Venn diagram of their own. Students gathered around the incubator carefully studying it to ensure their own drawings and labels were accurate. Some students wrote addition and subtraction problems that involved duck wings, chick legs, and duck friends.

All of my students gathered daily as a class on the carpet to discuss topics and ideas about our baby birds, to sing songs about ducks, to share duckling and chick books, and to dramatize, read, and write stories and projects about our small ducklings and chicks. We engaged with critical and reflective thinking, having deep discussions as the students grappled with the serious issue about what to do with an egg that had not hatched. This real-life classroom experience fueled incredible writing and learning. Students were involved in shared writing and learning with their peers, grade 6 [ages 11–12] partners, as well as family members. It was an exciting and inspirational place to be and became a model of how to engage students and families in meaningful learning for all.

Different routes to the destination (and sometimes, different destinations!)

I once had a student declare, "if people actually died of boredom, schools would be deadly!" I prayed he was talking about his homeroom teacher's classroom! It reminded me, though, to always look at tasks and con-sider how to give all learners choice, challenge, and support. Students who encounter executive functioning barriers do better when they are engaged, interested, and aware of the relevance. So how to not kill joy and curiosity? Here are some ways to differentiate content and/or pro-cess in small or sometimes bigger ways, selectively, as it makes sense for the unit or lesson:

- *real-life accessibility tools*, such as manipulatives or calculators
- *tangible ways to experience concepts*, such as artifacts, videos, or roleplay to make learning visceral and relevant

- *highlighting what is important* via organizers, charts, and mind maps, which can help learners with slower processing or smaller working memory capacity—these are skills to explicitly teach learners and challenge them as you progress throughout the year to take ownership over identifying main ideas, spot what's important, organize their own thoughts, and so on
- providing more *practice opportunities* with various options, such as a table where learners can come if they want to review with teacher support; independent challenges; small group problem-solving; or explain-to-your-partner prompts
- *fewer questions* to reduce cognitive overload and working memory demand, especially if they have shown mastery or if the method of answering causes them greater frustration than peers—if they can do it four times, why do it eight times?
- class activities to *access content in various interactive ways*, both individually and in groups (e.g., learning centers; audiobook center; giving cue cards of fractions equations; having students solve theirs and then attempt to sequence as a class from smallest to largest on a clothesline)
- group activities where students *prepare a specific role in advance* (e.g., different roles in literature circles; reading different materials before a jigsaw where students teach each other; debates; various stakeholder perspectives in social studies or geography)
- a *choice board* of options, such as a choice of writing prompt or math challenge; different types of problems that may appeal to faster or more deliberate processors—rather than more questions, which could be seen as a punishment (Oakley et al., 2021)
- a *choose-your-own-adventure sequence of performance tasks* to build a portfolio (my grade 8 [ages 13–14] teacher posted a list of leveled tasks assigned a numerical value. We had to add up to a certain number, which could be earned through any combination. We could do multiple small tasks, a medium and a small task, or a very large task. For science and math marks, my partners and I researched a class fish, and presented care and maintenance needs along with a budget of related costs and required items. We were later tasked with going to pick up a fish that someone donated to us!)
- options for *acceleration*, such as lengthier and more informative sources or readings

- building in *guided problem-solving*, such as packages of clues of varying complexities to guide inquiry
- optional *access points* in downtime—videos, graphic novels, picture books, extension projects, books, etc. on the topics we're learning
- *project-based learning* where students can select their topic.

Predicting barriers

Whether backward planning a whole unit, creating week plans, or throwing together a last-minute activity, I use the proactive strategy of thinking through each domain to remind myself of learner variability, potential barriers, and how to adjust. From there, I can more easily plan ways to enhance access or embed agency. To review:

- Those with *activated attention systems* likely need supports around down-regulating or up-regulating emotions and coping through transitions or any challenging learning moments.
- *Alternative communicators* need alternative ways to participate and to provide feedback besides speech.
- *Specialized processors* need aids to absorb information.
- *Distinct decoders* may have a different relationship to text and will benefit from experimenting with voice-to-text, text-to-speech, and other accessibility tools.
- *Measured movers* may benefit from similar assistive technology, especially if they struggle to convey ideas on paper. They may need more time to practice motor tasks (e.g., more time at a particular gym station), or you may choose to reduce motor skills required (e.g., pre-cut tissue paper for art projects for those students who don't want to cut their own).

Regardless of category, students who are reluctant during particular subjects or activities may need *gradual entry points*. For example, for a learner who struggles with dramatic tasks, we could find a way for them to observe first until they feel they understand what is being asked; we could ask them to act as a "reviewer" and give feedback on the meaning of nonverbal cues or make suggestions on how to make a message even clearer; we could ask them to take on a very specific role, such as creating a sign introducing the skit and being the person to call action—and then we can work on building comfort and community so they can take on a greater challenge next time.

Also regardless of category, many learners will need *executive functioning supports*. Consider what skills are required and how you can scaffold these. The tips throughout this chapter can help you!

Nerd alert: More executive functions that help students get things done

Many of the challenges that arise in the classroom come down to difficulties with EFs. The greater the complexity of a task, or the more tasks we have to do at one time, the more we rely on EFs. Those of us whose EFs don't work as reliably will struggle more under these conditions (Barkley, 2020). Patrice and Santana, from the beginning of this chapter, both struggled with different EFs. Many students with and without ADHD will need support to develop EFs, which don't fully mature until the mid-twenties to thirties. Students with ADHD will need particular patience and attention from you, as ADHD research shows that our brains aren't coordinating across areas that need to work together and our prefrontal cortex (EFs), hippocampus (memory), and amygdala (emotions) may be smaller. Another difference is in our default mode network (DMN), a function of the brain that, for all people, shows high activity when we are daydreaming. People without ADHD can easily stop this activation and switch on their attention using another part of the brain—their task-performing network—when needed. Take a guess whose brains can't stop activating their DMN? Yep, we ADHDers continue to show activity in our DMN (Wilkins, 2023).

So, how do I work with my ADHD? It's hit or miss, some days. Generally, I use knowledge of my brain, workarounds, and assistive technology. In the classroom, I teach my students about their EFs and some tools that might help, as well! I gathered some awesome information on EFs (e.g., Delahooke, 2019; Faith et al., 2022; Hammond, 2015; Oakley et al., 2021; Shanker, 2020) to introduce vocabulary, explore concepts, and nuture an understanding of students' relationship to their own EFs.

While this chapter may talk more often about ADHD given my personal experiences, executive functioning difficulties also impact people who have experienced trauma, who have learning disabilities, who have mood disorders or extreme stress, and/or who have damage to areas of the brain involved in EFs. We've already talked about working memory, sustained attention, and response inhibition; now, let's talk a little about the others (Faith et al., 2022) and when you might address them at school.

Metacognition

Metacognition is your insight into your own learning, behaviors, performance, and needs. You use metacognition when you think through how something went, how you could improve, what was easy or hard, and set goals for yourself.

Metacognition also helps us explain what we're thinking or how we solved a particular problem. Metacognition doesn't just happen—it helps to be prompted, especially since our brains are not as practiced at it, demonstrating significantly less brain activity when thinking about ourselves compared with when we think about others (Cozolino, 2013). In a study of medical students learning new surgical skills, the group that focused on learning goals, such as creating a memory strategy to remember the steps, looking for patterns, practicing to mastery, and focusing on the part that is hardest, demonstrated better metacognition, task engagement, and outcomes than the group given outcome-oriented goals, such as speed of suture tying or being in the top three in the class (Gardner et al., 2016). Another study showed that surgeons who mentally walked through the procedure in advance performed better and also were better equipped to handle any challenges that arose than those who did not mentally rehearse (Louridas et al., 2015). Those who excel at metacognition tend to be quite accurate in their self-assessments. This skill is vital to self-directed learning!

Metacognition is woven throughout the fabric of my classroom. It is actually one of the last EFs I teach, but the first I implement. Long before I name it, I have students setting their own goals and thinking about their thinking. I verbalize my own thinking, modeling my own metacognition. I conference with a few students each day and get them verbalizing their own. I give students exit tickets with reflective prompts. We talk as a group about how an activity went and what we learned from it. My students also complete Google Forms self-assessments on their overall learning and individual goals before report cards are due. After receiving a major assessment back, they also reflect on what their goals are on the next task of the same type. There is rarely a lesson in my classroom that doesn't incorporate some form of self-reflection.

When I finally introduce the vocabulary and give a mini-lesson on metacognition, students can spot innumerable ways they have already practiced metacognition. If they can't, I'll ask them to tell me how they beat their last video game level. "Aha, do you know what you just did? You were using your metacognition!" Even better, I'll ask them to look at our chart of executive functioning skills and identify which helped them. "Goal-oriented persistence and sustained attention!"

Here is an example of how another educator taught metacognition in their classroom.

INSIDER'S PERSPECTIVE

Megann Roberts, Special Education Resource Teacher, learning disability and ADHD

I've found metacognition one of the hardest expectations to assess; I can have all the conferences in the world, but encouraging students to engage in metacognition without a guide (educator) had proven elusive... until I invited our Awareness Journals! Each page is a different color (purple, green, and yellow) and they are stored in bins on a countertop or shelf. I start by introducing the concepts one at a time. For example, we'll work on one Assessment of Learning for a week, with me prescribing which task they will use for reflection and which prompt they will use. Then, I begin to "open the table" for students to pick a page of their choosing and reflect on a prompt of their choosing. Eventually, students are selecting their own prompt page (Assessment of Learning, Metacognition, or Mindset) and responding to a task of their own choosing.

When I write feedback to students on assigned tasks, I've never had any write back to me... except in their Awareness Journals. Back-and-forth, back-and-forth, over and over. My students love telling me about their learning, their thinking, and their mindsets. It's been a beautiful addition to our classroom routine!

Many EFs are used together, especially as academic demands grow in complexity. Here are a few others to keep in mind:

- organization
- cognitive flexibility
- task initiation
- time management
- planning and prioritizing
- goal-oriented persistence
- emotional control.

Organization

Organization is the ability to sort and classify materials (physical) or ideas and actions (mental) in space and time.

Tidy desks, neatly written agendas, color-coding, and essays that flow logically are examples of top-notch organization. Those of us with ADHD often struggle with physical and mental organization, finding it hard to keep in mind what we were supposed to do with that worksheet just handed out (working memory); we have difficulty noticing time passing (time blindness); and because we forget about tasks or objects we can't see (object impermanence), things get lost in the desk or backpack and instructions get lost in the ether. It's really overwhelming to keep everything in mind! We will get to some ideas for mental organization momentarily, but for now, let's think of some of the physical organization strategies and routines you can teach.

Desk organization

I teach students how to create a pile, sorted from largest on the bottom to smallest on the top, for each side of the desk. I recommend one be all the things you write in (notebooks, workbooks, folders, paper). The other can be texts and textbooks. Organizing it by size makes it easier to see everything. We also talk about the physical check—looking while you put material back to make sure it goes back where it needs to! We learn to check the schedule and try to put away materials at the end of one subject just before the next one begins.

Filing papers

I also have students practice what method of filing is easiest for them: three-ring binders, folders with metal tabs, or pocket folders. Sometimes, we introduce a pocket folder as a placeholder to sort later. We consider what times in their class schedule make the most sense for organizing materials.

Packing up

Some students may benefit from packing their bag with anything outstanding from the morning and then a second pack up before home time. Visuals of what they need or explicitly cross-referencing with the agenda (if recorded correctly) can help.

Agenda writing

This idea may be confronting, if you think writing in the agenda is important for responsibility. Assistive technology, like the student or teacher taking a photo of the homework board and posting it to Google Classroom, makes this comparatively stress-free, especially for learners with smaller working memory capacities or fine-motor difficulties, or who have already hit that point of cognitive overload for the day. We adults frequently take photos of slides during presentations rather than write them all down! Why not allow students the same option? Is our end goal exhausting them with writing, or getting the information home? With a photo, all the information is accurate and available to students from home. They are still responsible for what they do next. (No more signing 25 agendas for completion, either!) Another option is teaching agenda code: students come up with a legend of short forms for subjects (e.g., M = Math, L = Language Arts). They can simplify what needs to be written, using these short forms.

Cognitive flexibility

This is the ability to cope and regroup when something requires a change or is not going as expected.

We need this skill often as teachers, when lessons don't go according to plan or when students inspire us to go in an uncharted direction.

Students need it to accept feedback, to adjust to others' needs, to try a new way of solving a math problem, to change their initial hypothesis, to edit a story they thought they were done with, and to be patient in groupwork rather than beginning the project without input from others. I actually do a Lego challenge where students decide on a structure to build, like a spaceship, and then they have to take turns placing a single piece at a time. They have to try to inhibit comments (unless complimentary) and accept where their peers place the bricks. They can't move the pieces in this challenge, as they're working on sharing a vision and adjusting their plan as they go!

Task initiation

This is the EF that helps us to easily transition and get started on a new or different task.

Often, for neurodivergent folks, activating to get a task done can be the hardest part. It requires us to stop what we are doing or thinking about (response inhibition), think about the benefits of the new task, shift attention, and prepare to do the thing. For those of us with ADHD, our neurotransmitters don't make this easy for us the way it is for others. It can feel physically painful or distressing to have to stop and shift.

Students with ADHD do better with teachers who have flexible classrooms (Barkley, 2020)—classrooms where we can explore, choose our own tasks, and benefit from having our natural curiosity piqued, our interests harnessed, or a challenge to engage us. If the issue is boredom, here are some ways to help:

- *Flexible products*—Allow students to produce work in a format that works for them. My graduate students have submitted written text, charts, infographics, mind maps, audio notes, videos, and even podcasts reflecting on their takeaways from various classes. My elementary students have produced self-advocacy projects expressing their learning strengths and needs in slides, speeches, animations, comic books, raps, songs, and videos. It's way more fun for me, too, to receive projects where I can marvel at my students' strengths and creativity.
- *Flexible topics*—Allow students to select different prompts, essay questions, or topics to explore. I suggested many of my own essay topics in high school when I looked at the list of suggestions

and inwardly groaned. I worked so much harder on topics I was passionate about than on topics I was not interested in, and I was able to access hyperfocus rather than crying my way through an eternity (or so it felt) to complete the less desirable task.

INSIDER'S PERSPECTIVE

'Evelyn' (pseudonym), autistic High School
Teacher with possible ADHD

I love having multiple ways of showing my learning, including multimodal assignment options. Student choice is so powerful. There can be such a huge difference between slogging through an assignment you feel unconnected to, versus getting into a flow state and working with passion and excitement because the topic or genre or medium is exciting to you. If you're neurodivergent, you might have a harder time getting into a flow state, and you might find it impossible to do work unless it is interesting to you personally.

I also give students tips on engaging themselves and setting the work environment up to be more conducive to task initiation, such as:

- selecting a soundtrack
- adding a challenge
- body doubling
- self-awareness check-ins.

Selecting a soundtrack

I've had several students test out environmental dopamine hacks that use a surge in happiness neurotransmitters to help with transitioning, such as playing favorite songs to be able to get out of bed in the morning. In class, we experiment with different frequencies of noise, soundscapes, binaural beats, and genres of music. I will play a few minutes of different examples and ask students whether any in particular affected them. I'll challenge them to experiment at home, too, and to create a homework time playlist. Some of us actually focus better when we control background noise. I tend to only be able to listen to podcasts when I'm cooking or driving and seem to focus better on the main task when the highly active part of my brain is muted somewhat by the extraneous auditory processing.

Everyone has their own preference in these cases—I've had students who enjoy voices on TV or podcasts in the background, as long as they were episodes they'd already seen or listened to. Now, there are other processors who may find it hard to listen to music while working as it can take up working memory capacity (Oakley et al., 2021). The point of these conversations is to inspire student metacognition and better awareness of what personally works for them.

Adding a challenge

I will set the kettle to boil for tea and see how many dishes I can wash in the meantime, just to get me started. Once I've started, nine times out of ten I'll finish the task. Students can add time challenges (how many they can complete in *x* minutes), self-impose challenges to incorporate a silly word into a task, learn a new skill, add a fake time crunch, or agree to a challenge with a friend, such as adding as many hidden references to a favorite show as possible, and so on.

Body doubling

Have you ever gone to the library to get work done? You might have been using this strategy, where it's easier to get work done when you're around other people also getting work done. I zoomed with friends to write this book while they caught up on emails or organized their closets! To maximize the impact, teach students to talk through their work period plans with a partner.

Self-awareness check-ins

Do they need a snack, water, or stretch? Can they snack while doing their work for a mood and glucose boost? Maybe they need a short break to dance it out or stim. It is hard for any of us, adults included, to sit for 40 minutes. Honestly, we all deserve check-ins and movement breaks!

When we begin to think about extended work periods or projects managed over time, we are utilizing even more executive functioning skills. I'll introduce a few more and then talk about how to teach them in the context of a long-term assignment.

Time management

This is our awareness and accuracy in estimating how long something should take and where we are in managing that task over time.

Many folks with ADHD struggle to keep track of time passing. We might not be able to estimate how long something will take and tend to procrastinate chores or tasks that in our heads feel like they will take eons—even if it only takes a few minutes. I've worked with plenty of neurodivergent students with perfectionist streaks who just want to finish something in one sitting and who need to be explicitly taught that some tasks are meant to be managed over time, a little each day.

Planning and prioritizing

Going hand in hand with time management and organization, planning and prioritizing is how we divide up what we need and want to do over time and decide what is most important to attend to first.

It's vital to remember that knowing how to plan and prioritize isn't intuitive for most students. Students with ADHD may be less likely to coach themselves internally or to visualize an end product, which means they need more scaffolding to know how to proceed with a complex task (Barkley, 2020). Like dyslexic students, they're also less likely to use verbal rehearsal (Barkley, 2020; Smith-Spark & Gordon, 2022). It's hard for anyone with already maxed-out working memory to keep everything in mind to plan it out. And so, we must show students how to become mentally organized.

Goal-oriented persistence

This is our ability to keep in mind and work toward an end goal, over time.

Those of us with ADHD don't activate easily for tasks that aren't attention grabbers. As mentioned, folks with ADHD have differences in how our neurotransmitters function—including norepinephrine and noradrenaline, which impact our stress response, focus, memory, response inhibition, and activity levels; and dopamine, which helps people to develop motivation, regulate emotions, and take action. Dopamine gives other folks a feeling of satisfaction and reward after doing something hard, which then makes it easier for them to do that thing again. If you have less dopamine and it sticks around for a much shorter duration, let me tell you—everything feels like a slough. Instead of riding the high of "motivation" as others can, our brains don't value distant rewards with no immediate benefit (Barkley, 2020).

Emotional control

Emotional control is how we handle our emotions in order to achieve our goals.

Often, what gets in the way is our emotions. Procrastination is an emotional regulation problem, where we prioritize how we are feeling in the "now" at the expense of our future selves. Meanwhile, stress intensifies and ends up lasting longer over time as the deadline approaches and we don't consider how this will impact us later. We are people who hope against hope to wait for inspiration, which doesn't come; and then we bank on adrenaline and cortisol cocktails to willpower our way through it!

For me personally, there's never a time that basic tasks feel easy or automatic—where I don't have to think about them, talk myself into them, bribe myself, or otherwise try to make up for the missing internalized rewards. It's hard to motivate for a long-term future benefit, when everything feels painful and takes more effort than it appears to take others. The exception of course is when I'm really interested in something, and then my attention turns on at the exclusion of all else. Hyperfocus kicks in and I can lose hours. But that level of activation is unpredictable and unreliable.

Supporting and developing executive functions in the classroom

Let's look at how these related EFs can be supported and developed during ordinary classroom activities including:

- independent work
- homework
- long-term projects
- classroom discussions
- groupwork.

Independent work

Inevitably, some students who are novices to a subject or skillset will need more attention. You may wish to use some of the following strategies:

Review table

Normalize that students who want to go over the task instructions one more time can come to a special "review table." Students who are confident to get started will do so and those who want to ask a question or two can have a little more attention.

Multimodal instructions

Ensure you've gone over instructions orally and written them down or given a list of instructions. In my graduate class I post audio notes where I read out instructions that students can reference any time. Some have said they feel comforted by hearing my voice!

Chunk & Check-in (Dymond, 2020)

When a task requires greater working memory or other executive functioning demands, students may need it broken down to not feel so overwhelmed. How you chunk the work can vary, depending on age and stage.

- Check for understanding, then assign a few questions at a time. Check back in. Assign a few more. Repeat.
- Cut a worksheet into strips and provide the student with one strip at a time. Check in. Repeat. Reduce number of questions as needed as mastery is demonstrated.
- Put one task per page in a folder so nothing else is visible to overwhelm a student. Circulate and periodically check in.
- Check in with the student and ask them what part of the work they plan to start with and how long they think that will take, without pressuring for speedy results. Let them know you'll check back in shortly. Revise the goal, and repeat.

Homework

While I much prefer work students can complete in the classroom where they have access to support, sometimes unfinished work or projects spill over into home time. I try not to have key assessments completed at home, for a few reasons. If a student can't do it in your classroom, they are even less likely to be able to do it at home. Sometimes, out of frustration, adults may end up doing all of the work. Family labor should not be the solution. Parents or guardians are not always available to help and, even if they are, they may not know how you have taught something, which could be confusing to everyone. Conversely, some students have jobs or other responsibilities, do not have access to additional support or tutoring, and will not be able to complete homework. They've put in a full day at school, just as we have. Isn't it important to teach work–life balance? All students deserve a break, whether they've produced a masterpiece or struggled to produce at all. (The same is true for us, whether we accomplished all of our lesson goals or barely brushed the surface.) Rant over! If there will be homework, do your best to reduce it or to make it meaningful.

Chunk & Check-in at home

If parents report needing to sit with their child all the time, suggest that they gradually release responsibility to children using the Chunk & Check-in strategy. They can ask their child to pick the first subject they want to work on, review what to do, set a mini-goal, and then the parent walks away for a short period of time. They can check back in shortly to review, and then go over the next part. Over time, parents can see if their child can do more in one block and check in less frequently.

One of my coaching clients, a 14-year-old, would become emotional and argumentative at homework time. We unpacked this together and they revealed they struggled because, despite a visual schedule and predictable routines, they always assumed each piece of homework would take the entire evening and they imagined all their electronics time slipping away. Their procrastination and complaints were what was actually cutting into their free time! So, I helped to make it visual—while working on time management.

As part of the Chunk & Check-in, their parent helped them to fill out a chart.[1] They'd write down one homework task at a time and a prediction of how long it would take. Then they'd write the actual time it took after completing it and before proceeding to the next task, taking a short break between if needed. (Recording the actual time became a helpful

1   Template available on my website www.karadymond.com/blog/homework-helpers

reference for future homework sessions. "Remember how last time, you thought this number of math questions would take you 40 minutes, but it was half that?") At the end, they'd tally the actual on-task time needed for completion of all homework. Below, the parent would keep track of the time used up by delays like complaining or procrastinating and that was entered on the chart, beside "how much less free time was there due to delays?" Below this, they recorded the total homework time for that day (actual time needed and delays). It ended with reviewing how it went and setting a goal for the next homework session to help it to go more smoothly. After a few days of logging this together and visually noting the difference, homework time became remarkably more efficient—and less dysregulating for everyone!

Supportive environment, breaks, and self-care

When we talk about work completion at home, I have students think about:

- Where do they like to work and what conditions make it easier to work in?
- What is a self-care act that sets them up for success before home-work time, such as a snack, a glass of water, and/or an exercise break?
- How can they periodically reward themselves for getting parts done?

   For instance, if they finish homework for one subject, can they take a short YouTube video break (e.g., a video under 15 minutes) or play a round of Candy Crush? I ask students to brainstorm short break activities that are easy to transition to and from between blocks of work. They also identify any extremely moti-vating activities that take too long or are too immersive, because those are better rewards to save for after all their have-to-dos are done. I personally know not to turn on the TV or play a video game until I'm done with all my responsibilities for the evening!

If students get stuck on the break or have trouble getting started, this presents a good collaborative problem-solving opportunity to discuss barriers, brainstorm some strategies, and test it out, possibly with a reminder from a family member or friend next time. The process of reviewing homework time goals, even at school, can help strategies to be remembered. I've had students create their own posters or other visual cues to display at home to help them remember to set that alarm and transition back. We've emailed parents together to communicate the plan to try and whether the student wants any prompts or supports. It becomes a point of celebration when students manage it on their own, even when it isn't every time.

Meaningful learning connections

Communicating with families about what students are learning may help them to find real-life extension opportunities that help to link learning to what students already know. This leads to deeper learning and neural connections. If you had the time, you could even give families guiding discussion points. One of the benefits of teaching the same grade each year is that if you've developed this one year, you can roll out the same information for families the next year. Some forms of homework that may benefit everyone:

- reading for pleasure for a period of time
- playing math games
- practicing typing and a style of writing on a topic the student finds highly motivating (e.g., for procedural writing, how to create a monster spawner in Minecraft; for persuasive writing, a movie or video game review)
- creating a mind map or chart of what they know about a topic and still want to explore
- identifying a question they have for the next day's class
- asking family, friends, or neighbors about their experience with the topic
- reporting on real-life or observed in TV/media examples of the topic
- writing or talking with family about how a new concept relates to their own life
- completing a virtual quiz game
- watching optional extension videos
- making flashcards of new words or concepts learned in the day
- identifying questions or concepts to add to a class-created study guide.

Long-term projects

When I assign a project that students are expected to manage over time, I build in EF mini-lessons prior to a work period that aligns with where they are in their planning. These tend to address common problems that can come up.

Planning, prioritizing, and time management mini-lesson

As we review a new assignment guideline, I explain how teachers expect students to use the time allotted to work on a project, a little at a time. We break down the stated and unstated assignment expectation into a big to-do list together as a class (and with later assignments, we might do this individually and then come up with a class version together). Unstated expectations can include everything from including your name and a title to building in time to edit or practice what you will say when presenting. Once we all agree we have broken down all of the steps, we assign a couple of sub-tasks to do each day. We might write these in the agenda or even map it out on a calendar. I want them seeing the value of the process, rather than attempting to do it all in one evening! We might also identify what executive functioning skills will be needed at various points.

Mental organization mini-lesson(s)

As we begin generating ideas for the project, I show them organizational strategies they already know and use, even if they don't think of it as organizing, like T-charts and Venn diagrams. Then, we learn how to make a basic mind map or concept map. I show them how I'd fill out a mind map using a debate topic that they might have opinions on, placing my main question at the center: e.g., Are uniforms in schools good or bad? All of my thoughts branch off from that, and I can use words, phrases, and images. Students help me complete the mind map. Next, I'll get them trying a mind map to brainstorm ideas for their project. Depending on the task and the stages, I might also challenge them to try strategies like:

- brain-dumping their thoughts on the topic in stream-of-conscious-style dictation (voice to text) or writing without editing to get ideas out
- alternating stream-of-conscious writing and mind mapping to refine connections

- writing ideas on post-its, which makes them easier to group and sequence
- opening a Google document, brainstorming potential headings, and then slotting in whatever information they already know
- creating an ideas bank before sorting into themes and weaving together.

If students have no background knowledge at all (which is hopefully unlikely by the time you assign a large assessment!), they will need a research work period and guided graphic organizer to collect information on the topic before they can mentally organize the project as a whole.

Task initiation and time management mini-lesson

Prior to one of our early work periods, we might talk about how hard it can be to get started, leading to a mini-lesson on task initiation. We look at or listen to initial brainstorms and then identify the next smallest step. I provide a graphic organizer for them to set a goal for today's work period. It also has a block to identify how the work period went, whether or not they met the goal and what might have been the barrier, as well as a block to set a starting goal for the next work period. This has two main benefits: students get better at realistic time frame goals as they see what they can accomplish in each period, *and* they may find it easier to get started if they've already set their intention the previous day!

Goal-oriented persistence and metacognition mini-lesson

In another session, we might use Faith and colleagues' (2022) Barriers & Strategies Protocol to get the class to come up with barriers that are common in a work period and solutions the class can try that might help. Then, we test it out. At the end of the work period, we review how it went without judgment. What helped? What was still hard? What might we try next time? I love having students teaching us all new strategies and solutions!

Emotional control mini-lesson

We talk about procrastination and what might cause it. We identify some of the feelings underlying it, such as anxiety, boredom, or overwhelm.

As a group, we look at a worksheet I developed for what to do when you're stuck,[2] and students highlight, star, or circle ones that might help them—or share their own ideas.

Classroom discussions

Throughout the unit, we continue the metacognitive work of discussing the task demands and problem-solving prior to work periods. Once students know executive functioning vocabulary and you have it posted somewhere visible, you can ask students before any activity or task what executive functioning skills might be involved, and which they might find easy, hard, or somewhere in the middle today. You can continue to have them suggest strategies to try, activating their metacognition. This can be done as a class or during individual conferences or reflective organizers.

We also talk about how none of us at any age have perfect executive functioning skills. Faith and colleagues have a great EF Checker for parents, teachers, and students to find out their executive functioning profiles.[3] You can even have students fill the teacher survey out for you and talk about your and their perceptions!

After I began explicitly teaching EFs, it was incredible to see how quickly we all began recognizing when we were using our EFs in real life. I'd point out when I saw EFs in action, and pretty soon, students could do the same. We also discussed how we can be really good at EFs in some contexts but not in others. Students would tell me they used emotional control, sustained attention, and goal-oriented persistence during their soccer game or when working through a video game level. I would also model talking about how I was struggling with organization (one look at my desk could tell you that) and needed to carve out some organization time, and students followed suit in sharing their challenges. "I'm having trouble getting started. I guess I can figure out the next smallest task." "I can feel I'm not sustaining attention very well—maybe I need a fidget tool!"

My favorite moment last year was when an autistic video game designer came to visit my classroom. A student chimed up, "What executive functioning skills do you use in your role?" I took the visual list off

---

2   www.karadymond.com/resources/what-to-do-when-youre-stuck
3   Downloadable from https://activatedlearning.org/index.php/teacher-created-materials

the wall and our guest proceeded to talk through how each is important to his job, times he had experienced executive functioning challenges on the job, and how he had improved his executive functioning skills over time. It was inspiring—and a beautiful reminder for us all that adults don't start out with all the skills, necessarily. We are on a journey, developing new capabilities as we go, and we're all works in progress.

Groupwork

Many people, neurodivergent or otherwise, can find groupwork hard to manage. The social components can be anxiety-producing or more energy-draining for those with activated attention systems or who might be alternative communicators. For instance, ADHDers communicate in a less organized way during groupwork (Barkley, 2020). Specialized processors may need more time to formulate thoughts. Distinct decoders can do very well in groupwork, especially if they can use their strengths and others can handle the other areas. But the biggest challenge? Groupwork is like a theme park's tallest, fastest rollercoaster, and every executive functioning skill is involved, like a series of loop de loops! It's not for the faint of heart. So, how do we graduate students from the teacups and kiddie rides? Teachers can help everyone by structuring groupwork, just a little!

Some of the considerations:

- Do students need help finding a group?
- Do they need to do it in a group, or can it be an option?
- Do they have a friend in the group?
- Do they know what to do?
- Is there a way they can shine?
- Does the group know how to solve problems/include all voices?

While it's wonderful to select one's own group when you have friends or peers who are equally academically inclined, you always have to be vigilant when it comes to social dynamics. Finding a group was a dreaded experience for me in middle school. No one wants to be the last person standing, especially when others practically stampede across the room to solidify their group. Find ways of creating groups so it doesn't become a popularity contest. You might randomly draw names on Popsicle sticks, though sometimes it's better when we stack the deck a little. You could select a group leader and let them select a peer; and you select the next peer for the group, and so on. Assigning groups can be helpful to those in the room with fewer connections in the class, although making some groupwork optional can give students a break from the intense social demands. Provide options for students who may opt out and agree on a nonverbal signal or way of communicating this, so they do not need to draw attention to themselves. Because you are flexible some of the time, you can challenge students at other times to join a group.

Ask them their preferences for role or group members and see if you can work something out to increase their comfort. Assure them that their preferences and reasons (if given) are private and will not be shared with peers. Ideally, this can be done in a reflective prompt, journal, or Google Form. This may build the opportunity for greater metacognition, as you can ask students questions to get them to think about not only who they like, but who might be the best to enable them to get work done or which conditions enable them to learn the most.

Scaffolding groupwork with roles, jobs, organizers, and/or very clear procedures can also decrease opportunities for confusion, disengagement, or bickering. I also teach mini-lessons to help increase the success of these interactions, such as generating a class list of qualities of groupwork look-fors. We'll review after a groupwork session how we did and set goals for next time (there's that metacognition again)! At times we might discuss questions such as how do you divide work? How do you problem-solve if you and someone else have different ideas? Build in time afterwards to orally reflect on how it went and what strategies might help next time. After completion of a group project, have students complete individual reflections on how well the group collaborated, if everyone did their fair share, and so on. Once, I was abandoned the night before a project was due to finish my two group members' unfinished parts. I had already interviewed a neighbor about life in Australia and written a report. With my two partners backing out (they were also my bullies), I stayed up all night doing a visual display, and my mother had to make a dish we could pass off as being "Australian" using bananas and maraschino cherries we had in the fridge.

All this to say, it's not groupwork and go. Groups need check-ins, monitoring, and skill-building to ensure inclusion and problem-solving.

Common individual challenges that may arise

Proactively planning in opportunities for skill-building and other supports may reduce the number of students requiring supports over time. It may also lead to some positive peer coaching opportunities. You may still have students who need a little more help to problem-solve some common challenges during projects or larger tasks.

Problem: Difficulty conceptualizing the project

Many neurodivergent students will struggle to imagine what the end product should look like. They may give up because it feels futile or because they don't understand what is asked. Maybe they are overwhelmed in other ways, by their senses or too many ideas.

I can relate—my thinking is like a race car, with related ideas pinging off all the cell phone towers as feelings, concepts, words, and images as I zoom along the superhighway. Sometimes, we might have all the good ideas in the world and no clue how to harness them effectively. The sheer idea of all the work ahead can shut us down! Here are some tips you could give to students to try out:

- Take deep breaths and re-read the instructions (in your head or out loud) or use a text-to-speech reader like Speechify to read the directions to you as you follow along.
- Highlight or underline key instructions.
- Ask for help on concepts you don't understand.
- Imagine what your final product will look like, if you are able to. Then, think through backwards what components are needed.
- Ask for clarification from a teacher or peer by putting into your own words what is expected.
- Ask to see an example.
- Picture or write out the steps you will take to finish the task.
- Ask your teacher to help you break it down.
- Set an earlier deadline and ask your teacher for feedback on your first draft.

Problem: Difficulty generating ideas

Not every student can easily translate thoughts into words. This process can cost considerable effort and energy.

INSIDER'S PERSPECTIVE

Rozarina Md Yusof Howton, Graduate
Student, AuDHD and physical disability

Sometimes, my ideas do not translate to words. It's like a series of overlapping/merging abstractions in my head. Then trying to find the right words to describe it accurately is very energy intensive, so I freeze. I also freeze when I have to type the ideas down. It feels like the typing mechanism is less capable to access my "nonverbal ideas and abstraction" compared to writing. Like there is a neurological "gap" between typing and what I am thinking. Ditto speaking up my ideas in meetings. Unless I rehearse the script exhaustively. Presentations, to me, are highly rehearsed performances, where I need to really think and synchronize thoughts and movements and breathing. I burnout without fail, after each presentation. So, I often end up having to write things longhand, then type it out. Which means it takes three times longer than other students.

Alternative communicators, distinct decoders, and some specialized processors may need more time or alternative ways to express themselves. You've probably encountered a few students who are brilliant orally but who struggle as soon as they have to write their ideas down (and I always suspect working memory as a potential culprit).

You may get an indicator of who might need some help getting thoughts out based on earlier conversations about how students think (e.g., Who visualizes? Who thinks in words? Who feels first and then translates feelings into words? Who experiences a combination? Who finds it easy to express thoughts in words, images, dance, song, etc.? Who finds some of those modalities more challenging?). These can be enjoyable and insight-filled conversations that help everyone to appreciate that there are other ways of doing things.

Here are some strategies you could suggest to students:

- Try to assess where your ideas are getting stuck. Do you need more familiarity with the topic in order to have an opinion? Are you forgetting what the question is asking? Do you have too many thoughts at once? Do you have a great idea but forget it as soon as you go to write it down?

- Ask someone to read out the prompt you are working on. Speak your thoughts out loud in response.
- Externalize as much of your thinking as possible by using different brainstorming templates, like mind maps, charts, or post-it notes.
- If you are holding back or discounting ideas, give yourself permission to write them all down. Get them out without judgment.
- Give yourself processing time. Try thinking about what you want to do or say while exercising or moving your body.
- Carry a pad of paper or cell phone with a note app with you in case you have an idea outside of a work period.
- Sketch out your ideas.
- Speak into a recorder or voice-to-text app to capture your ideas (you can always edit later).
- Ask your teacher if you can use AI as a generative brainstorming aid (so long as your final project is your own thinking and writing).
- Is there a part you *can* think about, generate an idea for, and easily start with?

Problem: Difficulty getting started

There are many reasons students don't get started right away. Activated attention systems may be too anxious, overwhelmed, or simply too exhausted because of lack of sleep, an illness, or a hidden disability. Alternative communicators, distinct decoders, specialized processors, and measured movers might need more time to process or express themselves and may require a format that works best for their brains. They might not know where to start, particularly if it's a big task. They might be bored or cognitively overloaded. They may not know how to use assistive technology to help to make and track decisions about what to do and when. We as adults sometimes intuitively figure out and come to rely on assistive technology without thinking of it as a productivity aid. If I took away your Google calendar or your to-do list, how would you manage to start your day? If students say they understand the project but are still stuck, you might consider suggesting the following to students:

- Take a short movement, snack, or water break.
- Listen to music on headphones, chew gum, or move to a different seat for a change of scenery.
- Think of the next smallest action you can take (e.g., get out a pencil) and do it. Then, continue to ask yourself, what's the next smallest step?
- Consult your to-do list (remember we learned how to break this project down into a to-do list and assign a little each day until the project is due).
- Review the goal you set for today in the last work period (and remember to set a new goal for tomorrow).
- Ask yourself how your favorite character might approach the task.
- Write down a few options you could start with on post-its and draw one out of a hat. Either start there, or if you have a strong "no" reaction, you might realize where you *do* want to start.
- Brain dump without editing your thoughts on the topic for two minutes.
- Review or make a mind map of the concepts related to your task or topic to clarify your ideas.
- Ask for a sentence starter or example.
- Ask for help with the first part.
- Remind yourself you can edit later.
- Use assistive technology or aids like voice-to-text, digital to-do lists, the Eisenhower Matrix,[4] and the Pomodoro Technique.
- Think of a break or reward you will give yourself afterwards.
- Cover up any of the questions or components you are not working on to reduce cognitive load and feelings of overwhelm.
- Give yourself credit—thinking is work, too!

Here is an example of someone who uses music and other strategies to help set goals to start tasks.

---

4   https://productivitypatrol.com/eisenhower-matrix

INSIDER'S PERSPECTIVE

Maja Toudal, autistic/ADD Psychologist

I only learned to use soundtracks in university, and I wish I'd learned sooner. I find that the soundtrack very much depends on the task, however. For studying—reading or writing—I need soft classical music, piano and violin, not orchestral. For writing fiction, a hobby of mine, I prefer something that reflects the mood of what I'm writing. Importantly, it has to be instrumental. If I am working with words, I simply cannot also process language in the music, too. My mind will instinctively sing along, and my focus on reading or writing is immediately gone. For tidying my study space (or anywhere else), I need upbeat music. In this case, vocals are welcome but not necessary. Different soundtracks for different purposes.

I used to set a timer for 20 or 40 minutes when writing academic assignments. Then my goal would be something ridiculous like... 1–200 characters. A sentence or two, basically. I'd usually get much more done than that, but the fact that the goal was more than achievable meant it was much easier to get started.

Problem: Difficulty sustaining attention during a work period

You can probably spot some students who appear distracted, either inwardly or outwardly. Some might fly so under the radar that only they can tell you if they are deep in thought on the topic or not. Sometimes, what looks like distraction might be fidgeting with a tool while they are indeed thinking. We can hypothesize, but we can't always know students' internal experiences! I try to find a balance between letting them self-manage and not micromanaging with a billion reminders to get back on track.

I usually turn to metacognitive conversations so they can become more aware of when it's easier or harder to focus. I might start with an observation such as, "It can be really hard in work periods to sustain attention. Is that something you're finding hard right now?" I would ask them whether those distractions are internal or external, and whether what they are noticing makes it harder to accomplish the next step. I might ask if they need my help—and then I accept their answer. We might discuss some options to manage different types of distractions, such as:

- setting mini-goals
- taking frequent short movement breaks, such as a few minutes to walk around, do a set of jumping jacks or wall push-ups, or go get a drink
- taking periodic brain breaks (if you're a visualizer, this could be a mindful moment to think of a happy place or vacation. If you prefer something more tangible, look away toward another spot in the room or gaze out a window)
- changing up your workspace location (if this issue occurs at home as well, you may experiment with different locations and seating, or even intersperse a work period with a shower to come back, literally and figuratively, fresh)
- using a fidget tool or doodling while thinking
- setting your workspace up for success by only having what you immediately need out in front of you
- controlling your environment by using noise-canceling headphones, a desk carrel or shades to block out visual distractions, or adjusting the lighting
- checking in with your body (e.g., a body scan, progressive muscle relaxation, a big stretch, a weighted blanket or weighted pillow on lap or shoulders, a textured chair topper)
- reminding yourself what makes a good mini-break in the setting and what does not
- doing your best to avoid the temptation to open other tabs on a device or to play games
- reminding yourself what your goal is
- estimating the length of time you can usually work for. (Use the Pomodoro Technique but adjust the timer from 25 minutes to your adjusted amount of time, and then give yourself a brain or body break until the next timer reminding you to get back to work goes off. Gradually challenge yourself to work for longer increments.)

Problem: Difficulty managing the project over time

Some students (and even teachers) want to get it all done as quickly as possible, because it feels uncomfortable to have work outstanding. This can be a teachable moment. Learning is a process! You may need to remind the student that it is okay and expected for some tasks to take longer to complete.

- Say, write, or draw self-affirmations (e.g., "I've done hard things before!" "It doesn't need to be done all at once!" or "One step at a time!").
- Review your project breakdown and remind yourself your work will be better for doing it slowly.
- Set a maximum time limit for working for the session (and even for the day). It is okay—and often more productive—to pace yourself over time.
- Use a reminder timer for breaks and body check-ins (but change the sound to something relaxing!).
- Use the Pomodoro Technique or a YouTube channel or app that structures work and breaktimes for you (but make sure your break activities are easy to stop when time is up!).
- Ask to do fewer questions, so long as you show you can do it (quality over quantity!).
- Remember "best" effort isn't meant for all tasks—save energy for what's most important. Allow yourself permission to put less effort in on daily homework!
- Use the Eisenhower Matrix.
- Ensure your project breakdown is in a format where you can check off completed items and get a little dopamine boost!
- Remind yourself that you deserve a break and that breaks are important to learning.

Essentially, by explicitly teaching students—both as a whole class and as individuals—a variety of skills they will need now and in the future, we can give them chances to practice and eventually take ownership of many of these skills. We are front-loading supports and then encouraging and stepping back to watch how they do, guiding as needed. We are doing what we can to set them up for success, even in other classes where teachers do not teach or structure things in the same way.

Assessing students in ways that benefit them

We want robust and authentic opportunities to see and celebrate what students know and how they have grown. Just like it's important to balance activities in the day, we also need to vary the types of assessments we use so we are not privileging one particular form of output over another. Some students may even shut down if we assess in ways that don't work for their brains.

INSIDER'S PERSPECTIVE

C., STEM Worker and Neurodiversity Consultant, late diagnosed AuDHD

Second to my last high school year, I was learning German. For some reason, the teacher wanted us to spend the whole year working on sports, which I hated at the time because I was the kid who was always picked last in PE. And even worst, she "really wanted us to speak" and was grading according to the number of times we were interacting verbally. This was not agreeing with the way I wanted to learn the language. Despite a very good level (and a really small group), I spent the year being silent, sabotaging my otherwise top-of-the-class grades.

Tests

I have mixed feelings about tests. I was someone who generally performed well, often finishing more quickly than my peers. However, I have met brilliant students and colleagues with activated attentions who simply do not perform well under pressure. I've known learners who chronically run out of time because they take more time to process what is being asked or to generate their answers. Don't get me started on the difficulties experienced by those with fine-motor issues, as most tests require written or typed answers. Despite my success rate, I still encountered stumbling blocks on tests, particularly with true-or-false or multiple-choice types of questions, which I have always spent more time on, worried the wording may be purposefully confusing. I used to waste so much time writing out a sentence to explain why I chose a particular answer because I thought the teachers were fiddling with language to make it trickier than it actually was. So much comes down to interpretation, especially if the test isn't clearly worded.

A colleague shared with me an aha moment when she was marking an autistic student's history test. The question was along the lines of "How did explorer Jacques Cartier come to be in North America?" The student wrote, "By boat." He was not technically wrong, and the teacher learned to look over every test for question specificity! (She now calls the student up to ask for clarification if he answered a question in a way she wasn't expecting and often finds by rephrasing her ask, he shows more of what he knows.)

Forgetting for a moment the potential problems with IQ metrics, research shows there are significant gains to students' IQ scores when measures are taken to reduce anxiety (Shanker, 2020). That tells us anxiety can really get in the way. On the flip side, I recently learned that some people have a gene that gives them an advantage when writing timed tests and are better able to perform under high-stress conditions, whereas some students do better in situations where increases in stress are incremental (as cited in Shanker, 2020). So, should high-stakes testing be the only form of assessment we use? Absolutely not!

We don't have to throw everything out the window, but we may need to open it up to add some fresh air! If I were to use tests, I would aim to make them as low-stakes as possible. There are strategies that can be used to set students up for success.

Designing the test and conditions

- *Word tasks and questions for clarity.* Does the question clearly state how much information you're looking for? Telling them something like "Give at least three examples" removes some of the guesswork. You might include a range, such as three to five examples, as without the upper limit, it's possible a student might spend all their time here, trying to include the totality of their knowledge in one question.
- *Re-read your test* and consider whether it's clear of clutter, adequately spaced for all learners, and if the questions leave any room for interpretation.

- Reduce the stakes by letting students know *tests give you information about your teaching* and whether you need more time on concepts.
- Allow *working memory aids*, like formula sheets, a page of notes, or an open book. Students still need to know how to apply information, but they don't need to try to cram it all into their working memories.
- Provide *calculators and other tools* as required.
- Write an *encouraging note* partway through the test reminding students to breathe (Salend, 2011).
- Do a whole-class *mindfulness exercise* right before to help those activated attention systems.
- When possible, provide *options for showcasing what students know*, such as different prompts or performance tasks on a test.

Let's hear from two students about what has helped them.

INSIDER'S PERSPECTIVE

Zack Segal, 14, ASD and ADHD

One of the things that helps me with tests is having extra time. During the test, I need breaks. After about an hour of focus, my brain can't take it anymore. I like it when they let me get up and walk around. Or, if they don't, I'll play with my fidgets. I wish they would let me watch videos on stuff I'm into, like artificial intelligence, electric cars, or construction. After a break like that, I feel like I can get back to work.

Anonymous, a 21-year-old University Student with autism

My accommodation allows me to book and take exams in the test center, which greatly helps my focus. As someone within the autism spectrum, I have sensory overload when there are a lot of people in an exam room, and I get more stressed and tend to lose focus when there are more people around me. Thus, in the test center, I am allowed to take my exam in a smaller room with fewer people, which helps bring my nerves down quite a bit. Also, I get 50% more time to finish exams, homework, and midterms. This helps me to get less stressed over completing it on time and getting good grades. Thus, it helps me to stay more focused and finish with more attention to detail.

Skills to build

- Teach students to *read over the test* once, consider what might be easy or hard, and divide their time accordingly. Remind them to prioritize questions of greater value.
- Review *retrieval tips* to aid studying. Many students think the best ways to study are re-reading and highlighting, which research does not support (Dunlosky et al., 2013; Oakley et al., 2021).
- Include students in *designing practice tests* and *study guides*.
- Tell students *what to study* and *what formats* will be on the test.
- Teach the benefits of *emotional regulation tools* like deep breathing and positive self-talk before and during tests, which can improve outcomes (Salend, 2011).
- Tap into *metacognition* and ask students what resources and methods will help them to study. Chen et al. (2017) found that college students who were prompted to consider their study resources and plan for their use performed better than peers who were not.
- After a test, teach students to *reflect on the results*. What types of errors did they make? What could they do next time? Do they understand where they went wrong? How did they study? Could they make any adjustments?

Building these skills is also a way of assessing students, as Megann reflects.

INSIDER'S PERSPECTIVE

Megann Roberts, Special Education Resource Teacher, learning disability and ADHD

We start by co-creating a list of what was covered during the unit, and then we co-create a list of resources that can be used to gather information. I purposefully use a gradual release of responsibility: I start by modeling how to find information for the first item in the list of what was learned, then I show how to create a section on the study sheet where I can write important information. Then, I partner students to work on one or two items that were learned. Finally, I have students work independently to complete their study notes. This explicitly teaches students the process for creating study notes, setting them up for more success as we move through subsequent units of the curriculum.

Differentiated assessments

As I became a more self-directed learner, I discovered that, even with teachers, topics, or classes that I found uninspiring, I could amuse myself by injecting creativity. I remember a dull computer typing course with prompts so uninspired I ended up crafting a choose-your-own-adventure story that directed The Reader to proceed to various paragraphs to find out what happened to the main character, Bob. I vaguely recall him on a volcanic island, attempting to outrun lava. In English class, I was assigned a presentation on a poet, Robert Frost. His body of work did not resonate with me at the time, but I and my friends combined the format of Charles Dickens's *A Christmas Carol* to have ghosts revisit various hypothetical parts of Robert Frost's life to come up with rather zany reasons why he wrote several of the poems he did. Fusing actual biographical details, Easter eggs that were lines from various poems, and Monty Pythonesque situations made this type of project right up my alley. I often created skits or filmed videos with friends, infusing inside jokes. The best part was, I usually ended up deep diving into the topic and learning way more as a result. Often, I ended up doing even more work than was expected. I barely noticed, as I was having a great time.

Not every student is as emboldened as I was. They may not know they can think outside of the box or ask for something different. Schools commonly privilege written products as assessments. I get it—they are tangible evidence of what a student knows. I always think about learners for whom writing is a significant barrier to showing what they know. The writing of students with dysgraphia will be brief due to how laborious it can feel, and output will be limited compared to the many ideas they may have in their heads. If, however, you let these measured movers tell you what they know *orally*, using *speech-to-text apps*, or through *groupwork*, you and they may find expressing what they know to be significantly less painful and more reflective of their understanding.

There are many ways to open up assessments—and some we've already normalized, such as science fairs, speech contests, dance performances, and egg drop challenges where teams have to construct a basket to protect an egg dropped from a height. Some other ideas:

- speech or presentation, with the option to pre-record, present to a small group, or present to the class
- slides with audio notes embedded
- comic, story board, video game design plan, or other art response with some text or oral explanations
- song or song cycle
- diagram with labels and point-form written response
- a diorama or 3-D model with some text or oral explanations
- infographic
- skits or short films
- animations
- creative writing, such as stories or writing "historical" letters or diaries
- their choice, with your permission.

It's even possible to have different learning goals, tasks, and deadlines developed collaboratively with different students. One high school Media teacher I knew would have students set goals for the course. He then used these to differentiate the performance portion of the final test. If a student wanted to become a better editor, they had to edit provided footage together. Another student might want to improve their screenwriting and had a task that showcased that ability.

You might not be ready to give students ultimate freedom, just yet, and may prefer to provide a few targeted options. You will want to consider what is comfortable and in what ways students prefer to express their knowledge. Can you adjust the product as long as students are meeting criteria? When you really break down what you're actually assessing (usually the expression of ideas and *not* the mechanics of writing), other options are entirely feasible. This might include:

- working alone, in partners, in small groups; flexible groupings
- oral options like audio notes, slides embedded with voice notes, talking to you to explain the concept
- writing or typing
- sketching and labeling ideas to reduce writing (e.g., sketch science procedures).

As you get more and more comfortable, you may add more options or flexibility the next time around. You can begin asking students how they prefer to show what they know and whether they have any interests that relate to the topics or skills they could bring into their work. Is there a way—familiar or new—they'd like to explore to express their knowledge?

I've opened up culminating tasks so students have maximum flexibility. They can show me what they know through any format. My favorite part of teaching is when students leave me absolutely gobsmacked at their talents. We want assessments to celebrate student growth—and get students excited to show us what they've learned. It's a bit like having a map with many possible routes to the destination. When you give students the agency to choose how they will produce their knowledge, you are creating opportunities to showcase talents and inject interest. This helps everyone!

How do we make flexible projects—where students can select how they want to show what they know—work?

Clear goals

Students need to know what you will be assessing. You can show a pre-existing rubric or co-construct criteria for success together. A friend of mine photocopies the entire grade curriculum and has students design their own assessments using the overarching criteria!

Give enough guidance
Some students can fly with the freedom to choose, and some will need targeted choices, exemplars, and more frequent check-ins.

Emotional safety
Relationships or positive rapport with teachers always helped my learning and inspired me to take on more demanding challenges.

Self- (and peer-) assessments
Build in self-assessments at various stages. Students can report their progress and goals to you and also grade themselves on a rubric before handing in their final assignment. Depending on the group, you may include peer-assessments, scaffolding for positive and constructive comments.

Ongoing descriptive feedback
Conference regularly so you and students are on the same page in terms of how they are progressing. These are opportunities to harness student metacognition and to learn about how they are experiencing aspects of the task.

Neurodivergent educators like Aidan often make effective teachers for neurodivergent students, because they understand the need for ongoing and clear communication with students.

INSIDER'S PERSPECTIVE

Aidan Gowland, autistic/ADHD and multiply-disabled Grad Student and Educator

I didn't get diagnosed with ADHD and autism until I was almost 30, but I grew up in a well-off liberal pocket of an already liberal city, and so I was generally just treated as different, on my own terms, without a diagnosis beyond "gifted." I've also lived with mental illness my whole life, which has sometimes complemented and sometimes compounded my neurodivergent traits and experiences. From kindergarten to grade 12 (ages 16–17), with a few exceptions, I generally had teachers who recognized, and catered to, my unique needs without feeling like they needed a diagnosis, permission, or an Individualized Education Plan (IEP) to do so. However, the one thing I almost never received, and always wished for, was the ability to reconcile my ways of learning with instructors' ways of evaluating. Too often I received grades back that struck me as wildly unfair, even as a child, because it was evident that I was being tested more on my ability to understand an assignment (which were sometimes poorly written!) rather than on the actual content or learning outcomes. Understanding instructions has been an extremely challenging skill for me throughout my life—at school, at work, at home with my parents and now my partner, and in social gatherings—as it is for many neurodivergent folks. What happens when we take away the barrier itself—instructions—rather than trying to adapt the barrier to make it shorter? Surely asking someone to run over even a single, low, hurdle while their competitors run a flat 100-meter sprint is definitively unfair. By asking students how they can demonstrate their knowledge to us, we're flattening the terrain. I've gotten a long way by asking the following, and adapting accordingly:

- "What kind of thing do you best learn from? Podcasts? Magazine articles? YouTube videos? TikToks/reels? Could you make one of those to explain what you've learned to me?"
- "If you were in my shoes, how would *you* ask the class to show they've learned x, y, and z?"
- "I know you struggle to find the words for things when you have to write them down. Why don't you explain what we talked about today in class to me right now, instead of completing the weekly written reflection?"
- "I read your paper, and I can see you have a clear understanding of what we've been discussing and reading about for the past few weeks, but because of the requirements of the assignment (around writing, formatting, grammar, style, traditional arguments, etc.), you'd currently get a grade that I don't think

reflects that. The curriculum requires that I grade you on your critical thinking, ability to connect concepts, and ability to succinctly state an informed opinion. Can you think of a better way for you to do that than this assignment?"

If you're adapting the assignment based on the rubric and expected learning outcomes, make sure you explain what things like "critical thinking" or an "informed opinion" mean. And make sure to ask if there's any other part of the assignment they want clarification on.

Challenges we don't anticipate

Inevitably, some challenges with assessments can come up unexpectedly and may be very specific. Sometimes, students will tell us on their own and sometimes they won't, requiring our keen observation and curiosity. So, if you see a student who is shutting down, acting out, or headed to the bathroom every project work period, it may give you a clue it's time for a conversation to find out how you can both remove barriers. As Alfie Kohn (1993, 2006) might say, it could be time to ask yourself, "What's wrong with the task?"

Remove the guesswork by conferencing with all students and directly asking them how things are going—one of the most invaluable forms of assessment!

Conferences as assessments

Conferences can provide powerful evidence of student learning. They also present opportunities to reframe academic challenges for students. You may have already taught the whole class about the Learning Pit (Hammond, 2015) or about how everyone has different strengths and developing areas. It can take some time for this message to sink in. Individualized conversations can help you to personally connect and work on low self-esteem and self-efficacy. Other students will need to be engaged doing work that they can manage on their own, and you can dedicate this time to calling over several students in sequence. Use these conferences to ask students directly about how things are going—and what is easy or hard. This may give them a chance to shed light on their barriers so you can understand and support them better. It's also a chance to jointly come up with ideas to try for next time. I use Ross Greene's Plan B approach to guide these conversations (Greene, 2008, 2018).[5]

There are some students who may not know what part is hard or how to express it. You may have to do some detective work! Similar to backward planning, you can deconstruct the task and consider what parts might trip a student up. For instance, if the student incorrectly answered all the math questions of a certain type, it's important to disentangle the reason from the many skills embedded into the task. If they were word problems, is there a language barrier? Issues with decoding text or comprehending what is asked? Is it simply a computational error? Perhaps it is more of a working memory issue, and they forget what formula or procedure is required. Maybe they lose the steps or can't keep the numbers straight in their heads. Is it another EF barrier, like difficulty sustaining attention or initiating? Maybe it's a visual-spatial problem and they didn't line up numbers correctly. They could have fine-motor issues, rendering it nearly illegible, sometimes even to themselves (I have some first-hand experience with this). It could also have been a simple mistake.

Either way, you can see how a student's language understanding, fine-motor skills, working memory capacity, or other issues could prevent you from seeing how much they actually know. This is why—I'll say it again!—students are our best resource. Ask them about specific parts and see if they can identify for themselves where they encountered hurdles.

When conferencing with a student who can't express their challenges by spoken word, you can bring in other options. I once created a collaborative slide and had a student underline statements that were true for him, which helped me to figure out he might need more support with working memory. Other methods might include:

- Allow them to type their answers or write them on a whiteboard.
- A student who isn't speaking or writing yet may be able to show you whether or not they agree with a statement by showing a thumbs up, in between, or down. You could ask them yes or no

---

5   Learn about it at https://livesinthebalance.org/educators-tour

statements such as, "I'm going to suggest parts of writing you might find difficult. Show me with a thumbs up, in the middle, or down which are true for you... You find it hard to come up with ideas... You find it hard to remember your ideas in order to write them down... You find it easier to speak your ideas out loud..."

- Pre-write a variety of options on a piece of paper or in a Google document. Have students underline or highlight statements that are true for them.
- Give the student questions in advance to think about and process and then ask them how they want to answer.

From there, you can delve more deeply into why that task or activity is hard, and what might help. Allow students to be the first to pose solutions. It may feel uncomfortable for you but do your best to avoid swooping in to solve too soon. You're jeopardizing the burgeoning meta-cognition, expressive language, self-advocacy, and problem-solving skills if you deny students the chance to speak for themselves.

If you've given them processing time and they aren't yet suggesting any ideas, you could give a potential solution and ask what they think. Remember to honor what they think about your posed suggestion. Strategies are much more powerful when they come from the student themselves. They don't have to be perfect, but they are something to try and then review again in a future conference. You want students to walk or roll away from the conversation feeling like they were truly seen and heard. You both should leave with something specific and practical to try to make the environment or task more comfortable for next time. To give our conference a familiar and predictable structure—and the sense of comfort that comes with those things!—I wind down conferences by reviewing what they've set as a goal for the next week or so. I often ask if they have anything else to share and follow their lead. Our closing ritual is to talk about anything they have to celebrate and what they will do later on to relax or for their own self-care.

On a cautionary note, make sure you're problem-solving at a time when students and you are calm and ready to talk about challenges. While talking about challenges is important for self-advocacy, humans have a hardwired negativity bias which requires three times more positive experiences to offset one negative experience (Hammond, 2015). Students who have felt heavily criticized may experience this even more intensely—these may be neurodivergent students or students who are marginalized in other or multiple ways. So, expect that working on areas of need can trigger that amygdala and increase defensiveness (Hammond, 2015).

You can talk to them about how you know positive or negative feedback can feel triggering and remind them that your role is to support them and push them, just a little, out of their comfort zone so they can truly learn. Students may resist your compliments or deny evidence of progress. Don't stop, but make sure you're specific and accurate in the feedback you give. Direct them to evidence they cannot challenge—"I noticed how your artwork is progressing. It now has techniques like stippling and shading. That is really cool!" Find ways to interrupt their negative self-talk, which can contribute to learned helplessness (Seligman, 2006, as cited in Hammond, 2015). Provide written feedback on a post-it or to a group they are in, if direct verbal praise is too uncomfortable (Dymond, 2020). Give them processing time and don't expect an enthusiastic response or eye contact. I've seen the most resistant-to-compliments students get slight smiles, blush, and even begin to report on their own progress in our conferences. Know that, over time, your honest observations of their growth may trickle down, reshaping the story they tell about themselves.

Here's a creative example for how to structure conferences in the primary classroom.

INSIDER'S PERSPECTIVE

Amy Craze, Elementary (Primary) School Teacher

Student conferencing is essential for mapping out each student's next steps. This is the time to help students reflect on their learning and think metacognitively about areas for improvement. In an elementary school classroom, it can be challenging to meet with students one-on-one when there are so many demands from other students.

I have a fun solution to this challenge. During Writer's Workshop, I wear a flower necklace as a visual cue to all students that I am "invisible" except to the student I am conferencing with.

Before implementing this, we problem-solve as a class, discussing which issues can be solved by asking a classmate and which require immediate attention from a teacher.

During Writer's Workshop, I move from student to student, one table group at a time, spending about 10 minutes with each student to carve out their learning goals. By the end of the period, I can meet with at least five students and move to the next group the following day. Beside each learning goal, we add a blank circle. At the end of the workshop, students reflect on their progress by drawing a happy face if they met their goal, a neutral face if they almost met it, and a sad face if they did not.

During our next conference, we reflect on which goals were met, which were challenging, and why. This helps us shape new goals together.

Strategies for helping students to show what they know

We've covered a lot! Here's an at-a-glance of important considerations to plan for and scaffold steps students can take toward greater independence and success.

Effective unit planning:

- Plan for learner variability.
- Backward plan units.
- Identify the goals.
- Consider what needs to be assessed.
- Think of how to build capacity.
- Predict potential barriers.

Effective lesson planning:

- Incorporate engagement and participation access points.
- Provide language supports.

- Build in expression options.
- Add processing aids.
- Make movement-based adjustments.

Effective day planning:

- Balance the day's activities and modalities used.
- Include breaks.
- Highlight links between concepts.
- Build in a variety of ways for student metacognition and feedback.

Direct instruction in access points:

- Teach each executive functioning skill in the context they will use it—metacognition, organization, cognitive flexibility, task initiation, time management, planning and prioritizing, goal-oriented persistence, emotional control.
- Give instruction on:
  - how to organize desk and materials
  - how to pack up and record agenda information
  - how to set up their work environment
  - how to identify good mini-breaks and self-rewards
  - meaningful homework learning connections
  - groupwork look-fors
  - different brainstorming techniques
  - how to manage a project over time by breaking it down and mapping out on a calendar
  - strategies to help conceptualize projects, generate ideas, know where to start, stay on task in work periods, and manage emotions
  - how to study and create a study schedule
  - how to use tests and teacher feedback to grow.
- Teach a Tool of the Day or Week, such as:
  - various brainstorming techniques
  - background noises that may help during work periods
  - the Pomodoro Technique
  - the Eisenhower Matrix.

Encourage metacognitive talks:

- "What EF skills does today's task require? Will any be harder for you?"
- "What barriers can we anticipate may come up in a work period? What strategies might help?"
- "Is any part of this task becoming easier? Why or why not? Are there any parts that are still hard?"
- "What makes it easier to sustain attention during a work period?"
- "What types of questions do you like on tasks or tests? Which tend to stump your brain?"
- "What helps you when you're stuck on a difficult question?"
- "What do you think will be on this assessment?"
- "What can you do to help yourself in that subject/task? What can I do to help you?"
- "How do you find it easiest to get out your ideas? What helps?"
- "What is a good mini-break that is easy to transition back from? What's better to save for a reward later, when everything is done?"
- "What did you want to celebrate about your growth this week? What is your goal for next week?"
- "What are you planning to do today for your own self-care?"

Conclusion

Intentional planning can help us figure out what we hope to assess and exactly what skills and EFs we expect students to use when we do. From there, we can think through how to build capacity and support students to show us what they know and gradually take responsibility for their learning. It's nice to sit back and celebrate when they do!

CHAPTER 4 HIGHLIGHTS

✓ Expecting learner variability means teachers can build in different access points, choices, supports, instructions, and executive functioning mini-lessons, right from the outset.

✓ Thinking in terms of access, agency, and wellbeing helps in lesson planning.

✓ It is necessary to think critically about how we perceive effort, predicting barriers that may come up and weaving direction in EFs throughout lessons.

✓ Students can be taught skills to manage on their own when they encounter challenges working independently.

✓ Assessment should be in ways that benefit and celebrate students.

Questions for the reader:

✓ How do you already scaffold and support students to show their knowledge in more complex ways?

✓ What can you add?

✓ What could you substitute or get rid of?

✓ What amazing showcases of learning have you created for students? What contributed to that?

How We Plant Seeds for Change

Reflecting on how and why we teach

As teachers, we often teach how we were taught. We've absorbed the many hidden and ubiquitous beliefs underlying what and how we do things in schools. A lot of "shoulds": How listening should look. How working should look. How students should defer to teachers. How we should motivate struggling students via external rewards.

I want to give you permission to throw those "shoulds" out. In place of them, I want you to question things and to determine what makes the most sense to you, in your classroom. To really think about what you want to help students to become—and reflect on whether the things you are doing in your classroom are actually a means to that end (Kohn, 2006). This question is vital because how we think about our role, and the roles of students and education, influences what happens in our room (Kincheloe, 2003). Time to put ourselves and our thoughts under the microscope for a moment.

Chances are, if you're reading this book, you're really keen on developing your teaching. You may be the kind of teacher who goes above and beyond, and who puts all of themselves into the job. (Bless you!) I want to make you aware of your thought pattern: That teaching is sacrificial. That you have to be a superhero. (It's not, and you don't!) It becomes a pattern to swoop in to try to solve all the problems. We do everything we can to set students up for success—buying them organizers and different colored notebooks and folders with our own money. We give them more work periods in class so that students don't have to do work at home and the playing field is a little more level than when some students have parents helping them complete tasks and others do not (this is really important to remember!). We implement reward systems. And even then, they aren't living up to our expectations.

Can I confess something here? I always thought these things made the difference; that, if I just tried harder or made the work more desirable to the student, that it would be enough.

Unfortunately, when we think like this, it can also lead us to feeling that students are ungrateful or undeserving of the amount we put in, and teaching feels that much more thankless. If we then fail to do our own metacognitive work, we may miss that our solutions have been ineffective on their own because they aren't addressing where the student is stuck. And you know what we do next if these quick fixes haven't worked? We act like our students. We may give up. We accept that it just is what it is. We shame-spiral that we're not a good teacher. We vent to our colleagues about how the problem lies elsewhere.

We can embrace these moments as a call for self-reflection, so we can reconnect with our purpose and bravely question how we might grow as a teacher and ally.

INSIDER'S PERSPECTIVE

Karen Timm, Autistic Advocate, Educational Leader, and Founder of Neurodivergent Infinity Network of Educators

One of the most significant ways to ensure neurodiversity-affirmative or neurodiversity-affirming practice in our schools is to afford opportunities for continuous reflection, learning, and unlearning from and with autistic and otherwise neurodivergent educators. Representation truly matters. Our neurodivergent perspectives matter. For those of us who are autistic or otherwise neurodivergent educators, we have often peeled back the layers of our own identities, while simultaneously recognizing our own complicity in causing harm to neurodivergent students, and potentially neurodivergent colleagues, simply because we had been doing what we were trained to do as professionals. After all, so much of what we are trained to do is not based on what actually works for our neurodivergent neurologies, and it is certainly not based on our unique sensory systems. By ascribing to standards of practice which have been based on neuronormative standards, we have internalized ableism and masked our neurodivergent traits, but we have also impacted neurodivergent students and likely colleagues negatively as well by holding them to these same standards. When we realize this, it is something we can never unsee or unfeel, and the drive to make amends can be very strong.

Sometimes, we have a listening problem in schools. I'm not talking about the students. Let's shift gears here for a moment and imagine the similar feelings and experiences of students:

- 9-year-old Philip becomes upset when his group doesn't listen to his ideas. He eventually runs to the coats where he cries and tries to take deep breaths like he'd learned from a special education teacher. When his classroom teacher approaches to ask him about it, Philip repeatedly says, "Go away!" growing increasingly loud until his teacher buzzes the office for support. When the principal arrives, Philip thinks about how much trouble he'll be in at home and collapses, sobbing, on the floor in front of the class.
- Azadeh, 5, is in her first year of school. She is still learning how to make friends and often grabs toys or people. Words come a little more slowly than actions. She has been working hard with a teacher's aide to learn how to ask classmates to play. They role-played, drew out the steps, and reviewed before recess. Azadeh tries exactly what has been taught, and the other girls run away. She becomes angry and throws sand from the sand box at them. Her parents are called, and she has to sit in the calm down chair.
- 13-year-old Lamar wins the regional track meet. It's the first time at school he's felt accomplished or like he's done anything right. It's the first time he gets called to the principal's office for something good! His principal congratulates him and promises

to make an announcement to celebrate his huge success the next day. Lamar eagerly awaits the announcement that doesn't come. When the principal finishes the next day's report without a word, Lamar slams his book down, swears—at a volume meant to be to himself but is a little too loud—and gets sent to the office.

Just like for us, sometimes, the best-laid plans don't work. Philip and Azadeh both tried to use strategies they'd been taught. Philip was trying to calm himself and, even if the teacher didn't like the tone, he was self-advocating for space to calm down on his own. In the end, the problem escalated, leading Philip into a meltdown in front of peers. What would the impact on peer relationships be? Was the original problem—communication issues in groupwork—solved?

Azadeh wasn't prepared for other possible outcomes of asking friends to play or the reactions of other students. The recently taught expectations of how students "should" respond gave her a very narrow window for success and set her up for confusion and disappointment—not to mention getting in trouble with adults and being isolated from her classmates. (Calming areas are better when used electively, as it undermines the purpose to send students there as a punishment!) Has anything been done to help Azadeh meet her social goals next time?

Lamar was let down by a forgotten promise and punished for his reaction. Lamar's principal missed an opportunity to build a relationship and engage a learner whose school experiences thus far had not been positive. The event only further tarnished his reputation with staff and peers. Were his feelings addressed? Was his success celebrated? Will he care, now, if they do it a little too late?

We feel a lot of pressure to solve problems quickly, especially with so many eyes on us. Unfortunately, there are a few tactics adults sometimes default to which, unequivocally, don't work. If we made a wish list for our students' futures, punitive practices would achieve the exact opposite. There is a whole body of research that shows that repeatedly punishing or excluding students—whether taking away recess, banning from a club, restricting from a fun school experience, giving detention, suspending, expelling, or some other creative way of making students feel bad—is linked to lower academic achievement, poorer school attendance, lower likelihood of post-secondary education, and higher rates of engagement with the juvenile justice system or incarceration as adults, and disproportionately impacts racially marginalized and/or neurodivergent students (Balfanz et al., 2014; Gilliam, 2005; Gopalan & Nelson, 2019; Gregory & Roberts, 2017; Huang, 2018; James & Turner, 2017; Lacoe & Steinberg, 2018; Losen & Martinez, 2013; Okonofua & Eberhardt, 2015; Skiba et al., 2002).

None of us wish this for students. The research is bleak enough, but another is that punishments and suspensions don't build skills. They don't help us build rapport or capacity. And I've learned the hard way that it doesn't feel good getting into power struggles or losing my cool. (I'm certainly guilty of raising my voice and taking away privileges, particularly in my early years when I didn't know how to plan proactively and collaboratively.)

I've come to realize, no one likes to feel powerless—neither us nor our students! It's agonizing for us when a lesson falls apart, when a student takes a step backward, or when we are asking for help and not receiving it. But the implications of things falling apart for a student at school are potentially more devastating for them than they are for us. Peers pull away from them. Teachers dread having them in their class. We continue the cycle of punishing them for their "disrespectful attitude" without ever addressing student concerns. And the student may disengage from school entirely. We could do so much better, for all involved.

Growing as a teacher

So, how do we handle those stressful moments—when we're also in need of support—in a way that helps break these cycles? I'm not advocating for hand-holding or doing everything for students, which wouldn't be much help at all. I am advocating for helping students to become more aware of when and why they experience challenges, validating their feelings, recognizing their nervous system cues, and helping them to develop the agency to change their responses and to speak up for what might help them. I'm advocating for listening to students.

Here are some things I've learned that have helped me to grow as a teacher and person, which the rest of this chapter will expand on:

- Don't expect students to self-regulate better than the adults.
- Be aware of and manage your own triggers.
- Change the story you are telling yourself.
- Your best tool is relational safety.
- We don't need to prepare them for the "real" world—we need to prepare them for a better one.
- Question all your ideas about student motivation.
- Goals should be about making students' lives easier, not ours.

Being realistic about self-regulation
Don't expect students to self-regulate better than the adults.

There is an interconnectedness between our reactions and beliefs and those of students. In my first book, I shared a story of a student I found difficult to connect with. I didn't know what to do besides raise my voice or threaten to call his parents. I knew that wasn't sustainable and didn't feel great. It certainly didn't make me feel like the teacher I wanted to be (Oh, Captain! My Captain!). I knew I had to manage my reactions better. I started practicing the things I was teaching students. I tried breathing more. I brought mindfulness into the classroom to benefit everyone, myself included. Did I ever lean into that! At least once a day, I recited a mantra to help me develop greater patience that my favourite instructor in teacher's college had shared: "The children who need love the most will always ask for it in the most unloving ways" (Barkley, 2000, p.5). It gave me a goal to keep in mind.

I also began naming my feelings, calmly, and expressing what I needed, "I'm feeling impatient right now and I need to take a few deep breaths..." I remember a student's jaw dropping as he said, "You use strategies?!" He was convinced self-regulation was only something he needed to work at, rather than something that can feel difficult for many of us. I explained how we all work on finding strategies to help with big feelings. Those of us who have lived longer hopefully have a few more strategies under our belts. I realized the value of talking out loud to model taking a break, shaking out big feelings, stretching, and checking in with my body. Students need to see and learn healthy coping mechanisms, as the following anecdote suggests.

INSIDER'S PERSPECTIVE

'Evelyn' (pseudonym), autistic High School Teacher with possible ADHD

I'm glad that teacher education now includes a focus on mindfulness/self-awareness and student agency/self-advocacy. I'm still overcoming the idea that one of my main jobs is to endure discomfort without letting on that I'm uncomfortable. The idea that I can be mindfully aware of things bothering me in my environment and take steps to address them... that feels radical. It's important to be able to develop this skill because noticing things early gives you more control over how you respond. Think about visiting the mall with your family or friends: there's a certain pressure to stay together and keep to a certain pace and generally be ruled by the needs of the group. If I'm drinking water when I'm thirsty, having a snack when I'm hungry, sitting down when my feet hurt, plugging my ears when I pass loud noises, and expressing my emotions when they bother me (even if that might inconvenience others), then I'm less likely to suddenly and unexpectedly find myself crying and collapsing to the floor because I'm thirsty, hungry, in pain, and experiencing difficult feelings that I'm not processing.

I've come to learn that self-regulation abilities don't develop at specific ages (Delahooke, 2019). In the ideal world, children first learn how to handle their emotions in relationship with their trusted adults—which is known as co-regulation. After that, they may develop their emotional control, but this is shaped by their experiences and sense of safety, occurring on their own timeline.

According to Delahooke (2019), learners who are bottom-up emotions processors tend to have automatic and intense feelings and responses. They need their basic safety and relationship needs met. They also tend to regulate more from somatic experiences to soothe their emotions like massage, sensory items, favourite toys, headphones, movement, and music. They may not be able to label the feeling in name or in their body, especially in the moment. (Some neurodivergent people, including myself, find this hard as well, which is called *alexithymia*. I often work backwards, taking conscious note of my body clues, to try to figure out my feelings and the reasons behind it. Did I drink too much coffee today, or is my heart racing because I'm anxious? So while pulling a feelings word out of the air may take me a long time, ask me to share my feelings in a gif or a song, or even to select from a list of emotions words, and I more easily have an access point!)

Top-down processors have more intentional responses to their feelings. They have more access to their prefrontal cortex and can think through feelings and make choices about their reactions, often in the moment. They can engage in metacognition on what's happening in their brains and bodies, relate to and apply messages in books, name their feelings, and problem-solve. They may benefit from labeling feelings, journaling, and listening to socioemotional stories, which activate the PFC logic center and soothe an activated AMY. Some learners fall somewhere in between, or pinball between bottom-up and top-down processing, depending on the context (Delahooke, 2019). Very few adults have mastered top-down processing!

Try to harness the power of co-regulation for teaching how to handle big feelings. In your classroom, you can incorporate aspects of top-down and bottom-up emotions processing and verbalizing your own processes. Teach these strategies when everyone is calm, and practice with them. Whole-class regulation strategies are mutually beneficial! Then, if you find yourself butting heads, stop. Get quiet. Take a few steps back and slow your body down. Try some bottom-up strategies. Place a hand on your chest and breathe deeply. Hold yourself to a higher standard of self-regulation than is reasonable to expect of all students. Don't think of the situation in terms of winning and losing. No one wins unless you both figure out how to handle things more smoothly for next time.

Minding your triggers
Be aware of and manage your own triggers.

I once heard of a teacher who kept sending a student to the office for "disrespect." When asked to critically examine her definition of "disrespect," she realized it included being questioned. She had grown up in a household where she didn't have a voice (Marcellus & Speidel, 2023).

Like many of us, she held an unconscious belief that went unexamined and could easily trigger her when a student inevitably questioned her.

We make so many flash decisions as teachers that they aren't all going to be our best calls. We are allowed to be human. But here's the kicker: If no one had probed to find out the why, that teacher might still be reacting in ways that were not helping her or her student. If that's not an invitation for all of us to look inward, I don't know what is!

Think about what really bugs you in the classroom, and why. I have sensory issues and would love it if all of my groups remembered to use indoor voices at all times. When I notice my teeth gritting and body bracing, I try not to snap. I take a few breaths.

When I slip up and have moments that I know in retrospect I could have handled better, I spend time thinking about why. What was the trigger for me? It helps me to become more mindful when I'm in that situation again or when I notice signs that I, too, have an activated attention system and need to model some strategy use! Here's a way another educator models self-regulation for students.

INSIDER'S PERSPECTIVE

Megann Roberts, Special Education Resource Teacher, learning disability and ADHD

I purposefully use I-statement phrases for my students. I had a couple students this year who loved to chat, and while I also love to chat... there is a time and a place! Instead of getting angry, I turned to statements like "I'm finding it really hard to focus on _____'s reading because your talking is distracting me." Soon enough, I started to hear other students using I-statements with each other. A highlight of the year was when a rather meek, but very kind, student said to another, "I'm not enjoying working with you. You're being very silly and if you don't stop, I'm going to ask to work alone." I was very proud; a year ago, he would never have stood up for himself. But with purposeful modeling, he learned that he could prioritize his learning and wellbeing in a respectful way.

Changing the story
Change the story you are telling yourself.

Lazy. Defiant. Irresponsible. Spoiled. Unmotivated. Disrespectful.

   Get rid of those words from your teaching vocabulary. Each of these words can lead us to believe students are willfully choosing to behave this way—and they aren't (Greene, 2008; Shanker, 2020)—9 times out of 10, they're experiencing limbic system reactions out of their control. The other time? They're still struggling, if that's how they're dealing with their problems. When you encounter a challenging moment and begin thinking of the student in these kinds of terms, change the story you're telling yourself. Try not to stigmatize their struggles or prioritize your struggle over theirs. You're both having a tough time! It's time instead to use a neurodiversity lens! Jo Maselli explains what that looks like.

INSIDER'S PERSPECTIVE

Joanna Maselli, secondary school drama, English, and special education teacher with ADHD and parent to a neurodivergent kindergarten student

If we think about something like emotional intelligence or even executive functioning, when we're looking at it through a neurotypical framework as opposed to a neurodiversity-affirming framework, we can see very, very different things and draw very, very different conclusions. So, for example, if I have a student who cries when we talk about something sad and doesn't have really great literacy skills and has been mostly nonverbal until age 12, we could assume that there is an intellectual or developmental delay that impacts their intelligence and their emotional functioning. But if we take a neurodiversity-affirmative approach, we might see that, well, actually, the evidence of what is happening inside that person's mind emotionally and intellectually is very, very limited. So, the conclusion we can draw about their ability to function is also very, very limited. A student demonstrating emotions in a way that we might associate with a student who's much younger than they are physically could still have the level of emotional complexity as same-aged peers, but what is expressed out on the surface is something you might associate with a younger age group.

If we take a neuronormative framework and we look at a student who is not able to stay seated, not able to calm themselves, not able to stay on task, and we say, "Well, this is what a normal school environment is. All of these other students are able to do these things in this environment, so the problem is with you. You have low executive function." That's the neuronormative way of looking at it. The neurodiversity-affirming way of looking at it is saying, "What might that person's internal experience be? Have we been able to do enough or gather enough evidence, again, based on how this person communicates or doesn't, to understand what's going on inside of them?" A student who's able to sit still for five minutes under bright lights, in a busy room, in a loud environment that's very visually, emotionally, and mentally stimulating might actually be demonstrating more executive functioning capability than the student for whom that environment is not overwhelming and who is able to sit still for 20 minutes.

So, those are sort of the big questions that I think we need to ask and that we need to start understanding: "What evidence do we have of what this student is or is not capable of? How is that informing the judgments we're making about their developmental needs? How is that informing the way this student is treated?" Because what I saw personally were teenagers who were more developmentally on track than they were estimated to be, given low expectations, and it was taken for granted that students couldn't understand what the adults around them were saying while they were speaking about them in front of them. These are demoralizing to experience at any age, and that can become isolating and cause a student to further withdraw or to further lash out, just depending on their personality. And that's what I really want to see change when I talk about a neurodiversity-affirming approach or a neurodiversity-affirming framework to how we look at education.

Confession time: I encountered many more instances of challenging behaviors—and much greater intensities!—when I interpreted students through that deficit lens. Without meaning to, my reactions escalated these moments into power struggles. I was externalizing the problem—it's *all* the student, or it's because the family does x, y, and z. I realized that, in thinking this way, I was rendering myself powerless to change anything about the situation. This kind of thinking wasn't helping me, and I kept having the same disciplinary issues, over and over—until I brought in Dr. Ross Greene's Plan B approach (Greene, 2008; 2018). In this method, when a student is having a problem of some kind, you identify the unmet need. This helps you to laser in on an area that you can help with and frames it in more objective language.

Dr. Ross Greene's Plan B approach

The old lens: *Jimmy refuses to come to the carpet for read-alouds and will either raise his voice to protest loudly or stay at his desk, playing with erasers and not acknowledging the teacher or aide requests.*

Now, remove assumptions, value judgments, interpretations, and keep the context and main difficulty.

The new lens: *At read-aloud, Jimmy experiences difficulty when asked to transition to the carpet.*

1. Empathy stage

Here, you spend the most time and you listen and nonjudgmentally ask questions to find out all of the student's concerns and what was hard for them. This is where we distinguish between the symptoms (what you observed) and the real problem (what the student is reacting to). Open the conversation with an observation, like, "I've noticed you have difficulty coming to the carpet for read-aloud. Can you tell me about that?" As you explore, try not to ask, "Why did you do that?", which may shut down a student pretty quickly, and, truthfully, they may not know why they reacted that way! A more helpful question might be, "What was it you wanted to have happen?" You might ask questions like:

- "What's hard about coming to the carpet?"
- "I'm hearing that there isn't much room between your desk and

your classmates, and you don't like being bumped when everyone rushes to the carpet. Is that about right?"

- "Is there anything else that makes it difficult?"
- "Show me, from 0 to 5 fingers, with 5 fingers being absolutely true and 0 fingers being not true at all, how true what I'm about to say is... It is hard for you when you don't know where to sit at the carpet."

Before you transition to the next stage, you will want to make sure you've discovered all of the parts that feel hard for the student, summarized it, and gotten their agreement.

2. Define adult concerns

Now you can bring up the concerns from your perspective. How was the difficulty the student having affecting them and/or others?

"My concern is, I want you to know where to sit and to not feel distressed, so you and other students can all enjoy our story together. I know it doesn't feel good to feel overwhelmed by everyone moving all at once, and you told me it also doesn't feel good to sit out."

3. The invitation

You invite them to collaborate on solutions that are mutually satisfactory to try for next time. Try not to swoop in to impose solutions unilaterally. See what they can come up with. You can always come back to the drawing board if those ideas don't work.

- "What do you think might help you feel comfortable coming to the carpet?"
- "Is there anything I can do to help?"
- "Okay, we can adjust the desks, so you have more room to move. What might help about the noise, which you also said bothers you?"
- "Well, I can remind the class to try to come to the carpet more quietly. If they don't, is there anything you can do?... Would you like to wear headphones? No? No problem, if you don't think it'll work, we don't have to try it."
- "You're telling me you think, as long as you don't feel bumped and

there's more space, you can probably cope with your classmates talking. I'll do my best to remind your classmates to transition quietly, and I agreed you could sit at your desk for a little bit longer before you come to the carpet. Does that address your concerns about getting up from your desk? That part of the plan works for me too. Now, what should we do so you know where to sit?"

Let me tell you, the Plan B approach has transformed my classroom. I don't have huge issues anymore. A large part of this success is because I learned to look through another lens. I began to get curious and make compassionate assumptions. Evelyn explains why these can be transformative to your classroom.

INSIDER'S PERSPECTIVE

'Evelyn' (pseudonym), autistic High School Teacher with possible ADHD

Assuming the best about student intentions is a powerful thing. I'd rather assume the best and be wrong sometimes than assume the worst and be wrong sometimes. I can think back to times when I have broken a social rule that was extremely obvious to others but that I had never come across. For instance, yawning loudly during storytime because that's how my mom yawns, so I assumed that's how most people yawn. The teacher was so angry so quickly. That sudden switch to furious can happen when another person feels like you should know better. Sometimes it's people giving hints (that a more literal person might miss) then exploding because they feel ignored, while from the neurodivergent person's perspective, they are getting yelled at out of nowhere for something they didn't know was an expectation.

In my practice teaching, I have had good results from assuming the best when interacting with high school students. Leading with nonjudgmental curiosity and calmly explaining what the problem is... it's like giving a gift I have always needed (and still need) but don't always get. It helps me preserve a respectful relationship with students. I've seen some students flip a switch when they feel disrespected and misunderstood, and 1 aspire to do everything 1 can to ensure that my students feel like I'm dependably on their side.

It's important to listen with empathy, rather than swooping in to suggest unilateral solutions or consequences. Even if we can't solve a problem because it's at home or related to systemic barriers, students appreciate being heard and having someone share the weight of their concerns, even if only for a time. I'm a big believer that students and families never forget the dignity with which you treated them, even if challenges require longer periods of time than that during which you have students in your care.

There are so many positives from this approach! This helped me to change the story. 1 remember they need help. When a student is upset, it's a skill-building opportunity for both of us. 1 can now check my triggers in order to respond in a way that builds, rather than damages, rapport.

Some of the challenges that may come up:

Students aren't yet ready to talk

You can wait and revisit at another time. Everyone being calm is important. Sometimes, students aren't ready to talk because they're not used to adults really listening. It may take some time to get the buy-in. They may be waiting for the other shoe to drop, as if suddenly you're going to yell, "SURPRISE! You're going to the office!" They may need to go through the process once or twice and see that you mean what you say and that you follow through on the agreements made. I'll also say this: students have a much harder time continuing to argue with someone who speaks to them calmly and truly wants to listen. Wait it out, stay patient, and remember the human in front of you is struggling. Eventually, you'll have students who know they can bring problems to you.

Students aren't communicating in words

Use yes or no statements, thumbs up and thumbs down, or the five finger approach I learned from Dr. Ross Greene, above.

You want to swoop in and solve!

Please do not swoop in with suggestions of your own, as asking students to share their insights and solutions develops so many skills for both of you. Talking about what feels hard and what helps builds expressive and receptive language, metacognition, self-advocacy, perspective-taking, cognitive flexibility, planning, and problem-solving—to name a few! You will also come away with a greater capacity for understanding and supporting that student, and hopefully others who come along.

In necessary cases where administrator intervention and support are needed, remember that sending to the office—like other punitive practices—does not teach skills. One or more conversations will need to be had. Don't rob them of these opportunities. We're also changing the story for students—they can see themselves as problem-solvers, and not as problems to be solved. (It's also less work for me, because I don't need to generate all the solutions!)

The time factor

Many teachers are concerned about the time it eats out of their day. A related problem is adults might try to rush parts, like the Empathy step—don't do this. So often, what I thought was the problem wasn't even close to what the student was reacting to. We can't solve problems if we don't know what they are, and so often we have no idea about all of the stressors students are carrying into our classrooms with them. Think of it this way: In one or two conversations, you can deeply solve a problem collaboratively with a student, rather than getting into daily power struggles or spending the time it takes to constantly remind, dole out rewards, or use other methods to try to "motivate" a student to do it your way. I promise you that in the long run, it saves you time and energy and feels good for both of you.

By using a neurodiversity lens, I became open to other possibilities and experiences besides my own. I began to think of triggers students might encounter, and not just my own. In conjunction with this approach, I gradually changed our classroom environment to model breaks, whole-class self-regulation tools, mindful moments, free-access sensory tools and instruction on using them as a tool not a toy, a calm area students could use to cool off undisturbed, and gentle or playful instructions and redirections. All of these things, together, changed our classroom from a pressure cooker to a more comfortable climate.

I've changed the story for myself so much that, I daresay, I even appreciate these moments. Each experience is another reference point that helps me to navigate future situations with greater grace and clarity. I no longer feel alone or powerless when confronted with a difficult moment. I have a problem-solving mindset, and so do my students.

Using your best tool
Your best tool is relational safety.

Time to clean out the tool chest of anything that no longer serves you!

In your own life, have there been any people who you've had to address a problem with that have made this process easier? What qualities or techniques did they use? Conversely, what sorts of methods made solving problems impossible? I think we can all agree—none of us like being yelled at, belittled, publicly embarrassed, or denied a voice.

Break the cycle and make real change! You want students to feel safe to approach you with a problem. Students should feel like your responses will be measured, will validate their feelings, and will come from a place of compassion—even when they've done something wrong.

Relational safety makes everything else we want to achieve possible. Once student nervous systems are calm and regulated, they willingly share (Shanker, 2020). Their brains are able to learn, and you can make headway, helping them to be kinder to themselves by explaining amygdala hijacks and how hard it is—verging on impossible!—to choose a different response when dysregulated. You can make plans for how to identify when feelings are intensifying, and what strategies students think might help them, next time. You can normalize big feelings, talking about them, and finding ways to feel more comfortable. Communicating, via our words and actions, our commitment to student wellbeing can make all the difference.

INSIDER'S PERSPECTIVE

Maja Toudal, autistic/ADD Psychologist

Throughout my schooling experiences, before and after my diagnoses, one thing was always consistent; I always performed much better in the subjects in which my teacher seemed to genuinely show an interest in my wellbeing and believed in my potential. The teachers that cared, made me care too. When I felt included and welcome, I put in everything I could. Community is everything.

What power we wield! Every student should know that, even when they experience their worst challenges, you are truly in their corner.

Preparing for a better world

We don't need to prepare students for the "real" world—we need to prepare them for a better one.

Systems are restrictive and rigid and assume there is one standard way. I hear everyone feeling the pressure to prepare students for that kind of cruel and closed-minded world. Just because these systems exist, doesn't mean we have to replicate them. I'll bring it back to you again: If you or a colleague you cared for needed support at work, how would you want HR to respond? Would you want them to respond to your individualized needs and unique situations, or respond with a one-size-fits-all Band-Aid that doesn't even wrap around your finger?

Teaching needs to be less HR and more H-E-A-R-T. We get further with asking students what they need and building capacity than punishing or shaming them. We should not have policies like doubling the length of the assignment for each day it is late. These misguided forms of "motivation" don't make them hand it in faster. They don't make them want to come to our class. A student who is encountering barriers in the first place will only feel buried under the growing mountain that is the task.

We also don't need to use shame, which leads to greater issues with emotional regulation and self-esteem and inhibits the neuroplasticity that brains need to learn (Cozolino, 2013; Schore, 1998). Many neurodivergent folks already internalize so much shame in the form of *internalized ableism*—all those insidious "shoulds" we hear from others and then believe we "should" also be capable of, even when we have a disability in that area. For example, many ADHDers experience self-stigma in response to criticism or comparing themselves with peers (McKeague et al., 2015; Wiener et al., 2012). A study by Davidson, Vanegas, and Hilvert (2017) found that autistic adults are more likely to internalize a mistake as shame (e.g., "I'm a bad person"), rather than guilt (e.g., "I made one mistake, one time"). We already have a hard time forgiving ourselves or making choices that help us to stave off stress and burnout. It's exhausting!

Students should see there are other, better ways, so they can become the kind of adult who responds to others with empathy. I want them to be able to notice and speak out when policies are unjust. I want them to question things. I want them to help to build a more accessible world. So, remember, we can teach so that the students we teach today will become the adults who are better able to recognize and explain their challenges, regulate themselves, and problem-solve individually and collectively. We can help them grow into the kind of people this world needs.

Questioning what motivates students
Question all your ideas about student motivation.

Full disclosure: I've used reward systems and even recommended ways to implement some in my first book. More recently, I've abandoned them completely. It's the best thing I've ever done.

Somewhere between reading Alfie Kohn's *Punished by Rewards* (1993) and multiple perspectives on reward systems and behaviorism in general, I realized that, even though I said I believed differently, I was still teaching with an internalized, unchallenged belief that students were lacking the motivation to do well. That they needed carrots to be dangled.

And so, I interrogated this belief.

I've seen students overwhelmed by too many goals, from too many people, decided by everyone—but them. They come to believe they need "fixing." Their self-esteem takes hit after hit. Having other people assess them and dole out rewards if they pleased them or met their metrics didn't seem to bring joy to the students, nor did it lead to lasting change in many cases. If anything, it created bigger problems, with students growing older and expecting the world to be transactional, offering rewards for anything deemed "good" by others. I'd have students on edge, begging me to tell them they had a good day and to be sure to report that to their parents. That wasn't the intrinsic motivation or calm nervous systems I was hoping for. Coupled with the voices in the autistic community sharing in public forums about the dangers of compliance training and the risk it poses to their safety and wellbeing, I knew I needed to shift things.

I was terrified! I envisioned all the ways throwing out reward systems might backfire. I thought there was no way students would want to work on goals without a reward. (This is not to be confused with doing fun things as a class! You can still decide to go outside and enjoy the sunshine, or bring in a treat, so long as it's for everyone and it isn't contingent on pleasing you.) All the theory helped bolster my resolve to just try, for a little. At the same time, my program requirements needed adjusting due to the brief school closure period during the spring of 2020. We shifted to virtual group lessons, and I was given the gift of time to conference 1:1 online with each student every week, sometimes for up to an hour. I learned a ton from these conversations!

This context enabled me to try two things at once:

- I asked students to pick a single goal for school and another for home and walked them through how to self-assess their goals. I shifted into the role of a coach, helping them meet their goals and find new strategies or ways of advocating with the adults around them. I'd check in with parents/guardians and teachers for their perspectives, but I wasn't bringing in charts of data and snarky comments by others and reviewing them with the student.
- Rewards just weren't possible the same way, nor were they equitable. Everyone was dealing with a lot. Why should only the ones who met a goal perfectly, a few times, get a break or a goodie? As an adult, I give myself time to watch my favourite show or eat an ice cream cone, even if I haven't accomplished everything I wanted. So, I just asked them to mark their charts. I didn't make

promises or tell them they needed to get a certain number of Level 4s (the highest mark). I just listened and asked questions. I switched to focusing on "What are you doing for your own self-care?" I thought about the messages I was unintentionally sending, and I chose to send different ones. I wanted to fight productivity culture that makes us think our worth is our work. I hoped they would learn that they deserved to focus on their wellbeing, which should never be conditional on my or someone else's approval.

There were surprises at every turn! Students picked good goals for themselves, all on their own. Most of them marked their goals regularly, without me hounding them. Not one student asked for a reward. When I checked in with parents or teachers, I was told students were mostly accurate in their assessments. Students reported appreciating this new method, because they had control of their learning and could pick goals they felt ready for and that were truly meaningful. They also had the power to change goals when they felt like it, and we ended up working through many more goals than if I'd had parents and teachers marking four goals each at a time, as we had before. Their growth was exceptional and exponential, and they learned they could set and achieve goals for themselves.

Making students' lives easier

Goals should be about making students' lives easier, not ours.
If I'd really thought about it, I might have come to the conclusion sooner that this is what goals should be for. When I was in elementary school, I was pulled out of class for some typing lessons and some direct instruction to help correct my unusual pen grasp and illegible penmanship. I resisted the intervention, as I was a quick typist with my two pointer fingers and my right thumb for the spacebar. (We had a computer at home long before most of my friends, and I had been typing up stories for almost as long as I can remember.) The instructors showed me proper keyboard finger positions and gave me typing exercises. Whenever they looked away, I went back to the way that worked for me. Guess how many fingers I used to type this manuscript? Only three!

I've heard from many parents and teachers wondering about

individualized school plan goals that take away students' right to protest; that expect students to greet every teacher and student indiscriminately (something we'd never expect for other students); or that are deeply neuronormative, like demanding eye contact. When I hear about goals like these, I have to wonder, who are they serving?

I could write a whole book on this topic, but for now I'll just say that when you have to set goals for alternative programming, include the student. Ask what they want to learn and work on. Consider how they can use their strengths. That chatty student doesn't need to work on being quieter in the classroom! Instead, he could facilitate groupwork and use his social strengths to include the voices of everyone in the group!

Here are three essential questions I ask myself:

- What are my long-term goals for students?
- Am I giving them the opportunity to develop in those ways?
- Are their individualized learning goals designed to help them access what they need, understand themselves better, and be able to self-advocate?

At the end of the day, those are my real long-term goals for students! I now try to include goals like:

- expressing how they listen best
- identifying their learning and classroom communication preferences
- identifying a strength, need, and a strategy to try
- practicing a variety of self-regulation tools and identifying ones they enjoy
- deciding what tools work best for them in different contexts
- identifying and assessing their own personal school goal
- sharing their feelings through any format (e.g., orally, pointing to a word, finding a gif, drawing a picture, finding a song)
- communication skills in groupwork, rather than forced recess socializing (they may need a break!)
- selecting a format they wish to use for an assignment.

This is not an exhaustive list, but I hope it serves as some inspiration!

Conclusion

Our classroom is a delicate ecosystem. We are gardeners, tending to its rich diversity with our ongoing attention. This chapter illuminates the critical importance of reflexively examining our deeply rooted beliefs—about students and about your role as a teacher. Something I didn't realize until I had my own classroom—and my own garden!—is how intertwined are student and teacher wellbeing! I hope you glimpse some of the ways we can also be nurtured, if we are so willing to grow alongside those in our care.

CHAPTER 5 HIGHLIGHTS

✓ Throw out the idea that your teaching should reflect how you were taught.
✓ Punishments and suspensions don't build skills.
✓ Don't expect students to self-regulate better than the adults.
✓ Be aware of and manage our own triggers.
✓ Change the story you are telling yourself.
✓ Your best tool is relational safety.
✓ We don't need to prepare them for the "real" world—we need to prepare them for a better one.
✓ Question all your ideas about student motivation.
✓ Goals should be about making students' lives easier, not ours.
✓ Ultimately, students are our best resource!

Questions for the reader:

✓ What is one small change you can make to what you're already doing well?
✓ How can you make your classroom a microcosm of the world as you wish it to be?
✓ How are you going to plant seeds for a kinder, more comfortable world for everyone?

Concluding Thoughts

My Ultimate Secret Weapon

I've come to realize the two most powerful elements in the classroom. Can you guess? These two elements come together like an unstoppable force, like Godzilla with a light saber: the combined power of teacher and student self-reflection!

Listening has changed everything in my classroom. Even though challenges come up from time to time, they are far less frequent or intense. I feel empowered to take them all on, knowing I am not alone. The added bonuses are that I'm calmer, I have more fun, and I have energy in spades, since I don't waste all my time trying to get students to do what I've asked. I spend more time enjoying and hearing what students have to say—and they've taught me so much! At times I sound like a broken record, thanking them for teaching me strategies I can share with other students. They've given me feedback on things I can do better, and I've used them to improve. I can confidently say it's because of my students that I've come to center my pedagogy around access, agency, and wellbeing. In doing so, I hope students can envision and experience a world where their ideas and opinions are important, and where they can find solutions, individually and collectively. Where all kinds of minds can work together.

If it sounds like a formidable task, let me remind you that I've made these changes in baby steps, over time, and continue to make more. So, I invite you to do the same. Give yourself permission to test out one new idea from this book. Just one. Test it out for a while and see how it fits. Then, when you're up for a new challenge, add something else. Each change will lead to another, and another. Over time, you can make your classroom a microcosm of the world as you wish it would be.

If you're like me, you're going to want to do it all, all at once.

Indulge me, once more, in a final tangential anecdote. There are times when I stand outside on a clear night and look up at the stars. Often, in the voice of Mufasa from *The Lion King*, I am reminded that I am only one small part of things. An essential part, but not the only part. This helps me release the burden I feel to solve it all, all at once. I hope it helps you, too. Do what good you can, and trust that others are also working toward a kinder, more equitable system.

You are one of many, planting seeds.

Thank you for caring—and thank you for sharing in this work with me. We're in it, together!

Themed Glossary

Less commonly known neurodivergent experiences

Alexithymia: Difficulty pinpointing and describing internal experiences, especially emotions.

Aphantasia: Difficulty calling to mind sensory information, especially referring to visualization, but which may also apply to recall or imagination of touch, smell, taste, and/or sounds. "Aphants" may experience a partial or total absence of sensory imagination although they can remember facts about sensory information.

Apraxia: A condition where there is a disjunct between the brain and a part of the body that the brain is trying to control. This makes it difficult or impossible to coordinate on demand, to speak or perform motor tasks. Apraxia means there is total loss of movement/control. Dyspraxia means there is some loss of movement/control.

Dyscalculia: A learning difficulty in understanding arithmetic and numeracy in general.

Dysgraphia: A learning difficulty with the physical act of handwriting and writing mechanics, usually without any oral language difficulties.

Dyslexia: A learning difficulty involving spelling and reading, often thought to be difficulty with phonological processing (sound–symbol correspondence).

Dyspraxia: See Apraxia.

Echolalia: The repetition of a vocal phoneme or phrase of another's speech or sound effect. It is often a soothing action, a temporal placeholder allowing the brain to "catch up" with the other person's thoughts or questions, a mental association, or a stim.

Gestalt language processing: Rather than learning a word at a time, the learner combines and processes larger units of speech or sounds, which can mean it takes much longer to generalize the associated meanings or to recognize words on their own.

Hyperlexia: Hyperlexic readers easily decode (identify sounds of language) and appear to read well above the expected age range. This is sometimes accompanied by a corresponding difficulty in comprehension and/or oral expression.

Hyperphantasia: Extremely vivid visualization abilities, which often also include touch, smell, taste, and hearing.

Visual processing disorders: Many different types of visual processing differences exist that may present in different ways, such as difficulty differentiating between letters, shapes, objects, or backgrounds; coordinating motor or visual-spatial skills; remembering visual information; etc.

Brain structure and nervous system

Amygdala (AMY): A part of the limbic system that aids with danger detection; processes emotional information, especially related to fear; and uses that information to survive in the future.

Autonomic nervous system: A network of nerves managed by the limbic system that connects throughout our bodies, controls automatic functions of the body, and picks up information about the world around us to keep us safe.

Basal ganglia: Brain structures related to movement, cognition, and rewards.

Cerebral cortex: Multiple brain areas that help to process our sensory experience of the world into ideas and mental representations and are responsible for visual processing, auditory processing, awareness of body in space, and language.

Default mode network (DMN): A brain network that shows high activity when we are resting, introspective, or daydreaming.

Hippocampus: A part of the limbic system that helps with memory formation, emotional regulation, and learning.

Hypothalamus: A part of the limbic system producing hormones that help our body functions to regulate.

Limbic system: A group of structures in the brain that are responsible for emotions, memories, motivations, and behaviors.

Prefrontal cortex (PFC): A brain region associated with top-down processing, critical thinking, and executive functioning abilities.

Reticular activating system: A network of nuclei and neurons in the brainstem that scans for threats or rewards and helps us react quickly when it is alerted to danger. See also Neuroception under "Memory and attention."

Task-performing network: A brain network that activates when we pay attention to something external to us or perform a task.

Thalamus: A part of the limbic system that takes in sensory information.

Memory and attention

Declarative memory: Information learned and retrieved explicitly through conscious recall of fact (semantic) and event-based (episodic) knowledge in long-term memory.

Limbic braking (Shanker, 2020): An unconscious autonomic response whereby the limbic system starts limiting various brain functions due to overwhelm or an excess of stressors. This can often be perceived as a person giving up on a task, when it is a safety mechanism.

Long-term memory: The potentially infinite amount of information and memories we store and can recall at will.

Neuroception (Porges, 2004): The process of the limbic system constantly scanning for signs of threat or safety below our level of awareness.

Neuroceptive overdrive (Shanker, 2020): Some limbic systems are in a state of heightened sensitivity, reacting to threats even when there is no physical danger. This results in greater stress, reduced working memory, and negative impacts on learning.

Neuroplasticity: The idea that brains can change, grow, form new links, and strengthen through experience.

Procedural memory: Information learned implicitly through doing, practice, etc.

Short-term memory: A component of memory that retains information very briefly (i.e. seconds).

Working memory: A component of memory that allows us to keep information in mind temporarily to use and process it, which aids with memory formation. It is also considered an aspect of executive functioning.

Executive functions

Executive functions (EFs) comprise a set of cognitive skills that let us think things through, give our ideas language, and carry out goal-directed behaviors. Many experts have slightly different lists of skills. This book refers to the skills identified by Faith, Bush, and Dawson (2022):

Cognitive flexibility: An executive functioning skill that helps us to cope and regroup when something requires a change or is not going as expected.

Emotional control: An executive functioning skill that helps us to handle our emotions in order to achieve our goals.

Goal-oriented persistence: An executive functioning skill that helps us to keep in mind and work toward an end goal, over time.

Metacognition: An executive functioning skill that helps us to think about our own thinking, learning, behaviors, performance, and needs.

Organization: An executive functioning skill that helps us to sort and classify materials (physical) or ideas and actions in space and time (mental).

Planning and prioritizing: Executive functioning skills that together help us to divide up what we need and want to do over time and decide what is most important to attend to first.

Response inhibition: An executive functioning skill that keeps us from getting up or shifting our attention to something else because we're bored or a whim occurs to us.

Sustained attention: An executive functioning skill that helps us direct our focus, ideally toward what is deemed important in the situation so that we can make meaning out of it.

Task initiation: An executive functioning skill that helps us to easily transition and get started on a new or different task.

Time management: An executive functioning skill that helps us to have awareness and accuracy in estimating how long something will take us and where we are in managing that task over time.

Working memory: see Working memory under "Memory and attention."

Key concepts related to neurodivergent learners

Ableism: Discrimination (overt or covert) against a person with a disability, rooted in the belief (conscious or unconscious) that disability or a disabled person is in some way deficient or "lesser than."

Burnout: In the context of autistic people, this refers to excessive fatigue, greatly enhanced sensory reactivity, and loss of executive functions. Distinct from meltdowns or shutdowns, this lasts for a long time (days, weeks, or even months) and is usually the result of stress caused by excessive masking (hiding autistic traits).

Double empathy problem/double empathy (Milton, 2012): The idea that, when a miscommunication occurs between a neurotypical and a neurodivergent person, the breakdown is often seen as caused by neurodivergent communication differences, rather than it "taking two to tango." This also refers to the common misperception by neurotypical people that neurodivergent people lack empathy because they may not show empathy the way a neurotypical might (empathy showing is variable across neurotypes).

Internalized ableism: Disabled/neurodivergent people can develop a feeling of discrimination against themselves due to the way that others treat them, internalizing that they "should" be able to function the same way as nondisabled/neurotypical people.

Monotropism (Murray et al., 2005): A theory developed to explain the autistic ability to become fully absorbed for extended periods of time in a flow state by the things that fascinate us, which can be to the exclusion of noticing anything else—needing to eat, drink, go to the bathroom, or get up and move. I think of this as an interest-based attention system, making it easy for an individual to shift attention and stay on task when the topic is appealing and a significant struggle when it is not.

Neurodivergent: A term referring to a person or people (identified, self-identified, or unidentified) whose brain(s) is/are wired differently than what is conceptualized as the "standard" or "average" way, which is called neurotypical. In this book, neurodivergence is inclusive of all neurotypes besides "neurotypical." When considered this broadly, people who are neurodivergent may comprise a larger collective than traditionally conceived, or than when they are counted as falling under individual neurotypes. This positioning calls into question the validity—and the helpfulness—of presuming a "standard" or "superior" way of functioning. However, as long as society conceives of and marginalizes some forms of human variability as "abnormal" relative to a culturally constructed idealized "norm," there will be a need for terms like neurodivergent and neurotypical. Neurodivergent people, especially within neurotypes, may have commonalities in how they see and experience the world. For instance, neurodivergent people may encounter systemic barriers and misunderstandings more often in day-to-day interactions and settings than neurotypical people, especially if they are multiply marginalized due to discrimination against additional aspects of their identity. A neurodivergent person may also be multiply neurodivergent, relating to or falling under one or more neurotypes (see also Neurotype).

Neurodiverse: A term meaning made up of many types of brains, which includes neurotypical brains, as all people fall under the umbrella of neurodiversity. Society is neurodiverse!

Neurotype: A collective embodied experience of a form of neurodivergence, which may be from birth or acquired (e.g., autistic, ADHD, bipolar, depression, anxiety, giftedness, traumatic brain injury, Parkinson's). Given the complexities of neurodivergent experiences, there is no consensus on what constitutes a neurotype in research literature; this is also because definitions of neurodivergence are arbitrary, as they are based on behavioural descriptors which are culturally constructed and subject to revisions in successive editions of diagnostic manuals (John, 2018; Leong, Hedley, & Uljarević, 2019). Similarly, there is no consensus on whether to view multiply neurodivergent presentations (e.g., autism and ADHD) as their own neurotype (e.g., auDHD), or to consider their lived experiences through the lens of interactions between intersecting neurotypes. For the purposes of this book, "neurotype" is used in the sense of a ""neuroculture" (Hillary, 2020), as in, a group of individuals who share common experiences due to the similar ways their brains and nervous systems influence processing and perspective. Neurodivergent neurotypes—any brain that is not "neurotypical"—have unique potential for community identification and support to navigate societal misconceptions, stigma, and self-stigma as well as for collective resistance to ableism and disablism. In this book, the neurotype or "label" is positioned as less important than a more holistic understanding of the specific strengths and support needs of the individual, and none is positioned as the "ideal".

Neurotypical: People who are commonly thought to learn and process information in what is seen as the "standard" way—though there is tremendous variety in how anyone learns and processes! "Neurotypical" is one neurotype of many, and this book challenges its mythical superiority. Given that many systems and structures are designed with neurotypical people in mind, they generally find it easier to navigate the world on a day-to-day basis when compared with neurodivergent people.

Teaching lingo

Differentiated instruction: An approach to teaching that considers individual learner needs, strengths, and interests when designing instruction. Teachers vary aspects of the environment, content, process, product, and/ or assessment with specific students in mind.

Schema: A cognitive framework for organizing and understanding a concept and related information and skills.

Universal Design for Learning: An approach to teaching that incorporates multiple means of engagement, representation, action, and expression in order to support all students.

References

Baglieri, S. & Lalvani, P. (2019). *Undoing ableism: Teaching about disability in K-12 classrooms*. Taylor & Francis Group.

Balfanz, R., Byrnes, V., & Fox, J. (2014). Sent home and put off-track: The antecedents, disproportionalities, and consequences of being suspended in the ninth grade. *Journal of Applied Research on Children, 5*(2), 13. https://doi.org/10.58464/2155-5834.1217

Barkley, R. A. (2000). *Taking Charge of ADHD: The Complete Authoritative Guide for Parents* (2nd edn). Guilford Press.

Barkley, R. A. (2012). *Executive Functions: What They Are, How They Work, and Why They Evolved*. Guilford Press.

Barkley, R. A. (2020). *Taking Charge of ADHD: The Complete, Authoritative Guide for Parents* (4th edn). Guilford Press.

Boeltzig, M., Johansson, M., & Bramão, I. (2023). Ingroup sources enhance associative inference. *Communications Psychology, 1*(40), 1–13. https://doi.org/10.1038/s44271-023-00043-8

Chapman, R. (2020). Neurodiversity, disability, wellbeing. In H. Bertilsdotter Rosqvist, N. Chown, & A. Stenning (Eds.), *Neurodiversity Studies: A New Critical Paradigm* (pp.57–72). Routledge.

Chapman, R., & Carel, H. (2022). Neurodiversity, epistemic injustice, and the good human life. *Journal of Social Philosophy, 53*(4), 614–631. https://doi.org/10.1111/josp.12456

Chen, P., Chavez, O., Ong, D. C., & Gunderson, B. (2017). Strategic resource use for learning: A self-administered intervention that guides self-reflection on effective resource use enhances academic performance. *Psychological Science, 28*(6), 774–785. https://doi.org/10.1177/0956797617696456

Cherry, K. (2024, May 20). What it's like to have aphantasia: Many people can't visualize images in their mind. Verywell Mind. www.verywellmind.com/aphantasia-overview-4178710

Cozolino, L. (2013). *The Social Neuroscience of Education*. W. W. Norton & Co.

Crompton, C. J., Ropar, D., Evans-Williams, C. V., Flynn, E. G., & Fletcher-Watson, S. (2020). Autistic peer-to-peer information transfer is highly effective. *Autism, 24*(7), 1704–1712. https://doi.org/10.1177/1362361320919286

Crouch, E., Radcliff, E., Strompolis, M., & Srivastav, A. (2018). Safe, stable, and nurtured: Protective factors against poor physical and mental health outcomes following exposure to adverse childhood experiences (ACEs). *Journal of Child & Adolescent Trauma, 12*(2), 165–173. https://doi.org/10.1007/s40653-018-0217-9

Davidson, D., Vanegas, S. B., & Hilvert, E. (2017). Proneness to self-conscious emotions in adults with and without autism traits. *Journal of Autism & Developmental Disorders, 47*(11), 3392–3404. https://doi.org/10.1007/s10803-017-3260-8

de Groot, A. D. (1978). *Thought and Choice in Chess*. De Gruyter Mouton. https://doi.org/10.1515/9783110800647

Delahooke, M. (2019). *Beyond Behaviors: Using Brain Science and Compassion to Understand and Solve Children's Behavioral Challenges*. PESI Publishing & Media.

Deniz, F., Nunez-Elizalde, A. O., Huth, A. G., & Gallant, J. L. (2019). The representation of semantic information across human cerebral cortex during listening versus reading is invariant to stimulus modality. *Journal of Neuroscience, 39*(39), 7722–7736. https://doi.org/10.1523/JNEUROSCI.0675-19.2019

Donaldson, A. L., Corbin, E., Zisk, A. H., & Eddy, B. (2023). Promotion of communication access, choice, and agency for autistic students. *Language, Speech & Hearing Services in Schools, 54*(1), 140–155. https://doi.org/10.1044/2022_LSHSS-22-00031

Dunlosky, J., Rawson, K. A., Marsh, E. J., Nathan, M. J., & Willingham, D. T. (2013). Improving students' learning with effective learning techniques: Promising directions from cognitive and educational psychology. *Psychological Science in the Public Interest, 14*(1), 4–58. https://doi.org/10.1177/1529100612453266

Dymond, K. (2019). *Teacher Insights: Self-efficacy and Professional Development Needs Related to Supporting Children with High-functioning Autism*. ProQuest Dissertations & Theses.

Dymond, K. (2020). *The Autism Lens: Everything Teachers Need to Connect with Students, Build Confidence, and Promote Classroom Learning*. Pembroke Publishers.

Faith, L., Bush, C., & Dawson, P. (2022). *Executive Function Skills in the Classroom: Overcoming Barriers, Building Strategies*. Guilford Press.

Fleming, S. (2014). The power of reflection. *Scientific American Mind, 25*(5), 30–37. https://doi.org/10.1038/scientificamericanmind0914-30

Gallichan, D. J., & Curle, C. (2008). Fitting square pegs into round holes: The challenge of coping with attention-deficit hyperactivity disorder. *Clinical Child Psychology and Psychiatry, 13*(3), 343–363. https://doi.org/10.1177/1359104508090599

Gardner, A. K., Jabbour, I. J., Williams, B. H., & Huerta, S. (2016). Different goals, different pathways: The role of metacognition and task engagement in surgical skill acquisition. *Journal of Surgical Education, 73*(1), 61–65. https://doi.org/10.1016/j.jsurg.2015.08.007

Gilliam, W. S. (2005). *Prekindergarteners Left Behind: Expulsion Rates in State Prekindergarten Systems*. Yale University Child Study Center.

Gopalan, M., & Nelson, A. A. (2019). Understanding the racial discipline gap in schools. *AERA Open, 5*(2). https://doi.org/10.1177/2332858419844613

Greene, R. W. (2008). *Lost at School: Why Our Kids with Behavioral Challenges Are Falling Through the Cracks and How We Can Help Them*. Scribner.

Greene, R. W. (2018). Transforming school discipline: Shifting from power and control to collaboration and problem solving. *Childhood Education, 94*(4), 22–27. https://doi.org/10.1080/00094056.2018.1494430

Gregory, A., & Roberts, G. (2017). Teacher beliefs and the overrepresentation of black students in classroom discipline. *Theory Into Practice, 56*(3), 187–194. https://doi.org/10.1080/00405841.2017.1336035

Hammond, Z. (2015). *Culturally Responsive Teaching and the Brain: Promoting Authentic Engagement and Rigor Among Culturally and Linguistically Diverse Students*. Corwin/Sage.

Hillary, A. (2020). Neurodiversity and cross-cultural communication. In Bertilsdotter Rosqvist, H., Chown, N., & Stenning, A. (Eds.), *Neurodiversity studies: A new critical paradigm* (pp.91–107). Routledge.

Huang, F. L. (2018). Do Black students misbehave more? Investigating the differential involvement hypothesis and out-of-school suspensions. *Journal of Educational Research, 111*(3), 284–294. https://doi.org/10.1080/00220671.2016.1253538

Hudson, R. F., High, L., & Al Otaiba, S. (2011). Dyslexia and the brain: What does current research tell us? *The Reading Teacher, 60*(6), 506–515.

James, C. E., & Turner, T. (2017). *Towards Race Equity in Education: The Schooling of Black Students in the Greater Toronto Area.* York University, Toronto.

John, Y. (2018). Answer to: Can you list all the different neurotypes? *Quora.* https://www.quora.com/Can-you-list-all-the-different-neurotypes-I-m-struggling-to-find-them-but-I-know-of-the-neurotypical-brain-psychopathic-brain-autistic-brain-dyslexic-brain-and-ADHD-brain-What-other-brains-are-there/answer/Yohan-John

Kendle, A. (2017). *Aphantasia: Experiences, Perceptions, and Insights.* Dark River.

Kincheloe, J. (2003). Critical ontology: Visions of selfhood and curriculum. *Journal of Curriculum Theorizing*, Spring, 47–64.

Kirschner, P. A., & Hendrick, C. (2020). *How Learning Happens: Seminal Works in Educational Psychology and What They Mean in Practice.* Routledge.

Kohn, A. (1993). *Punished by Rewards: The Trouble with Gold Stars, Incentive Plans, A's, Praise, and Other Bribes.* Houghton Mifflin.

Kohn, A. (2006). *Beyond Discipline: From Compliance to Community* (10th anniversary edn, 2nd edn). Association for Supervision and Curriculum Development.

Lacoe, J., & Steinberg, M. P. (2018). Rolling back zero tolerance: The effect of discipline policy reform on suspension usage and student outcomes. *Peabody Journal of Education, 93*(2), 207–227. https://doi.org/10.1080/0161956X.2018.1435047

Leong, D., Hedley, D., & Uljarević, M. (2020). Poh-tay-toe, poh-tah-toe: Autism diagnosis and conceptualization. *Journal of Child Neurology, 35*(3), 247–248. https://doi.org/10.1177/0883073819887587

Lindt, S. F., & Miller, S. C. (2017). Movement and learning in elementary school. *Phi Delta Kappan, 98*(7), 34–37. https://doi.org/10.1177/0031721717702629

Locke, J., Ishijima, E., Kasari, C., & London, N. (2010). Loneliness, friendship quality and the social networks of adolescents with high-functioning autism in an inclusive school setting. *Journal of Research in Special Educational Needs, 10*, 74–81. https://doi.org/10.1111/j.1471-3802.2010.01148.x

Losen, D. J., & Martinez, T. E. (2013). Out of school and off track: The overuse of suspensions in American middle and high schools. The Civil Rights Project/Proyecto Derechos Civiles. https://civilrightsproject.ucla.edu/resources/projects/center-for-civil-rights-remedies/school-to-prison-folder/federal-reports/out-of-school-and-off-track-the-overuse-of-suspensions-in-american-middle-and-high-schools

Louridas, M., Bonrath, E. M., Sinclair, D. A., Dedy, N. J., & Grantcharov, T. P. (2015). Randomized clinical trial to evaluate mental practice in enhancing advanced laparoscopic surgical performance. *British Journal of Surgery, 102*(1), 37–44. https://doi.org/10.1002/bjs.9657

Magimairaj, B. M., & Nagaraj, N. K. (2018). Working memory and auditory processing in school-age children. *Language, Speech & Hearing Services in Schools, 49*(3), 409–423. https://doi.org/10.1044/2018_LSHSS-17-0099

Manning, C., Hassall, C. D., Hunt, L. T., Norcia, A. M., et al. (2022). Visual motion and decision-making in dyslexia: Reduced accumulation of sensory evidence and related neural dynamics. *Journal of Neuroscience, 42*(1), 121–134. https://doi.org/10.1523/JNEUROSCI.1232-21.2021

Marcellus, L., & Speidel, A. (Hosts). (2023, September). Changing perceptions to address the school to prison pipeline. [Audio podcast episode]. Real Talk for Real Teachers by Conscious Discipline. https://open.spotify.com/episode/otbD1BNVTi102Hn46Z2KlC

McKeague, L., Hennessy, E., O'Driscoll, C., & Heary, C. (2015). Retrospective accounts of self-stigma experienced by young people with attention-deficit/hyperactivity disorder (ADHD) or depression. *Psychiatric Rehabilitation Journal, 38*(2), 158–163. https://doi.org/10.1037/prj0000121

Milton, D. (2012). On the ontological status of autism: The "double empathy problem." *Disability & Society, 27*(6), 883–887. https://doi.org/10.1080/09687599.2012.710008

Mind Tools. (2024). The Roman Room System. www.mindtools.com/adc3q6y/the-roman-room-system

Murphy, S. L. (2019). *Fostering Mindfulness: Building Skills that Students Need to Manage Their Attention, Emotions, and Behavior in Classrooms and Beyond.* Pembroke Publishers.

Murray, D., Lesser, M., & Lawson, W. (2005). Attention, monotropism and the diagnostic criteria for autism. *Autism, 9*(2), 136–156. https://doi.org/10.1177/1362361305051398

NeuroQ. (2022, June 15). Living with hyperphantasia. https://neuroq.com/blog/living-with-hyperphantasia

Oakley, B., Rogowsky, B. A., & Sejnowski, T. J. (2021). *Uncommon Sense Teaching: Practical Insights in Brain Science to Help Students Learn.* TarcherPerigee.

Okonofua, J. A., & Eberhardt, J. L. (2015). Two strikes: Race and the disciplining of young students. *Psychological Science, 26*, 617–624. https://doi.org/10.1177/0956797615570365

Pastor-Cerezuela, G., Fernández-Andrés, M.-I., Sanz-Cervera, P., & Marín-Suelves, D. (2020). The impact of sensory processing on executive and cognitive functions in children with autism spectrum disorder in the school context. *Research in Developmental Disabilities, 96*, 103540. https://doi.org/10.1016/j.ridd.2019.103540

Perrachione, T. K., Del Tufo, S. N., Winter, R., Murtagh, J., et al. (2016). Dysfunction of rapid neural adaptation in dyslexia. *Neuron, 92*(6), 1383–1397. https://doi.org/10.1016/j.neuron.2016.11.020

Porges, S. (2004). Neuroception: A subconscious system for detecting threats and safety. *Zero to Three, 24*(5), 19–24.

Reeves, E., Miller, S., & Chavez, C. (2016). Movement and learning: Integrating physical activity into the classroom. *Kappa Delta Pi Record, 52*(3), 116–120. https://doi.org/10.1080/00228958.2016.1191898

Ringer, N. (2019). Young people's perceptions of and coping with their ADHD symptoms: A qualitative study. *Cogent Psychology, 6*(1). https://doi.org/10.1080/23311908.2019.1608032

Salend, S. (2011). Addressing test anxiety. *Teaching Exceptional Children, 44*(2), 58–68. https://doi.org/10.1177/004005991104400206

Schore, A. N. (1998). Early shame experiences and infant brain development. In P. Gilbert, & B. Andrews (Eds.), *Shame: Interpersonal Behavior, Psychopathology, and Culture* (pp.57–77). Oxford Academic. https://doi.org/10.1093/oso/9780195114799.003.0003

Shanker, S. (2017). *The Self-Reg View on: Schools as "Self-Reg Havens."* The MEHRIT Centre. https://self-reg.ca/wp-content/uploads/2020/06/Infosheet_Schools_as_Self-Reg_Havens.pdf

Shanker, S. (2020). *Reframed: Self-Reg for a Just Society.* University of Toronto Press.

Shaw, S. C. K., Fossi, A., Carravallah, L. A., Rabenstein, K., Ross, W., & Doherty, M. (2023). The experiences of autistic doctors: A cross-sectional study. *Frontiers in Psychiatry, 14*, 1160994. https://doi.org/10.3389/fpsyt.2023.1160994

Shaywitz, S. E. (2005). *Overcoming Dyslexia: A New and Complete Science-Based Program for Reading Problems at Any Level.* Alfred A. Knopf.

Singh, A., & Alexander, P. A. (2022). Audiobooks, print, and comprehension: What we know and what we need to know. *Educational Psychology Review, 34*(2), 677–715. https://doi.org/10.1007/s10648-021-09653-2

Skiba, R. J., Michael, R. S., Nardo, A. C., & Peterson, R. L. (2002). The color of discipline: Sources of racial and gender disproportionality in school punishment. *Urban Review, 34*, 317–342. https://doi.org/10.1023/A:1021320817372

Smith-Spark, J. H., & Gordon, R. (2022). Automaticity and executive abilities in developmental dyslexia: A theoretical review. *Brain Sciences, 12*(4), 446. https://doi.org/10.3390/brainsci12040446

Toudal, M. & Attwood, T. (2024). *Energy accounting: Stress management and mental health monitoring for a better quality of life.* Jessica Kingsley Publishers.

Vermeulen, P. (2012). *Autism as Context Blindness.* AAPC Publishing.

Vermeulen, P. (2018, October 25). Autism and the Predictive Mind [Keynote presentation]. Geneva Centre for Autism Symposium, Toronto, ON, Canada.

Vermeulen, P. (2023). *Autism and the Predictive Brain.* Routledge.

Visu-Petra, L., Cheie, L., Benga, O., & Miclea, M. (2011). Cognitive control goes to school: The impact of executive functions on academic performance. *Procedia: Social and Behavioral Sciences, 11*, 240–244. https://doi.org/10.1016/j.sbspro.2011.01.069

Vygotsky, L. (1986). *Thought and Language.* MIT Press.

Waltz, M. (2020). The production of the 'normal' child: Neurodiversity and the commodification of parenting. In H. Bertilsdotter Rosqvist, N. Chown, & A. Stenning (Eds.), *Neurodiversity Studies: A New Critical Paradigm* (pp.15–26). Routledge.

Wiener, J., Malone, M., Varma, A., Markel, C., et al. (2012). Children's perceptions of their ADHD symptoms: Positive illusions, attributions, and stigma. *Canadian Journal of School Psychology, 27*, 217–242. https://doi.org/10.1177/0829573512451972

Wilkins, F. (2023). How is the ADHD brain different? Child Mind Institute. https://childmind.org/article/how-is-the-adhd-brain-different

Williams, K. (2022, October 3). Dyslexia and phonological processing. Dyslexia UK. www.dyslexiauk.co.uk/dyslexia-and-phonological-processing

Zheng, R. Z., & Gardner, M. K. (2020). *Memory in Education.* Routledge.

3